Preconcentration and Drying of Food Materials

Process Technology Proceedings

Process Technology Proceedings, 5

Preconcentration and Drying of Food Materials

Thijssen Memorial Symposium — Proceedings of the International Symposium on Preconcentration and Drying of Foods, Eindhoven, The Netherlands, November 5–6, 1987

Edited by

S. Bruin

Unilever Research Laboratory, Vlaardingen, The Netherlands

ELSEVIER – Amsterdam – Oxford – New York – Tokyo   1988

ELSEVIER SCIENCE PUBLISHERS B.V.
Sara Burgerhartstraat 25
P.O. Box 211, 1000 AE Amsterdam, The Netherlands

Distributors for the United States and Canada:

ELSEVIER SCIENCE PUBLISHING COMPANY INC.
52, Vanderbilt Avenue
New York, NY 10017, U.S.A.

ISBN 0-444-42968-9 (Vol. 5)
ISBN 0-444-42382-6 (Series)

D
664. 0284
INT

This book is to be returned on or before
the last date stamped below.

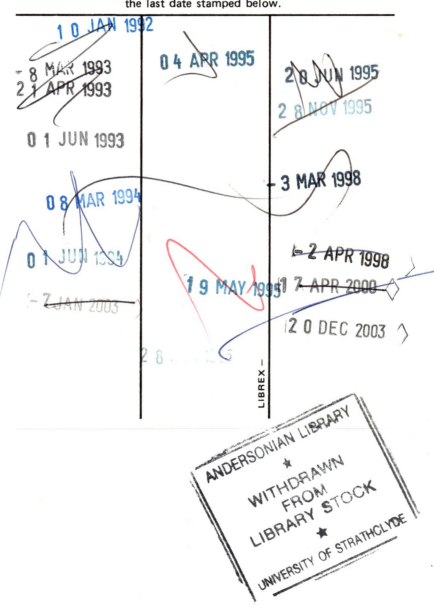

Thijssen Memorial Symposium

International Symposium on Preconcentration and Drying of Foods

ORGANIZING COMMITTEE

S. Bruin (chairman)
P.M. Baalman (secretary)
W.J. Coumans
J.W. van Heuven
J.M. van der Kamp
P.J.A.M. Kerkhof
K. van 't Riet
H.G.J. de Wilt
H.A.J. Wouda

SCIENTIFIC COMMITTEE

S. Bruin (chairman) – Unilever, The Netherlands
J.J. Bimbenet – ENSIA, France
C. Cantarelli – University of Milan, Italy
B. Hallstrøm – Lund University, Sweden
C.J. King – University of California, USA
K. van 't Riet – Agricultural University,
The Netherlands

SYMPOSIUM SPONSORS

Douwe Egberts, Utrecht

Eindhoven University of Technology, Eindhoven

Gist-brocades, Delft

Grenco Process Technology, 's-Hertogenbosch

Netherlands Association of Engineers (NIRIA),
Department of Process Technology

Royal Institution of Engineers in the Netherlands
(KIvI), Department of Process Technology,

Royal Netherlands Chemical Society (KNCV),
Division of Process Technology

TNO, The Hague

Unilever, Rotterdam

Prof Dr. Ir. H.A.C. Thijssen
14 October 1927–19 September 1986

PREFACE

Following the sudden death of Prof. Ir. H.A.C. Thijssen on September 19, 1986, the idea of organizing a symposium to honour his memory quickly gained favour, and the venue was soon chosen: Eindhoven University of Technology, with which he had been associated for twenty years. Just over a year later, on November 5–6, 1987, the Thijssen Memorial Symposium was held in Eindhoven, and it was attended by some 170 delegates from all parts of the world.

Professor Thijssen was one of the most creative and stimulating advocates of applying chemical engineering principles to food process engineering. His scientific work focussed on preconcentration and drying of food materials, so the topic of the memorial Symposium was clear from the outset.

The symposium was organized under the auspices of the European Federation of Chemical Engineering as its 374th Event, the Roytal Netherlands Chemical Society (KNCV), the Royal Institution of Engineers in the Netherlands (KIvI) and the Netherlands Association of Engineers (NIRIA). A total of 41 papers were presented, most of them written by individuals and groups who had worked with Professor Thijssen at some point in his career.

The financial support of KNCV, KIvI, NIRIA, Eindhoven University of Technology, the TNO Organisation and the following industries: Douwe Egberts, Gist-brocades, Grenco Process Technology and Unilever is gratefully acknowledged.

Wageningen, January 1988   S. Bruin

TABLE OF CONTENTS

XII

OPENING LECTURES

Preconcentration and Drying of Food Materials, edited by S. Bruin
Elsevier Science Publishers B.V., Amsterdam, 1988 — Printed in The Netherlands

THIJSSEN LECTURE: INTRODUCTION TO THE SYMPOSIUM TOPIC

Dr ir S. Bruin*
*Unilever Research Laboratorium, P.O.Box 114, 3130 AC Vlaardingen
(The Netherlands)

Mrs Thijssen, Ladies and Gentlemen,

The two arts of Preconcentration and Drying: two important operations in the food industry have always been in the centre of Prof Hans Thijssen's professional endeavours. It therefore is appropriate to have these topics as the core of our memorial symposium, paying tribute to an extraordinary man.

Here I take it you allow me to start on a somewhat personal note.

Almost exactly 22 years ago I first met Hans Thijssen, when I started a three year Ph.D. project at the Agricultural University of this country on the subject of concentration of aroma components from food liquids. Prof Leniger was my first promotor and Prof Thijssen was in principle prepared to act as the second promotor. He immediately made it quite clear to me it was not going to be an easy ride. He, as usual, kept his promise and how vividly do I remember his radiant, effervescent and contageous enthusiasm for the, at that time, relatively unexplored area of application of chemical engineering principles to food processing. In this country at that time, Prof Thijssen at the Eindhoven University of Technology and Prof Leniger at the Agricultural University in Wageningen were pioneering the area, with markedly different approaches that turned out to be complementary to each other. Leniger with an empirical approach to research, teaching a balanced and systematic coverage of all technical aspects of food production operations. Thijssen selecting a few research topics that looked amenable to chemical engineering analysis (drying of food liquids, freeze concentration), teaching courses that were somewhat systematic, sparkling with enthusiasm and a proof of his theme that chemical engineering analysis <u>can</u> be applied fruitfully to food processing. Despite his high standards and sense for quality I eventually succeeded in getting

also his approval for my thesis. If the concept of a godfather also extends
to the transfer of science from the older generation to the next I
certainly would call Hans Thijssen to be mine.

Now, what I want to do in this short introductory lecture is to give an
overview of the scientific work of Hans Thijssen, and indicate links with
the programme of our Symposium of today and tomorrow, in particular with
some of the keynote lectures.

Keenly he started his professional carreer in the years between 1952-
1954 with a thesis on the influence of the composition of binary mixtures
on the tray efficiency in distillation [ref. 1-4]. This thesis is a fine
piece of technical work, ranging from developing a measuring system for
tray efficiencies on a small distillation column, via an improved test on
thermodynamic consistency of binary vapor-liquid equilibria to a very
plausible explanation of concentration dependence of tray efficiencies.
Apart from this we can read in the introduction, and I quote:
"When comparing the chemical industry with the food industry it is
remarkable that the relatively young chemical industry has surpassed by
far the much older food industry, especially in terms of knowledge of
the technological basic principles and control of processes" ....
"Because the food industry uses similar operations and processes as the
chemical industry, the food industry can profit from the know how
assembled by the chemical industry. So far this has not happened
sufficiently ...... One of the reasons being the fact that the food
industry also shows marked differences with the chemical industry:
several key unit operations of the chemical industry hardly are
important to the food industry, and the other way around, but especially
the nature of raw materials is completely different ....".
"The raw materials of the food industry have a very complicated structure
and chemical composition and show large variations over time. Also
biochemical and/or biophysical changes of the product occur. By applying
a processing method, which is in itself right and which is successfully
applied in the chemical industry, quality changes can occur that make
the end product unsuitable for consumption...."
"It is therefore clear that food technology is in many respects more
complicated and difficult than chemical technology. This does not take
away the fact that there are big advantages to apply the knowledge of
unit operations and unit processes to the food industry. However, it
must be done intelligently, taking into account the typical aspects of

the food industry...."

You realise that this quote, Ladies and Gentlemen, summarises Hans Thijssen's philosophy on food process engineering as much then, in 1954, as it did throughout his carreer. How intelligently indeed did he apply chemical engineering to the food industry, and how skilled in the arts he became!

On finishing his thesis Hans Thijssen joined the food industry in 1955 with P. de Gruyter & Sons in 's Hertogenbosch, not far from here, where he would stay for 9 years. De Gruyter was a grocery firm, with coffee as one of their major products. In this period he started to study preconcentration and drying with instant powdered coffee as the main product application. Those also were the days when James's and Martin's gas-liquid chromatography was developing rapidly as a tool for separation of food aromas, and characteristic for Hans Thijssen he contributed with a paper on the theory of chromatographic separation in capillary tubes, pushing the HTU concept rather than HETP as a measure of separation power of a chromatographic column, following the Van Deemter/Klinkenberg/Zuiderweg approach [ref. 5-6].

Upon being called to the position in 1964 he joined the Chemical Engineering Department of the then young Eindhoven University of Technology as a full professor. Even when he returned to industry in 1973 he retained his contacts with the University as an adjunct professor to this institution. Having settled he delivered an impressive inaugural address in October 1965 in which he again reinforced his philosophy on the interplay between technologies in the chemical and the food industries [ref. 7]. In this 9 year period in Eindhoven he worked with an enthousiastic, self juvenating group of graduate students and permanent staff on basically two topics: drying (in particular aroma retention during spray drying and freeze drying) and freeze concentration as a preconcentration method. This work led to many publications and a number of patents on freeze concentration technology.

However tempting, rather than discussing this work in detail I refer to the key note lectures to be delivered by Professors King from the University of California, Berkeley, and Karel from the Massachussetts Institute of Technology on concentration and (spray) drying of food liquids and volatiles retention tomorrow, and to the key note lecture of this afternoon by Mr Van Pelt from Grenco Process Technology on freeze concentration applications and economics. Suffice here to say that in both areas Hans Thijssen had really innovative contributions: e.g. the selective diffusion concept explaining the retention of very volatile aroma components in drying [ref. 8-19] and the key improvements of crystallisers and wash column technology to improve separation of mother liquor from ice crystals in freeze concentration [ref. 20-28]. One of the most significant honors bestowed on him, he undoubtedly considered to be the 1978 "Food, Pharmaceutical and Bioengineering Award" from the American Institute of Chemical Engineers [ref. 29].

A most striking feature of Hans Thijssen's work I always found to be his ability to simplify quite complex interaction patterns between variables in processes, partly by intuition, partly by simple application of balance equations; usually lumped-parameter approaches. But at the same time he knew the art of rousing the interest of very good, and mathematically well trained, graduate students in his field of research (e.g. Rulkens, Schoeber, Kerkhof) [ref. 30-32]. It was this mix of skills, or symbiosis, that has led to various new concepts.

Now, one example of this is the concept of Regular Regimes in calculating drying behavior of particles of simple geometries when the moisture diffusion coefficients are concentration dependent [ref. 32-34] which enables one to calculate the approximate drying behavior without the need to go into tedious numerical integration methods. This method is also a powerful technique to derive the concentration dependence of the diffusion coefficient of water from only a limited number of measured drying curves of a probe [ref. 34]. Coumans, in a Ph.D. study started under the guidance of Hans Thijssen, has recently refined this approach further to a useful tool [ref. 35-36] and we will hear more of this very recent work tomorrow morning. The concept of Regular Regimes could only have been created by a team in which advanced numerical mathemical approaches were continually confronted with Hans Thijssen's passion to understand the transport phenomena in drying and to achieve the simplest possible description.

Similar and a second example, linked to the Regular Regime concept in drying, is the calculation of sterilisation conditions of packed foods. Hans Thijssen realised that also in heat penetration into packed foods the temperature profiles would follow similarity patterns over time and he

stimulated some of his graduate students to think this through and simplify
the usual but cumbersome calculation methods of Ball and Olson [ref. 37],
Hayakawa [ref. 38] or Stumbo [ref. 39]. The result was a short cut
calculation method for sterilisation conditions yielding optimum quality
retention of conduction heating of packed foods [ref. 40-42].

A third example is the problem of mass transfer between two phases
moving countercurrently but both subject to axial dispersion naggingly
trying to destroy separation sharpness. Of course this problem was solved
by Sleicher at Shell Research Emeryville in California [ref. 43-44] and
Miyauchy and Vermeulen at the University of California, Berkeley [ref. 45]
in the late fifties and milked by Hartland and Mecklenburg from the
University of Nottingham in Britain about ten years later [ref. 46-47]. The
resulting equations of Sleicher and Miyauchi and Vermeulen were, however,
rather tedious to use and those of Hartland and Mecklenburg even more so.
In preparing lecture notes for a mass transfer operations course Hans
Thijssen stumbled upon this problem. He got the simple idea that axial
mixing in both phases could be described by the cascade of mixers model and
derived in two evenings the basic concept of a model that Kerkhof neatly
worked out. This extremely simple model [ref.48] results in a very
unsophisticated equation that completely predicts the effects of axial
dispersion in a counter current operation with only small deviations from
the Sleicher/Miyauchi/Vermeulen equations under most situations of
practical interest.

In 1973 Hans Thijssen moved back to industry, becoming a research
director for Douwe Egberts/Jakobs, a joint venture between two European
coffee manufacturers.

In 1977 the cooperation between the Douwe Egberts and Jakobs companies
was discontinued and he became director of R&D and Engineering for Douwe
Egberts. As I already mentioned he kept a close link to the Eindhoven
University of Technology as an adjunct professor in the Chemical
Engineering Department.

Also in this period he remained active in coaching graduate students and
also as a second promotor to Ph.D. projects at the Dept of Food Process
Engineering of the Agricultural University on topics like drying (Van der
Lijn, Liou and Luyben) and solid/liquid extraction (Spaninks), [ref. 49-
51]. My, necessarily subjective, view on this period of close co-operation

between the Departments at Eindhoven and Wageningen is that it was a true symbiosis which offered many advantages to graduate students at both Universities.

From 1981 to 1983 Hans Thijssen was a member of the Management team of the Division of Technology for Society (MT/TNO) of the TNO organisation in the Netherlands with special responsibility for biotechnology in an "across-departments" organisation. From 1983 onwards he was a member of the management team of Gist Brocades NV in Delft for the bio-process technology area. End 1985 he established himself as an independent consultant for Gist Brocades NV and for Grenco Process Technology.

In this period, from 1981 onwards, he contributed to bio-process technology in many ways and continued to improve the freeze concentration technology. An interesting review paper on the impact of biotechnology on the food industry written together with Roels [ref. 52] summarises their views: "....the trees of biotechnology do grow to heaven but, common to the more sturdy real trees, at a rather slow pace". About freeze concentration we will hear more in the lecture by Van Pelt this afternoon.

Throughout his carreer Hans Thijssen was very active in professional organisations. He was a long time member of the Food Working Party of the European Federation of Chemical Engineering which he chaired from 1977-1981. In this connection he advocated on numerous occasions his views on the needs for process engineers to become involved in the food industry [ref. 53-55]. In 1980 he was chairman of the Royal Netherlands Chemical Society (KNCV). The Symposium of today appropriately occurs under the auspices of, amongst other, these two organisations.

Let me conclude with a brief preview of the two days ahead of us.

Today we start with a key note lecture by Prof Loncin from the Technische Universität Karlsruhe, FRG, on the activity of water and its importance in preconcentration and drying of foods. Apart from his initial work on vapor liquid equilibria Hans Thijssen usually took it for granted that by some equation one could describe the sorption isotherm of water in foods, but he was of course keenly aware of the central role water activity plays in preconcentration and drying of foods and stimulated his students to fully think through its implications. Having had this look into the thermodynamics of equilibrium we move on to preconcentration.

A key note lecture by Prof Hallstrøm from the University of Lund, Sweden, will indicate new developments in the classical area of evaporation as a preconcentration process. Since most of the novel preconcentration processes will be compared in their economy and product quality with this work horse of the food industry it is appropriate to remain aware of major improvements in its economy and product quality effects. Hans Thijssen, together with Van Oyen and Van der Malen [ref. 56-58], put it this way:

"Unlike the concentration of most "chemicals", the dewatering of foods is a delicate affair. Even at moderate temperatures many of their constituents prove to be chemically unstable. At temperatures between 30 and 70°C, enzymatically catalysed reactions can alter food properties within a few minutes. To obtain good products, sanitary conditions must also meet strict standards. For many foods the quality is moreover strongly dependent on the concentration of odorous compounds. All aroma compounds are naturally volatile and can partly or even totally be lost by evaporation.

For the concentration of liquid foods, three different main groups of processes can be used, viz. evaporation with or without aroma recovery by stripping and/or distillation, reverse osmosis and ultrafiltration with or without aroma recovery from permeate by distillation, and freeze concentration ...."

In the papers with Van Oyen [ref. 56-57] the quality aspects and costs of concentration were analysed and compared between a number of evaporator types and configurations, freeze concentration, reverse osmosis and ultrafiltration. The paper with Van der Malen [ref. 58] focussed in particular on the effects that energy saving programs would have on product quality. The latter paper, naturally, was also meant to provide a sales pitch for Hans Thijssen's freeze concentration process technology.

Today's afternoon will see some novel approaches to preconcentration, the main triggers for their development being to maintain delicate product quality and/or product functionality such as: concentration of fruit juices while retaining the full taste, concentration of enzyme solutions while retaining full functionality or concentration of micro organism suspensions while retaining full viability.

Tomorrow we have devoted to drying: principles, modelling, processes, optimisation and measurements techniques. As I said before, Hans Thijssen's main contributions to the area of drying were the concept of selective

10

diffusion of water relative to volatile flavor components and the short
cut calculation approaches to drying. From the many contributions in
lectures and posters of this Symposium emerges a picture that confirms the
trail-blazing contribution that Thijssen's school at Eindhoven made on
understanding the heat and mass transport phenomena during drying of food
materials.

Mrs Thijssen, Ladies and Gentlemen,

I hope to have been able to give you a brief overview of the eminent
professional carreer of Prof Hans Thijssen and a view on how we, as the
Scientific Committee, arrived at the programme structure of this Symposium.
However, how deeply do I feel that - in limiting myself to his professional
work - only a small part of his personality came into focus. His personal
charm, warm friendship, his optimism and sense of humor were some other
extraordinary qualities that I will never forget.

I thank you for your attention.

REFERENCES

1. H.A.C. Thijssen, Effect of liquid composition on plate efficiency in the rectification of binary mixtures, Dissertation, Verslagen van Land-bouwkundige Onderzoekingen, no. 61.12, Staatsdrukkerij, Den Haag, 1955.
2. W.R. van Wijk and H.A.C. Thijssen, Concentration and plate efficiencies in distillation columns, Chem. Eng. Sci. 3, (1954), 153-160.
3. H.A.C. Thijssen, Distillation column for study of individual plate efficiencies, Chem. Eng. Sci. 4 (1955), 81-84.
4. H.A.C. Thijssen, Thermodynamic evaluation of binary vapor-liquid equilibria, 4 (1955), 75-80.
5. H.A.C. Thijssen, Gas-liquid chromatography. A contribution to the theory of separation in open hole tubes, Journal of Chromatography 11 (2), (1963), 141-150.
6. J.J. van Deemter, F.J. Zuiderweg and A. Klinkenberg, Chem. Eng. Sci. 5, (1956) 271-289.
7. H.A.C. Thijssen, Samenspel der Technologieën, Inaugural address, Technical University Eindhoven, 8 October 1965.
8. H.A.C. Thijssen, W.H. Rulkens, Retention of aromas in drying food liquids, De Ingenieur, Chemische Techniek 5, (1968), Ch 45-47.
9. W.H. Rulkens, H.A.C. Thijssen, Numerical solution of diffusion equations with strongly variable diffusion coefficients, Trans. Inst. Chem. Engrs. 47 (1969), T292-299.
10. L.C. Menting, B. Hoogstad, H.A.C. Thijssen, Diffusion coefficients of water and organic volatiles in carbohydrate-water systems, J. Food Technology, 5, (1970), 111-126.
11. L.C. Menting, B. Hoogstad, H.A.C. Thijssen, Aroma retention during the drying of liquid foods, J. Food Technology, 5, (1970), 127-139.
12. H.A.C. Thijssen, Flavour retention in drying preconcentrated food liquids, J. Appl. Chem. Biotechnol. 21, (1971), 372-377.
13. W.H. Rulkens, H.A.C. Thijssen, The retention of organic volatiles in spray drying aqueous carbohydrate solutions, 7, (1972) 95-105.

14. W.H Rulkens, H.A.C. Thijssen, Retention of volatile compounds in freeze drying of malto dextrin, J. Food Technology, 7, (1972), 79-93.
15. H.A.C. Thijssen, Prevention of aroma losses during drying of liquid foods, DECHEMA Monografieën, 70, (1972), 353-367.
16. J.L. Bomben, S. Bruin, H.A.C. Thijssen, R.L. Merson, Aroma recovery and retention in concentration and drying of foods, Advances Food Research, 73 (1973), 1-111.
17. P.J.A.M. Kerkhof, H.A.C. Thijssen, Retention of aroma components in extractive drying of aqueous carbohydrate solutions, J. Food Technology, 9, (1974), 415-423.
18. P.J.A.M. Kerkhof, H.A.C. Thijssen, The effect of process conditions on aroma retention in drying liquid food, Proceedings Int. Symposium Aroma Research, Zeist, (1975), Pudoc, Wageningen, pp 167-192.
19. P.J.A.M. Kerkhof, H.A.C. Thijssen, Quantitative effects of process variables on aroma retention during the drying of liquid food, AIChE Symposium Series, 73, (1977), 33-46.
20. H.A.C. Thijssen, M.A.G. Vorstman, J.A. Roels, Heterogeneous primary nucleation of ice in water and aqueous solutions, J. of Crystal Growth 3, 4 (1968), 355-359.
21. H.A.C. Thijssen, Recent developments in freeze concentration of food liquids, DECHEMA Monografieen 63 (1968), 153-177.
22. N.J.J. Huige, H.A.C. Thijssen, Rate controlling factors of ice crystal growth from supercooled water and glucose solutions, Proc. Symp. on Industrial Crystallisation, London, 15-16 April, 1969.
23. N.J.J. Huige, H.A.C. Thijssen, H.J.A. Schuurmans, Nucleation and growth of ice crystals in a continuous stirred tank crystallizer, Proc. 3d Congress CHISA, Marienbad, 15-20 September, 1969.
24. N.J.J. Huige, H.A.C. Thijssen, Production of large crystals by continuous ripening in a stirred tank, J. of Crystal Growth, 13/14 (1972), 483-487.
25. N.J.J. Huige, M.M.G. Senden, H.A.C. Thijssen, Nucleation and growth kinetics for the crystallisation of ice from dextrose solutions in a continuous stirred tank crystallizer with supercooled feed, Kristall und Technik, 8, (1973, 785-801.
26. M.A.G. Vorstman, H.A.C. Thijssen, Stability of displacement of viscous aqueous solutions by water in a packed bed of ice crystals, Proc. Int. Symp. on Heat/Mass Transfer problems in Food Engineering, Wageningen, 24-27 October, 1972.
27. H.A.C. Thijssen, Freeze concentration, in Advances in Preconcentration and Drying of Foods, Ed. A. Spicer, Appl. Sci. Publ. London, (1974), 115-151.
28. H.A.C. Thijssen, Freeze concentration, Shokuhin Kogyo 21, (1978), 41-52.
29. H.A.C. Thijssen, The Food Industry in a changing society, Chem. Eng. Progress, 75, (1979), 21-26.
30. W.H. Rulkens, Retention of volatile trace components in drying aqueous carbohydrate solutions, Ph.D. Thesis Technical University Eindhoven, 1973.
31. P.J.A.M. Kerkhof, A quantitative study of the effect of process variables on the retention of volatile trace components in drying, Ph.D. Thesis Technical University Eindhoven, 1975.
32. W.J.A.H. Schoeber, Regular Regimes in Sorption Processes, Ph.D. Thesis, Technical University Eindhoven, 1976.
33. W.J.A.H. Schoeber, H.A.C. Thijssen, A short cut method for the calculation of drying rates for slabs with concentration dependent diffusion coefficient, AIChE Symposium Series, 73, (1977), 12-24.
34. W.J.A.H. Schoeber, H.A.C. Thijssen, A step-by-step method for calculation of the concentration dependence of the diffusion coefficient from a single (de)sorption experiment, Int. J. Heat Mass Transfer 21, (1978), 1070-1071.

12

35. H.A.C. Thijssen, W.J. Coumans, Short-cut calculations of non-isothermal drying rates of shrinking and non-shrinking particles and of particles containing an expanding gasphase, Proceedings 3d Int. Symp. Drying, Kyoto, 1984, p 22-30.
36. W.J. Coumans, Power Law Diffusion in Drying Processes, Ph.D. dissertation, Technical University Eindhoven, 1987.
37. C.O. Ball, F.C.W. Olson, Sterilisation in Food Technology, Mc.Graw-Hill, New York, (1957).
38. K. Hayakawa, New parameters for calculation mass average sterilizing value to estimate nutrient retention in thermally conductive food, Can. Inst. Food Technology Jnl., 2, (1969), 165.
39. C.R. Stumbo, Thermobacteriology in Food Processing, 2nd Ed., Academic Press,New York, 1973.
40. H.A.C. Thijssen, P.J.A.M. Kerkhof, A.A.A. Liefkens, Short cut method for the calculation of sterilisation conditions yielding optimum quality retention for conduction type heating of packed foods, J. Food Science, 43, (1978), 1096-1101.
41. H.A.C. Thijssen, L.H.P.J.M. Kochen, Short-cut method for the calculation of sterilisation conditions for packed foods yielding optimum quality retention for conduction type heating at variable temperature of heating and cooling medium, Food Process Engineering, Vol 1, Food Processing Systems, Appl. Sci. Publ., (1980) pp. 122-137.
42. H.A.C. Thijssen, L.H.P.J.M. Kochen, Calculation of optimum sterilisation conditions for packed conduction type foods, J. Food Science, 45, (1980), 1267-1272.
43. C.A. Sleicher Jr., Axial mixing and extraction efficiency, A.J.Ch.E. Jnl, 5, (1959), 145-149.
44. C.A. Sleicher Jr., Entrainment and extraction efficiency of mixer-settlers, A.J.Ch.E. Jnl, 6, (1960), 529-531.
45. T. Miyauchi, Th. Vermeulen, Longitudinal dispersion in two-phase continuous-flow operations, Ind. Eng. Chem. Fundamentals 2, (1963), 113-125.
46. S. Hartland, J.C. Mecklenburg, A comparison of differential and stagewise counter current extraction with backmixing, Chem. Eng. Sci. 21, (1966), 1209-1221.
47. J.C. Mecklenburg, S. Hartland, Two phase counter current extraction with high backmixing, Chem. Eng. Sci., 23, (1968), 1421-1430.
48. P.J.A.M. Kerkhof, H.A.C. Thijssen, Simple model describing the effect of axial mixing on counter current mass exchange, Chem. Eng. Sci. 29, (1974), 1427-1434.
49. J. van der Lijn, Simulation of heat and mass transfer in spray drying, Ph.D. Thesis Agricultural University, Pudoc, Wageningen, 1976.
50. Jun Kong Liou, An approximate method for nonlinear diffusion applied to enzyme inactivation during drying, Ph.D. Thesis Agricultural University, Wageningen, 1982.
51. J. Spaninks, Design procedures for solid-liquid extractors, Ph.D. Thesis Agricultural University, Wageningen, 1979.
52. H.A.C. Thijssen, J.A. Roels, The impact of Biotechnology on the Food Industry, Engineering and Food, 2, (1983), 833-846.
53. H.A.C. Thijssen, S. Bruin, The need for technological Developments in the Food Industry, Proceedings Symposium Progress in Food Engineering, 3-5 June 1981, Milan, Forster Verlag, Küsnacht, Switzerland, 1983, pp 5-15.
54. H.A.C. Thijssen, Process Engineering in the food industry - a growing demand, Chemistry and Industry, 12 (1975), 501-504.
55. H.A.C. Thijssen, Stimulering van gerichte produkt en procesontwikke-ling in de Nederlandse voedingsmiddelenindustrie dringend gewenst, Farewell Symposium Prof.Dr.Ir. H.A. Leniger, Wageningen, 9 december 1977, Voedingsmiddelentechnologie 11, (1978), 21-25.

56. H.A.C. Thijssen, N.S.M. van Oyen, Analysis and economic evaluation of concentration alternatives for liquid foods - quality aspects and costs of concentration, J. Food Process Engineering, 1, (1977), 215-240.

57. H.A.C. Thijssen, N.S.M. van Oyen, Concentration alternatives for fruit juices: technical, economic and quality considerations. Int. Fruchtsaft-Union, Wiss.-Tech. Komm. 15, (1978), 87-114.

58. H.A.C. Thijssen, B. van der Malen, Implications on quality of energy savings in the concentration of foods, Res. and Conservation, 7 (1981), 287-299.

Preconcentration and Drying of Food Materials, edited by S. Bruin
Elsevier Science Publishers B.V., Amsterdam, 1988 — Printed in The Netherlands

ACTIVITY OF WATER AND ITS IMPORTANCE IN PRECONCENTRATION AND
DRYING OF FOODS

Marcel Loncin

Department of Food Process Engineering
Universität D 7500 Karlsruhe (W. Germany)

Summary

Activity of water is one of the most important factors influencing
growth and thermal destruction of microorganisms as well as enzymatic or purely chemical reactions. The purpose of this paper is
to emphasize its influence on freezing, boiling and drying phenomena. The influence of heterogeneous systems (superficial activity
of water) is also considered.

Activity of water and osmotic pressure

The activity of water (a_w) is defined as:

$$a_w = x \cdot \gamma = \frac{f}{f_0}$$

with x : Mole fraction of water

γ : Activity coefficient of water

f : Fugacity of water in the system

f_0 : Fugacity of water at reference conditions

and $\mu - \mu_0 = R \cdot T \cdot \ln \frac{f}{f_0}$

μ : Chemical Potential of water in the system

μ_0 : Chemical Potential of water at reference conditions

f_0 and μ_0 are chosen arbitrarily but at the same reference
conditions.

If the gas phases are considered as ideal, the ratio of fugacities
is equal to the ratio of pressures

$$\frac{f}{f_0} = \frac{p}{p_0}$$

with p : vapor pressure of water in the system

  p_0 : vapor pressure of pure flat liquid water at the same temperature.

The error due to this assumption is normally less than 1 % under the conditions usually encountered in the food industry.

The advantages of the expression a_w are that in complex, possibly polyphase systems the mole fraction x of water is unknown and the activity coefficient is not accessible, but that the ratio

$$\frac{p}{p_0} = a_w$$

can easily be measured. In addition, although p and p_0 are very strongly dependent on temperature, their ratio can normally be considered as constant for small temperature intervals.

It is obvious that in polyphase systems, under isothermic conditions, at equilibrium, the vapor pressure of water and therefore a_w is equal for each constituent. This is perhaps the reason why some authors replace the concept a_w by "Equilibrium Relative Humidity" which can be rather confusing in some cases! The fact that the partial pressure of water in a gas (air) in equilibrium with a product is equal to the vapor pressure of water in the product is the basis for most of the methods of determination of a_w. The last published consists of hanging a droplet of a polyol like Glycerol near the product and measuring its refractive index which is correlated with a_w (ref. 1).

It is easily shown that a simple relationship exists between a_w and the osmotic pressure π

$$a_w = e^{-\frac{\tilde{V}}{R \cdot T} \cdot \pi} \tag{1}$$

with R : Constant of perfect gases ($8.314 \ J \cdot K^{-1}$)

  $\tilde{V}$: Partial molar volume of liquid water ($\sim 0.018 \ m^3$)

  T : Temperature in Kelvin (K)

  π : Osmotic pressure in Pascal (Pa)

It should be pointed out that under normal conditions the order of magnitude of the osmotic pressure is considerably higher than the vapor pressures.

For a 0.1 molar solution of sucrose, the osmotic pressure is about 10^5 Pa and the difference of vapor pressures of water at room tem-perature about 10^3 Pa.

If we consider a perfect semi-permeable membrane, the osmotic pressure in the column of liquid, considered having the density ρ_1 of water, is equal to

$$\pi = h \cdot \rho_1 \cdot g$$

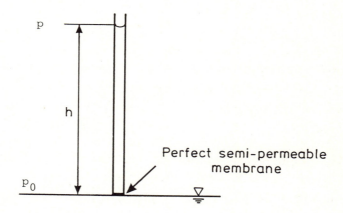

Fig. 1: column of liquid due to osmotic pressure

The vapor pressure at the top of the column (p) is lower than the vapor pressure (p_0) at the surface of free water. This difference ($p_0 - p$) is equivalent to a column of water vapor with a density ρ_g function of pressure and therefore of h.

$$dp = - \rho_g \cdot g \cdot dh$$

On the other hand

$$\rho_g = \frac{M}{V}$$

with   M : Molecular weight of water (18 kg/K·mol)
       V : Volume.

Considering that water vapor is a perfect gas (which is correct under normal partial pressures)

$$\frac{dp}{p} = - \frac{M}{R \cdot T} \cdot g \cdot dh$$

or after integration

$$\ln a_w = - \frac{\tilde{V}}{R \cdot T} \cdot \pi \qquad \text{with } \tilde{V} = \frac{M}{\rho_1}$$

which is identical with equation (1)

An approximation of eq (1) is unfortunately often used. It consists of assuming that the activity coefficient of water is equal to unity (which is completely false in concentrated solutions). In this case

$$a_w = \frac{n_w}{n_w + n_s}$$

with n_w : Number of moles of water

n_s : Number of moles (or ions) of solute

If, on the other hand, by truncating a well known series to the first term, one assumes that

$$\ln (1 - x) = -x \quad \Big| \quad + \frac{1}{2} x^2 - \frac{1}{3} x^3 \ldots\ldots$$

the following equation is obtained

$$\pi \cdot V = n_s \cdot R \cdot T \ .$$

This equation has the advantage of beeing similar to the equation of perfect gases, but is completely false in the case of concentrated solutions.

Osmotic pressure is, in the food industry, the main factor influencing a_w. This is the case for fruits and fruit juices, vegetables, bread and biscuits, jams, meat and fish products. Other factors of minor importance are:

- adsorption of water at solid-gas interfaces
- capillary condensation
- dissolution of water in the fatty phase and
- formation of crystals (α Lactose).

a_w influences enzymic reactions, the growth of microorganisms, germination of spores, chemical reactions like hydrolysis, oxida-

tion and nonenzymatic browning (Maillard Reactions), as well as
the thermal destruction of enzymes, microorganisms and spores.

It influences also important unit operations like

- freezing and freeze-concentration
- boiling
- drying and
- reserve osmosis.

Activity of water below 0 °C

In a partially frozen system at equilibrium

the chemical potential of solid water (ice) μ_s

is equal to the chemical potential
of water in the intersticial solution μ_l

It can be shown (ref. 2) that the activity of water in the solution is given by

$$\ln a_w = -\frac{\Delta h_s}{R \cdot T} \cdot (1 - \frac{T}{T_w})$$

$$+ \frac{\Delta c_p}{R} \cdot (\frac{T_w - T}{T})$$

$$- \frac{\Delta c_p}{R} \cdot \ln \frac{T_w}{T} \cdot \qquad (2)$$

with Δh_s : Molar melting enthalpy of water in $J \cdot Mol^{-1}$

or h_l : molar enthalpy of liquid water
minus
h_i : molar enthalpy of ice

T_w : Melting temperature of pure water
under 10^5 Pa   (273.15 K)

Δc_p : Difference between the heat capacity of liquid water
and ice in $J \cdot K^{-1} \cdot Mol^{-1}$.
It is assumed that Δc_p is a constant.

If, for the sake of simplification, Δh_s is considered as a constant

If the activity coefficient of water is taken equal to 1

If we assume again that ln $(1 - x) = -x$ and

If we approximate $T \cdot T_w \cong T_w^2$ we obtain the equation

$$\Delta T = \frac{R \cdot T^2}{\Delta h_s} \cdot \frac{n_s}{n_s + n_w} \tag{3}$$

which leads to acceptable results only for dilute solutions.

Approximation polynoms also exist which are much more accurate. The best known, proposed by CHIRIFE, is

$$-\ln a_w = 9.6934 \cdot 10^{-3} \cdot \Delta T + 4.761 \cdot 10^{-6} \cdot \Delta T^2$$

ΔT is the depression of melting point due to the presence of solutes dissociated or not (in ^oC or K).

The determination of a_w by cryoscopy or thermal differential analysis is very accurate for high a_w. It is one of the few practicable methods for products containing volatiles like alcoholic beverages. The figure obtained is only valid at freezing temperature but can be extrapolated to temperatures above 0 ^oC (refs. 3-4).

HARZ (ref. 2) has shown, that in aqueous solutions of carbohydrates, alcohol and organic acids encountered in beverages, mixed crystals never occur; the crystalline phase consists only of pure water even below what is supposed to be the eutectic point. Even at -63 ^oC an aqueous sucrose solution distinctly shows two phases (Fig. 2).

On the other hand glucose has been prepared by replacing protons of -O-H groups with Deuterium. A solution of this product in heavy water contains only protons linked to Carbon atoms. Every relaxation curve at -24.5, -26.7 and -29.0 ^oC can be approximated by a single exponential graph showing that no proton exists in the solid phase (Fig. 3).

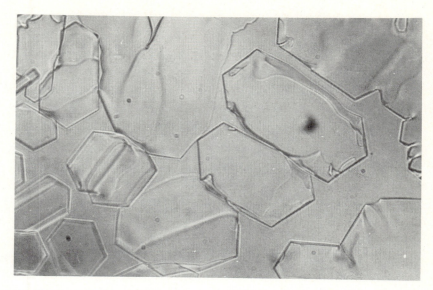

<u>Fig. 2:</u> Microscopic appearance of a 60 % aqueous sucrose
solution at -63 °C (ref. 2)

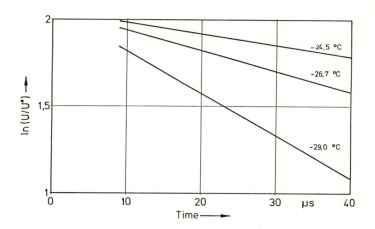

<u>Fig. 3:</u> Relaxation curves of deuterated glucose in heavy
water (ref. 2)

In a two phase system at equilibrium, the vapor pressure of water
as ice crystals and in the intersticial concentrated solution are
identical and a_w depends only on temperature.

$$a_w = \frac{\text{Vapor pressure of solid water (Ice)}}{\text{Vapor pressure of liquid, undercooled flat water}}$$

At -10 °C, a_w in an aqueous system at equilibrium containing ice crystals is equal to 260.0/286.6 = 0.907 and is independent of nature and initial concentration of solute(s) and of the presence of a third and possibly fourth phase, as in the case of ice cream.

The prediction of freezing behavior of aqueous solutions is important for freeze-concentration, for the storage of deep-frozen foods and for thawing. This is especially important in connection with use of microwaves which heat the solution but not directly the ice crystals.

Fig. 4 shows that the Margules, Wilson and UNIQUAC methods correlate very well with experimental data; the best agreement is obtained from the traditional 2nd order Margules equation.

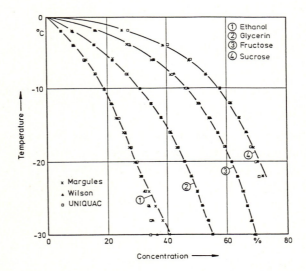

Fig. 4: Approximation of experimental freezing curves
(ref. 2)

On the contrary the UNIFAC method which includes no adjustment coefficient can not be used. It is also possible to predict the freezing curves of solutions containing several solutes like model wine or grapefruit juice (Fig. 5).

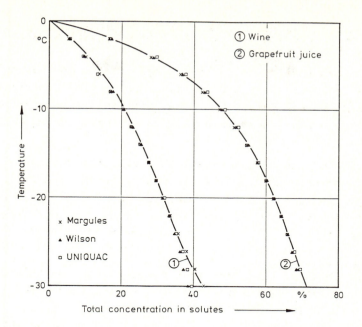

Fig. 5: Approximation of freezing curves for model solutions (ref. 2)

Here also the 2nd order Margules equation gives the best correlation.

Activity of water above 100 °C

If any substance initially containing an excess of water is heated in a closed vessel at a temperature above 100 °C and if the pressure is released in order to reach the atmospheric pressure (10^5 Pa), a_w is <u>only</u> a function of this temperature (Fig. 6).

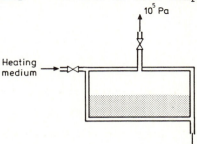

Fig. 6: Heating a product in a closed vessel above 100 °C at atmospheric pressure

The vapor pressure of water in the product is 10^5 Pa because it is in equilibrium with the atmosphere. On the other hand the vapor pressure of pure flat water is only a function of temperature e.g. $1.43 \cdot 10^5$ Pa at 110 °C.

In this case any product will have an

$$a_w = \frac{10^5}{1.43 \cdot 10^5} = 0.70$$

This does not depend on the binding forces between water and solute(s) or solid(s). The figure obtained is actually the a_w at the equilibrium temperature (above 100 °C); it can, however, be extrapolated to lower temperatures (ref. 3). This fact is very important in extrusion, where a_w at the outlet (and for a given product the water content) is a function of the temperature only.

The same is true in the case of solutions of electrolytes or non-electrolytes. A solution boiling at 110 °C under atmospheric pressure has an $a_w = 0.70$, it is not influenced by the composition and the possible presence of solids.

As in the case of freezing, sound thermodynamical equations can be developed relating the increase of boiling temperature with the concentration of solutes.

The Clausius-Clapeyron equation with finite differences can be written

$$\frac{\Delta p}{\Delta T} = \frac{p \cdot \Delta h_v}{R \cdot T^2}$$

with Δh_v : Molar enthalpy of vaporization of water in $J \cdot Mol^{-1}$.

because $\Delta p = p \cdot (1 - a_w)$

$$a_w = 1 - \frac{\Delta h_v}{R \cdot T^2} \cdot \Delta T$$

For dilute solutions the activity coefficient can be taken equal to one and the elevation of boiling point due to the presence of solutes is

$$\Delta T = \frac{R \cdot T^2}{\Delta h_v} \cdot \frac{n_s}{n_s + n_w} \tag{4}$$

which is very similar to equation (3).

It is obvious that these considerations are not limited to atmospheric pressure. The direct measurement of the vapor pressure of water at room temperature (after removal of inert gases) is probably the best method for the determination of sorption isotherms in the absence of volatiles (ref. 5).

It should be pointed out that drying in a system like Fig. 6 even under vacuum is extremely slow (even if a stirrer is incorporated) and inefficient. At 50 $^{\circ}$C at 10^4 Pa the final

$$a_w \quad = \quad \frac{10^4}{1.233 \cdot 10^4} \quad = \quad 0.81$$

corresponding for starch or protein (standard hygroscopy), to a residual water content of about 14 %!

At 50 $^{\circ}$C at 10^3 Pa the final a_w is still 0.08 and the residual water content 1.6 % for the same materials.

Very often, in modern evaporators, the increase of boiling point due to the presence of solutes is the limiting factor for the use of recompression of steam. Systems with high performance have only a temperature difference of 3 $^{\circ}$C, or even less, between condensing steam and boiling liquid. They require an energy of less than 10 kwh to evaporate 1000 kg of water; that means less than 1 % of the energy required by conventional drying.

It is hardly worthwhile recalling that besides membrane fouling, a_w (or the osmotic pressure of solutions) is the most important factor influencing the practical use of reverse osmosis (ref. 6). Let us mention the new "SEPARA" systems developed by F.M.C.-DUPONT which allow to concentrate fruit juices by reverse osmosis up to 65 Brix corresponding to several hundred bar.

Activity of water and drying rate

Water can be removed

by boiling off: in this case the vapor pressure of water reaches
the total pressure;

by diffusion: in this case the driving force is the difference
between the vapor pressure of water at the surface of the product
and the partial pressure of water in the gas (usually air) used as
drying aid.

Intermediate phenomena also exist where boiling and diffusion
coexist, especially the spray and drum drying of liquids and pasta
(ref.7).

In the case of *boiling*, the rate of drying is only a function of
the heat transfer between heating medium and wall, inside the
wall, between wall and product and in the product itself. When the
boiling temperature is reached, the solvent (water) boils off
(Fig. 6). Mass transfer influences only the drying rate of some
solids because of the possible migration of solvent from cold to
hot regions (ref. 8).

In the case of *diffusion*, the rate of drying is given by equation:

$$(H_2\overset{\cdot}{O}) = \frac{d(H_2O)}{dt} = A \cdot \beta \cdot (P_{solid} - P_{air}) \qquad (5)$$

$(H_2\overset{\cdot}{O}) = \dfrac{d(H_2O)}{dt}$ is the rate of drying in kg water$\cdot$s^{-1}

A $\qquad$ is the interfacial area between air and solid
or liquid to be dried

β $\qquad$ is the mass transfer coefficient, which can be
obtained from classical equations relating

Sh $\quad$ Sherwood Number $\quad$ to
Sc $\quad$ Schmidt $\qquad$ " $\qquad$ and
Re $\quad$ Reynolds $\qquad$ " $\qquad$ in
the case of forced convection or
Gr $\quad$ Grashof Number $\quad$ in
the case of free convection

P_{solid} $\qquad$ is the vapor pressure of water at the surface of
the product visualized as a solid

P_{air} is the partial pressure of water in the bulk of the gas phase

Equation (5) relates the drying rate to the gas phase. It is physically sound so are following assumptions:

A   does not depend on the water content except for the shrinkage which can easily be taken into account. However changes of shape and agglomeration phenomena can play an important role.

β depends only on the properties of air (Sc) and flow phenomena (Re or Gr) but not on a_w at the surface.

P_{air} is an average value outside the boundary layer. In a steady state it is function of the coordinates but not of the time. It results from mass balances and can be easily calculated for fluidized beds. For multilayers it can be more difficult to calculate because of channelling.

P_{solid} is basically a function of mass transfer inside the solid; its prediction is much more difficult mainly because the rate of mass transfer in solids is highly dependent on the water content.

                     The accumulation of solutes at the surface (case hardening) plays also an important role.

Basically P_{solid} can be taken equal to

$$P_0 \cdot a_{wo}$$

a_{wo} is the activity of water at the surface or interface

P_0 is the vapor pressure of pure flat water at the temperature of the surface of the product. It depends only on this temperature

a_{wo} can be calculated by three methods (ref. 9), which give excellent agreement as shown in table Fig. 7

1. method consists of measuring the "wet" bulb temperature of a sample
2. method consists of measuring the "wet" bulb temperature and the drying rate of a sample
3. method consists of measuring the drying rate only.

sample	drying time (R.H.$_{air}$= 0.30) ϑ_{air} = 32 °C	a_{wo}		
		1.method	2.method	3.method
agar	3 h	1.0	1.0	1.0
agar containing 30 % sucrose	0.5 h	0.77	0.77	0.76
agar containing 30 % sucrose	1.5 h	0.46	0.47	0.46
agar containing 30 % sucrose	2.5 h	0.41	0.41	0.41
peeled apples	1 h	0.90	0.88	0.85
peeled apples	3 h	0.62	0.61	0.58
peeled carrots	1 h	0.93	0.92	0.90

Fig. 7: Activity of water at the surface (a_{wo}) determined by
three different methods (ref. 9)

It should be pointed out that a_{wo} influences not only the drying
rate but also chemical and especially biochemical reactions like
the growth of microorganisms and enzymic browning.

It can also be easily demonstrated, that due to the fact, that the
Lewis number (Le) of wet air is not very different from unity a
simple relationship exists between coefficient of mass transfer
(β) and coefficient of heat transfer (α). In the international system of units this equation is

$$\frac{\alpha}{\beta \cdot \Delta H} = 64.7$$

ΔH is the mean enthalpy of vaporization of 1 kg water in the range
of temperatures considered.

Decrease of apparent interfacial activity of water

The activity of water at interfaces can be very different from a_w inside the product in various situations, which are summarized on Fig. 8.

a_w at the surface (a_{wo}) is different from

a_w inside

- if dry air is in contact with moist solids

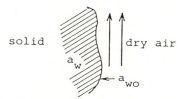

- if humidification occurs (e.g. before milling)

- if temperatures change or differ in packaged goods

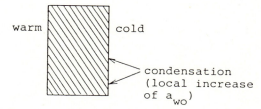

- if solubility suddenly changes (e.g. by heating of o/w-emulsions)

Fig. 8: Situations where an heterogeneity of water activities takes place (ref. 9)

As already shown on Fig. 7 a_{wo} is a function of the drying conditions and of the time. It is clear, that if the velocity of air is equal to zero (closed system) and if the air remains in contact with the product long enough, the relative humidity of the gas phase will be numerically equal to the activity of water of the product.

If the velocity of the gas phase increases and if its relative humidity is lower than the activity of water of the solid, the activity of water at the interface (a_{wo}) decreases (Fig. 9). If diffusion phenomena in the solid are slow enough compared to the rate of exchange between solid and air, they become the controlling factor and a_{wo} becomes equal to the relative humidity of the bulk of the gas phase.

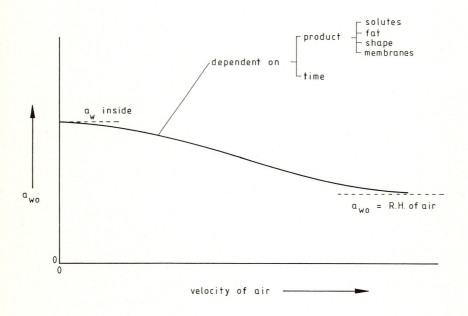

Fig. 9: Influence of the velocity of air on the activity of water at the interface (ref. 9)

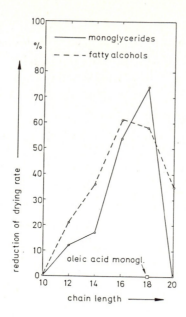

Fig. 10: Reduction of drying rate under standard conditions
        (ref. 10)

As already shown in 1965 with LENGES, some saturated Monoglycerides, decrease like Cetyl Alcohol, the rate of evaporation of water. In the case of solids this can be expressed as an apparent
decrease of a_{wo} in a dynamic system.

More recently ROTH (ref. 10) has confirmed, that this action is
maximum for Glycerol Monostearate (Fig. 10).

More important is the fact, that this retarding action is due to a
single monolayer of Monoglycerides. This has been demonstrated by
dipping on agar gel (98 % water) in a Langmuir Trough, covering
the surface of water with a monolayer and removing the gel slowly
while maintaining the film pressure constant. This is obtained by
decreasing the free surface of water in the Langmuir Trough; this
decrease is exactly equal to the area of the agar gel.

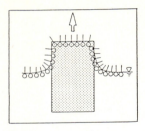

<u>Fig. 11:</u> "Transplantation" of a Monolayer of Glycerol
             Monostearate (ref. 10)

It is also remarkable that the inhibition of drying by Glycerol
Monostearate is much more important at low temperatures (Fig. 12).

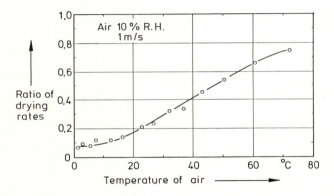

<u>Fig. 12:</u> Ratio: Drying rate with Monoglycerides / Drying rate
             of the untreated gel (ref. 10)

This can be explained by a sort of "crystalisation" or orientation
of the arrays of Glycerol Monostearate at low temperature. The selectivity of the C_{18} chain is probably due to the necessity of having a layer thick enough to decrease the rate of mass transfer
(lower limit) and to the "brittleness" of longer chains (upper limit) (ref. 11).

The use of Glycerol Monostearate reduces dramatically the loss of
weight during cooling and storage of meat, it improves the appearance of cheese slices and reduces the withering of lettuce. As a

monolayer the concentration calculated on the total mass is normally less than 1 p.p.m. This use is not patented.

Conclusions

The activity of water besides its influence on chemical and biochemical reactions plays an important role in various unit operations.

Sometimes a_w in the bulk of a solid or a liquid determines this influence. It is the case for freezing, freeze concentration, evaporation, reverse osmosis and for some kinds of drying. Mechanical properties like elasticity, rheological behavior are also influenced by a_w inside the product.

On the other hand most practical case of air drying, agglomeration, appearance depend on the activity of water at the interface (a_{wo}), which can be influenced under dynamic conditions by surface active agents like Glycerol Monostearate.

References   (Limited to 1985 - 1987)

1 R.J. Steele, Use of Polyols to measure Equilibrium Relative
   Humidity, Int. Journal of Food Science and Technol., 22 (1987)
   377-384.
2 H.-P. Harz, Untersuchungen zum Gefrierverhalten flüssiger
   Lebensmittel im Hinblick auf das Gefrierlagern, Gefrier-
   trocknen und Gefrierkonzentrieren, Dissertation Universität
   Karlsruhe (1987).
3 H. Weisser, Influence of temperature on sorption isotherms,
   in: M. Le Maguer und P. Jelen, Food Engineering and Process
   Applications (1986) 189-200.
4 C.S. Chen, Calculation of water activity and activity
   voefficient of sugar solutions and some liquid foods, Lebensm.
   Wiss. u. Technol. 20 (1987) 64-67.
5 A.L. Benado and S.S.H. Rizvi, Water activity calculation by
   direct measurement of vapor pressure, Journal of Food Science
   52 (1987) 429-432.
6 H.T. Chua, M.A. Rao, T.E. Acre and D.G. Cunningham, Reverse
   osmosis concentration of apple juice, Journal of Food Process
   Engineering 9 (1987) 231-245.
7 J. Vasseur, G. Trystram et F. Abchir, Modelisation du séchage
   sur cylindre, 1. Congrès National de Génie des Procédés, Edit.
   Lavoisier-Technique et Documentation, 1(1987) 279-294.
8 E. Tsotsas, E.U. Schlünder, Vacuum contact drying of
   mechanically agitated beds: The Influence of Hygroscopie
   behaviour on the Drying Rate Curve, Chem. Eng. Process. 21
   (1987) 4, 199-208.

34

9   T. Roth and M. Loncin, Superficial activity of water, in: D.
    Simatos, J.L. Multon, Properties of Water in Foods, Martinus
    Nijhoff Publ., Dordrecht (1985) 331-342.

10 T. Roth, Verminderung des Stoffübergangs an wäßrigen
    Oberflächen durch grenzflächenaktive Stoffe, Dissertation
    Universität Karlsruhe (1986).

11 G.T. Barnes, The effects of monolayer on the evaporation of
    liquids, Advances in Colloid and Interface Science 25 (1986)
    89-200.

PRECONCENTRATION

Preconcentration and Drying of Food Materials, edited by S. Bruin
Elsevier Science Publishers B.V., Amsterdam, 1988 — Printed in The Netherlands

PRECONCENTRATION: NEW DEVELOPMENTS

B. Hallström

Department of Food Engineering, Lund University, P.O. Box 124,
S-221 00 Lund (Sweden)

ABSTRACT

Recent developments are reviewed with special regard to design and energy conservation.

The falling film concept was introduced during the 40's and the different designs developed since then are presented. The most common falling film evaporators have cylindrical tubes as the heating surface; the advantages and drawbacks of this geometry are discussed. When the liquid to be concentrated flows through the cylindrical tube its amount diminishes. This leads to wetting problems if the feed is not increased which, however, results in a lower concentration ratio. Simultaneously vapour is formed along the tube resulting in an increasing volume flow. These two phenomena demand an evaporation channel with decreasing wetted perimeter and increasing cross-sectional flow area. These conditions seem contradictory and obviously a cylindrical tube is more or less a compromise. However, a recent design offers a way of overcoming this problem. This new evaporator is presented.

More than ten years ago, the cost of energy increased considerably and this forced manufacturers of evaporators to design arrangements with lower energy consumption. Evaporation and drying are two of the most energy demanding unit operations and therefore special effort was devoted to the problem. Multiple-stage evaporators, and thermal and mechanical compression were the solutions. These different arrangements are reviewed and analysed.

INTRODUCTION

In the past several state-of-the-art papers on evaporators have been issued. This unit operation has gained a lot of interest especially after the sudden increase in energy costs in 1973. In 1974 Thijssen wrote the paper "Fundamentals of Concentration Processes" (1) covering all aspects of evaporation as well as other concentration processes. In the same year, Mannheim and Passy produced the paper "Non-membrane Concentration" (2) which was more specifically directed towards evaporation. In 1977, Schwartzberg analysed "Energy requirements for liquid concentration" (3). An interesting analysis of concentration alternatives was made by Thijssen and van Oyen in 1977 (4). A later, important contribution was made by Wiegand in 1985 (5). Papers by Knipschildt (6) and Kessler (7) should also be mentioned.

In the following, mainly the falling film concept will be considered and some basic research in this field will also be referred to. Thus, several PhD theses should be mentioned (8,9,10,11). These theses are all mainly concerned with heat transfer problems.

TABLE I Literature overview

Author (Ref.)	Separation theory	Heat transfer	Design	Fouling	Energy
Thijssen 1974 (1)	x				x
Mannheim and Passy 1974 (2)			x	x	
Schwartzberg 1977 (3)					x
Thijssen and van Oyen 1977 (4)	x				x
Wiegand 1985 (5)			x	x	x
Knipschildt 1986 (6)			x		
Kessler 1987 (7)				x	
Chun (8)		x			
Persson 1978 (9)		x			
Papendieck 1984 (10)		x			
Fiedler 1985 (11)		x		x	

THE DEVELOPMENT OF THE FALLING FILM CONCEPT

The falling film concept was introduced by D D Peebles and P D V Manning in 1935 and the first patents are from this period (12). No real progress was then made until after World War II. Wiegand first introduced this design in Europe but soon falling film evaporators were being manufactured by several evaporator companies.

One important feature of the falling film principle is the very small amount of liquid contained in each tube during evaporation. In this way, a maximum concentration ratio can be reached in single pass flow. Further, due to the difference in function compared with the older, climbing film evaporator, a much smaller temperature difference was needed between the heating medium and the evaporating liquid. This made the design much more favourable for multiple-stage arrangements. These important features are the reason why the falling film evaporator soon became the dominating evaporator in the food industry, and still is.

Wetting figure

For many years the normal design consisted of 1½" or 2" tubes in 4 m length. An important role in the design procedure is the liquid coverage or wetting parameter, being the amount of liquid fed to each tube, sometimes calculated as the amount of liquid per metre tube perimeter (circumference). If this number is too small the tube will not be completely covered by the liquid and dry spots will occur, leading to crust formation and capacity losses. On the other hand, if a too high wetting figure is chosen the concentration ratio in single pass mode is lower and the required final concentration is not reached.

It is obvious that there is a close relationship between the length of the tube and the wetting of the surface. This has resulted in the length of the tubes today being in many cases, 12-15 m.

A drawback of the longer tubes - apart from the height of the apparatus - is the increased vapour velocity in the tube outlet due to the extra vapour formed. This may again result in dry spots - the concentrate in the outlet end of the tube may also be blown away. To overcome these problems modifications of the tube evaporator concept were introduced.

Modified designs

An attempt at a modified design was made by Wiegand (1976) who used a special climbing film "Drallstromrohr" in a falling film plant (13). This tube had an increasing area as vapour was formed along the tube, thus maintaining a film and accordingly minimizing the liquid content of the tube in comparison with a normal climbing or falling film tube.

The Finnish company MKT designed conical falling film tubes with the perimeter decreasing along the tube (14). This solved the wetting problem but the high vapour velocity at tube outlet was still a problem.

The opposite holds true for the Alfa Laval Expanding Flow evaporator (2). The heating surface consists of a stack of conical plates. The liquid to be concentrated is fed to alternate spaces through nozzles in a central spindle. As the liquid passes upwards and outwards in a channel of increasing flow area, it evaporates. The mixture of concentrated liquid and vapour formed leaves the cones at their outer peripheries. Primary steam is introduced at the periphery of alternate conical channels. In this design, wetting at the outlet became a problem while the vapour velocity could be controlled.

The falling film concept has also been applied to a plate design. A combined climbing and falling film concept was introduced by APV in 1957 (2). Several modifications have been made since then, and in 1974 APV introduced a plate evaporator with only a falling film. This type of equipment is still very successful for many applications. A similar design has been developed by Schmidt-Bretten (1983) (15). There is also similar Japanese equipment on the market. This equipment is characterized by an apparatus height much lower than the falling film tube equipment. However, as far as is known, they also all have evaporator channels with constant width and constant flow area.

Optimization

One important parameter in this type of evaporator is - as mentioned - the wetting figure (surface coverage). Each liquid at each concentration is characterized by a minimum figure below which the liquid film flowing along a surface will break up leading to the formation of dry spots and incrustation which will start to decrease the capacity. It is possible to estimate this figure through experiments. It is therefore possible to calculate the ideal width of the heating surface (circumference or perimeter) giving sufficient coverage at each length coordinate The diagrams (fig. 1) show an example: the perimeter and the concentration ratio versus the length of the surface are calculated based on the assumptions given in table II.

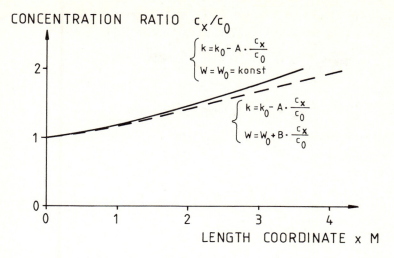

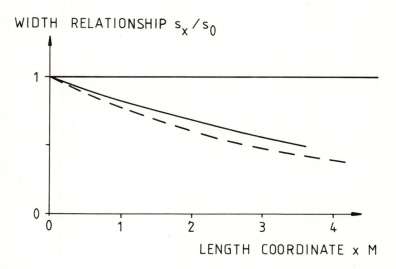

<u>Fig.</u>1

Width of heating surface and concentration ratio versus length
coordinate.

TABLE II

Comparison of channel lengths for different surface configurations.
Concentration ratio 2:1
Single pass flow
Temperature difference 5 K

1. Minimum wetting figure independent of concentration/viscosity

	Decreasing channel width		Constant channel width: cylindrical tube	
	Inlet	Outlet	Inlet	Outlet
Wetting figure, kg/m h	150	150	300	150
k_x/k_o	1	0.91	1	0.91
s_x/s_o	1	0.5	1	1
Length, m		3.61		5.19

2. Minimum wetting figure vs concentration/viscosity

Wetting figure, kg/m h	150	200	400	200
k_x/k_o	1	0.91	1	0.91
s_x/s_o	1	0.375	1	1
Length, m		4.15		6.91

In this table a comparison is also made with tubular cylindrical channels,
i.e. normal falling film tubes.

When constant wetting is required along the whole channel, we have
used the figure 150 kg/m h. The required length will be 3.61 m. Using the
same k value and the same k value decrease with concentration we need a
tube of length 5.19 m. In the second, more realistic, case a wetting
figure which increases with concentration/viscosity is used. We used the
same wetting figure at the outlet of the two channels to be compared, 200
kg/m h. For the tube we need a length of 6.91 m, while the ideal channel
requires only 4.15 m, a reduction of 40%. Practically, as will be seen
below, the tubular design needs a higher outlet wetting figure than the
channel and this makes the difference even more pronounced. The same heat
transfer coefficients have been used in both cases, but a true analysis
should also consider differences in this respect.

Obviously, it is possible to design an optimal evaporator heating surface with regard to wetting. By means of the diagrams one can find the minimum length necessary to reach a required concentration ratio.

However, there is one more condition to be considered and that is the vapour velocity. This velocity, especially at the tube or channel outlet, should not be too high in order not to blow away the liquid film. In tubular falling film channels this can be a problem, especially in very long tubes. These conditions therefore call for increasing area versus the length in order to avoid too high vapour velocity.

A new design

These two conditions - decreasing perimeter and increasing area versus channel length - seem to be contradictory. A channel with constant dimensions along the length coordinate, i.e. a cylindrical tube, certainly does not fulfil these criteria. However, geometrically it is possible to design channels which satisfy the conditions specified. Such an arrangement is covered by recent patents and has been on the market since last year (16). The patented design is such that the vapour space increases (working down from the top) so that a low vapour velocity is maintained. Similarly, the wetted perimeter, i.e. the heating surface width, decreases in order to maintain as constant a liquid film thickness as possible. Fig. 2 shows the design principle. Today's advanced workshop techniques make it possible to manufacture this type of heating surface. However, another important feature of this design is that all supporting points in the evaporation channel have been avoided. Earlier plate evaporators require supports between the plates in order to maintain a defined distance. Such supports disturb the flow, especially at low wetting figures. In the present design these supports are completely avoided by means of a special cassette design.

The next diagram (fig 3) shows a comparison of the performance of a conventional falling film tubular evaporator (van der Ploeg, tubes 4 m 35.5/38 mm) and the cassette design shown in the previous figure (Alfa Laval ACE Cassette Evaporator, channel length 2 m). The diagram shows the

44

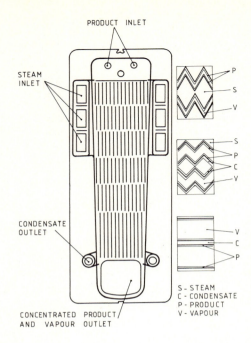

Fig 2

Principal design of the cassette evaporator. To the right sections
of the steam and vapour channels at the top, middle and bottom.

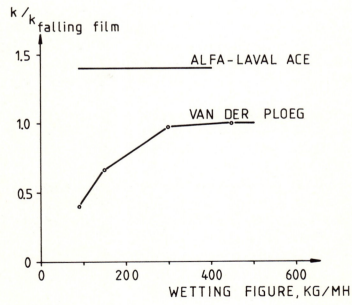

Fig. 3

Comparison of the apparent heat transfer coefficients for a falling
film tubular evaporator and the cassette evaporator.

k value under similar evaporation conditions versus the wetting figure. When the figure is decreased, i.e. when the feed is reduced, the whole heating surface is not covered, resulting in an apparent decrease in the k value. The diagram shows that it is possible to operate the new evaporator at a lower wetting figure than the tubular one, thus verifying the above-mentioned theories. Several plants are now operating at a wetting figure of about 100 kg/m h.

ENERGY CONSIDERATIONS

The principle, as well as the practical use of multiple-stage arrangements, is very old. In the food industry, especially in dairy and fruit juice processing, the number of effects increased after 1973.

The number of effects is limited by the total temperature difference available. The maximum temperature is defined by the thermal stability of the product (quality degradation, incrustation). The lower temperature is determined by available cooling facilities for the condenser and sometimes the viscosity of the product.

The principle of thermal vapour recompression (TVR) has been well known for many years and is already an established process in multiple-stage plants.

Mechanical vapour recompression (MVR) is also an old principle but was scarcely used before 1973. Due to the favourable cost of electric power compared with oil, MVR is common today in several countries. Both fans (ventilators) and turbocompressors are used. Fans are preferred for plants smaller than 20 t/h evaporated vapour. In this case, the pressure increase is limited to about 20%, corresponding to a temperature rise of about $4^{o}C$ in the range 60-70 ^{o}C (5). Turbocompressors are able to reach a pressure increase of about 80%, resulting in a temperature rise of about $14^{o}C$ (5). These are normally used for large plants.

Calculation of energy input

Depending on the concentration process used, either thermal energy, electrical/mechanical energy or, as in most cases, both are required. As these forms of energy are not directly comparable, the energy input must be transformed into an equivalent energy form.

Thermal energy is generated from oil at a very high efficiency, 80-90%. Producing electrical/mechanical energy from oil leads to a much lower efficiency, normally in the region of 30%. To add these energy forms together to form a total (steam-) equivalent energy input, electrical energy input has to be multiplied by a "heat-to-power" factor. Schwartzberg (3), in his calculations, used a factor of 3, while Thijssen (4), calculating his factor in slightly different way, reached a value of 2.84. Kessler (7), on the other hand used a figure of 2.5 by multiplying the specific electric power demand by 3 and the specific steam demand by 1.2. This figure varies since electricity is generated not only from oil but also from other sources (hydraulic power, nuclear power) and the relationship also varies from one country to another. However, what is of real interest to the processing industry is the price it has to pay per kg of water evaporated. So the sum of the costs of electrical power and steam is the figure of interest, or their relationship (4, 17):

$$\frac{\text{cost of 1 kWh}}{\text{cost of 1 kg steam}}$$

This relationship depends not only on how local energy is produced, but also on national taxes etc.

TABLE III
Comparison of energy requirements (17)

Type of plant	Direct energy input		Eq. energy input kWh/kg
	Steam kg/kg	Power kWh/kg	
Evaporation			
TVR 3 effects	0.20 - 0.25	0.003	0.17 - 0.20
5	0.13 - 0.17	0.003	0.11 - 0.14
7	0.077 - 0.13	0.003	0.07 - 0.10
MVR	0.02	0.010 - 0.030	0.046 - 0.11
RO		0.005 - 0.012	0.015 - 0.048

In this table a "heat-to-power" ratio of 3 has been used. For comparison reverse osmosis (RO) is also included.

Comparison of energy costs

The diagram (fig. 4) has been designed as follows.

S_E Cost of evaporating 1 kg water
S_s Cost of producing 1 kg steam
S_p Cost of 1 kWh
P_s Specific steam requirement
P_p Specific power requirement

$$S_E = P_s \cdot S_s + P_p \cdot S_p$$

$$= S_s \left(P_s + P_p \cdot \frac{S_p}{S_s} \right)$$

$$\frac{S_E}{S_s} = P_s + P_p \frac{S_p}{S_s}$$

In the diagram S_E/S_s is plotted versus S_p/S_s (fig. 4). This means that the cost of evaporating 1 kg of water is expressed in relation to the cost of producing 1 kg of steam. On the other axis, the relationship between the cost of 1 kWh and the cost of producing 1 kg of steam is expressed. Only the lower figures from table III have been used. The energy costs used are given in table IV.

TABLE IV

Energy costs used in figure 4 (1986)

	Power, S_p	Steam, S_s	S_p/S_s
France	F 0.29/kWh	F 0.135/kg	2.2
US	$ 0.07/kWh	$ 0.013/kg	5.4
West Germany	DM 0.20/kWh	DM 0.06 /kg	3.3
Thijssen 1974 (4)	–	–	7.0

48

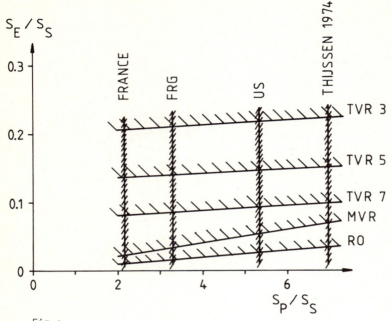

Fig.4
Energy costs for different concentration alternatives.

The influence of the increasing cost of oil is observable in the diagram. The European situation before 1973 is illustrated to the right in the diagram. As oil prices increase the conditions are moved towards the left. Accordingly, to the left we find countries with favorable prices of electric power while to the right the US are still producing steam at a rather low price.

The diagram also shows in which countries MVR and RO are in progress.

REFERENCES

1 H.A.C Thijssen. Fundamentals of concentration processes. In: A Spicer
   (Editor), Advances in Preconcentration and Dehydration of Foods.
   Applied Science Publishers Ltd London, 1974, 13-44.
2 C.H. Mannheim and N. Passy. Non-membrane concentration. In: A Spicer
   (Editor), Advances in Preconcentration and Dehydration of Foods.
   Applied Science Publishers Ltd London, 1974, 151-201.
3 H.G. Schwartzberg. Energy requirements for liquid concentration.
   Food Technol., March 1977, 67-76.
4 H.A.C Thijssen and N.S.M van Oyen. Analysis and evaluation of
   concentration alternatives for liquid foods. In Preprints: 7th
   European Symposium Food Product and Process Selection in the Food
   Industry. Eindhoven 1977.
5 B. Wiegand. Evaporation. In: R Hansen (Editor) Evaporation, Membrane-
   filtration and Spraydrying. North European Dairy Journal, Denmark
   1985, 91-177.
6 M.E. Knipschildt. Drying of Milk and Milk Products. In R K Robinson
   (Editor) Modern Dairy Technology. Elsevier Applied Science Publishers,
   London and New York 1986, 131-234.
7 H.G. Kessler. Multistage evaporation and water vapour recompression
   with special emphasis on high dry matter content, product losses,
   cleaning and energy savings. In Milk - The vital force. D Reidel
   Publishing Co. 1987, 545-558.
8 K.R. Chun. Evaporation from the liquids. Dissertation University
   of California.
9 L. Persson. Klentubsindunstaren - en experimentell och teoretisk
   undersökning. Dissertation Lund University 1978.
10 H. Papendieck. Strömung und Wärmeübergang in welligen Flüssig-
   keitsfilmen. Dissertation T U Braunsweig 1984.
11 J. Fiedler. Ansatzbildung durch Milchsalze und Molkenproteine
   beim Eindampfen von Molke und Ultrafiltrations-permeat in einen
   Fallfilmsverdampfer. 1985.
12 D. Peebles. US Patents 2090985 and 2168362, 1935.
13 B. Wiegand. Kombinierte Kletter- und Fallstromeindampfanlagen für
   die Milchindustrie. Deutsche Milchwirtschaft 23, 1976, 681-682.
14 MKT Tehtaat Oy. Brochure Evaporators. 1972.
15 M. Dimitrion. Sigmaster concentration plants with aroma recovery.
   Operation experience and new developments. Broschure. 1986.
16 U. Bolmstedt, B. Hallström, B.O. Johansson and O. Olsson. Swedish
   Patents 8008594-7 and 8008595-4. 1982.
17 B. Hallström. Energy Consumption in Membrane Processing of Foods.
   In RP Singh (Editor) Energy in Food Processing. Elsevier, 1986.

Preconcentration and Drying of Food Materials, edited by S. Bruin
Elsevier Science Publishers B.V., Amsterdam, 1988 — Printed in The Netherlands

MULTISTAGE EVAPORATION IN THE DAIRY INDUSTRY:
ENERGY SAVINGS, PRODUCT LOSSES AND CLEANING

S. Bouman, D.W. Brinkman, P. de Jong, R. Waalewijn.
NIZO, P.O. Box 20, 6710 BA Ede, Netherlands

SUMMARY
    In the dairy industry multistage falling-film evaporators are used to
concentrate skim milk, whole milk and whey. In recent years a great
development has taken place in evaporation plants to reduce the energy
consumption. A modern evaporator design will give a specific energy
consumption of 0.1 (kg steam per kg water evaporation).
    Energy savings can be achieved by increasing the number of effects. More
effects, however, also increase the heating surface area and the investment
costs. Larger heating surface areas also can cause an increase in the amount
of deposits and in the costs of product losses and waste water disposal.
    The results of experiments are discussed and recommendations are given for
minimizing total evaporation costs, including investment and energy costs, and
also costs of product losses and waste water disposal. Suggestions are given
of ways to improve the cleaning procedure.

INTRODUCTION

    In 1986 over 12 thousand million kilograms of milk were produced in the

Netherlands. Twenty-five per cent of this amount was used for the production

of milk powder, and forty-one per cent for cheesemaking. In the latter

process, for the Dutch situation, roughly the same amount of whey is produced,

which serves as a basis for making whey powder. The production methods for

skim milk powder, whole milk powder and whey powder are quite similar.

Concentration of the thin liquid takes place in a multi-stage falling-film

evaporator. The viscous concentrate leaving the evaporator is atomised and

dried in spray-towers. From the point of view of energy consumption it is more

economical to concentrate with evaporators to the highest possible dry matter

content, 70 % to 90 % of the water present in the thin product being removed

by falling-film evaporation.

    This article gives the results of research work carried out at NIZO with

the aim of reducing energy in production costs. The first part of this

contribution deals with what is possible in reducing the energy consumption.

It is based on a study carried out in the Dutch dairy industry by Jansen et

al. (1). The second part gives the results of the investigations to establish

the magnitude of product losses caused by fouling of the heat-exchanging

surface in falling-film evaporators for whole and skim milk.

EVAPORATORS IN THE DAIRY INDUSTRY

In the dairy industry falling-film evaporators are commonly used. The heat exchange surface consists of a bundle of vertical tubes. Figure 1 shows schematically the procedure in one tube. The liquid to be concentrated flows down inside the heating tubes as a film. The downward movement of the film is caused by gravity and is increasingly supported by the developing vapours flow in the tubes.

In recent years a great development has taken place in evaporation plants to reduce the energy consumption. Relatively small evaporators were replaced by 6 or 7 effects evaporators with thermal vapour recompression. In modern evaporators longer heating tubes also are chosen, up to 12 metres in length or even more. Fig. 2 shows a simplified flowsheet of a modern 6-effects evaporator with a specific energy consumption of only about 0.10. This means that only 0.1 ton of steam is needed to evaporate 1 ton of water from the product.

Figure 1. Falling-film evaporator

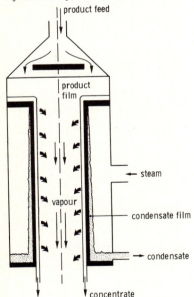

Product distribution

A uniform distribution of the product at the feed inlet is required to guarantee a sufficient supply of liquid to each of the tubes. The distribution device has to fulfil the following functions (2):
- to distribute the product uniformly between the tubes;
- to distribute the product evenly on the circumference of each heating tube.

Figure 2. Flowchart of a modern evaporator with 6 effects and thermal vapour recompression.

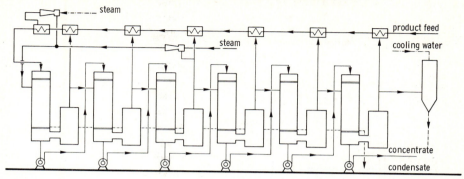

Figure 3 shows a possible way of distributing the product over the tubes. Pre-distribution is achieved by means of a distribution bowl. Also pre-distribution plates with product holes in the bottom are used. The flash vapour which develops in the headspace of an effect flows downwards through small tubes in the distribution plate. By these vapour tubes, which are placed just above the evaporation tubes, the difference in pressure over the distribution plate is reduced to a minimum and the desired level of the liquid on the plate can be achieved.

Energy savings

It is common knowledge that by increasing the number of vacuum units ('effects') of an evaporator the energy consumption decreases (3). In Figure 4 the relation between the energy consumption and the number of effects is

Figure 3. Liquid distribution in a falling-film evaporator.

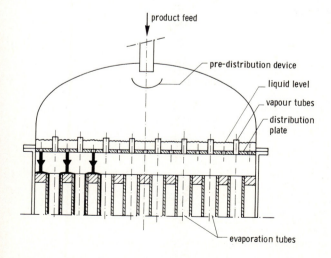

Figure 4. Energy consumption in relation to the number of effects.

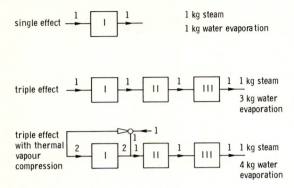

given. Recompression of a part of the vapours will also decrease the steam consumption. For the design of a plant the total temperature difference over the effects is depending on the properties of the product to be concentrated. The larger the number of effects at a given overall temperature range, the smaller the differences between the temperatures in the effects will be. This results in an increased heat-exchanging surface area.

Jansen et al. (1) have given the relation between the steam consumption and the heat-exchanging area for different lay-outs of the evaporation plant; see Figure 5. All the evaporators mentioned have the same capacity:
- feed: 30.000 kg/h, 9 % TS;
- concentrate: 5.400 kg/h, 50 % TS;
- water evaporation: 24.600 kg/h.

Figure 5. Energy consumption in relation to the heating surface area for different lay-outs of the plant.
D/S: ratio vapour/live steam; T_p: pasteurisation temperature;
p_s: steam pressure

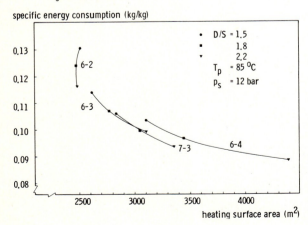

It appears that the energy consumption depends on the number of effects and the position and efficiency of the vapour compressor. Lower energy consumptions need larger heating surface areas and higher costs of investments.

PRODUCT LOSSES

Measurements

Several evaporators for whole and skim milk in the dairy industry were investigated. The operating conditions during the running time and the product losses during cleaning of the plant were measured. During the operating time the following parameters describing the evaporation process were measured: the product temperatures and the evaporating temperatures in the effects, the flow rate of the feed and the concentrate, the dry matter content (density) of the concentrate and the steam consumption.

After a production run of about 20 hours the cleaning was accomplished in the following sequence:
- rinsing with water;
- cleaning with sodium hydroxide;
- intermediate rinsing with water;
- cleaning with acid;
- rinsing with water.

At the end of production, water was admitted to the feed tank to drive out the product from the evaporator. When the water arrived at the end of the evaporator the outcoming flow was switched over from the concentrate tank to the sewage system. The quantity of milk solids still present in the rinsing

Table 1. Product losses caused by fouling in two evaporation plants.

number of effects		4	7	7	7
whole or skim milk		whole	skim	whole	whole
pasteurization temp.	(^{0}C)	89	85	85	108
rinsing losses	(kg)	50	280	400	560
burn losses in pré-heaters and heaters	(kg)	n. m. [1]	n. m.	330	440
total burn losses (as perc. of total losses)	(kg) (%)	370 (88)	1290 (82)	7250 (95)	9750 (95)
degree of pollution	(IE)[2]	310	890	7300	9270
specific losses (kg thin milk as perc. of capacity)	(%)	0.1	0.1	0.9	1.3
specific losses (kg thin milk per m^2)	(kg/m^2)	1.3	0.3	1.5	2.0

[1] n. m. = not measured
[2] IE = Inhabitant Equivalent = waste water disposal unit

water when it is switched over forms the so-called rinsing-losses. The product
residuals in the sodium hydroxide and acid cleaning solutions cause the
so-called burned-on losses. Both the rinsing and the burned-on losses were
measured by analysing the cleaning solutions. The results for two evaporation
plants are given in Table 1. The losses of milk components were converted to
kg thin milk. The losses of whole milk were 0.1 to 1.3 per cent of the feed
and expressed per m^2 heat exchanging surface area (the specific product
losses) 1.3 to 2.0 kg/m^2. For skim milk the product losses were 0.1 per cent
of the feed or 0.3 kg/m^2.

Inspection

From inspection of the evaporators, right after the end of production and
before cleaning, it appeared that in many cases the liquid was not distributed
uniformly over all tubes. In the photograph in Figure 6 the consequences are
seen: in some groups of tubes the amount of deposit is much higher than in
other ones.

It is recognized that a critical component in falling-film evaporators is
the distribution device. The product must be distributed uniformly at the feed
inlet to assure a sufficient supply of liquid to each tube. If a distributor

Figure 6. Fouling caused by a non-uniform distribution.

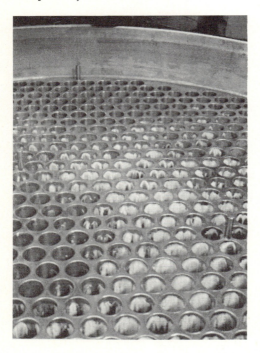

does not satisfy this condition adequately, individual heating tubes will not be provided with sufficient liquid and there is consequently the danger of deposit formation.

COSTS OF EVAPORATION

The total evaporation costs depend on the steam consumption, the specific surface area of the evaporator and on the specific product losses. In Figure 7 these costs are given in relation to the specific surface area, which is defined as the ratio of the heating surface area of the tubes and the evaporating capacity $(m^2/(kg/h))$. The measured losses are indicated by a + sign. In this figure only multiple effect evaporators with TVR are concerned, and the following costs are taken into account:
- capital costs (increasing with the size of the evaporator);
- energy costs (decreasing with the size of the evaporation);
- costs of product losses and waste water disposal.

It can be seen from the figure that the minimum of the production costs, indicated by the dashed line, depends on the fouling of the heating surface.

Figure 7. Costs of evaporation of whole milk. +: measured values.

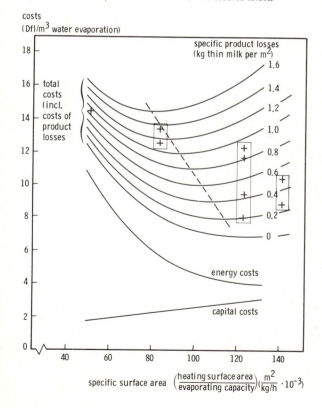

costs
$(Dfl/m^3$ water evaporation)

specific surface area $\left(\dfrac{\text{heating surface area}}{\text{evaporating capacity}}\right)\left(\dfrac{m^2}{kg/h}\cdot 10^{-3}\right)$

When the product losses decrease the optimum moves to evaporators with larger heating surface areas. Reduction of fouling will provide substantial savings. If in modern evaporators with a specific surface area of 120-140 $(10^{-3}, m^2/(kg/h))$ the fouling is reduced from 1.0 to 0.2 kg/m^2, the production costs will decrease by about 40 % for whole milk evaporation and by about 30 % for skim milk evaporation.

CLEANING PROCESS

Cleaning of modern multi-stage evaporators is an expensive, time-consuming and difficult process. Cleaning milk evaporators takes about 20 % of the production time. The daily costs of cleaning, being energy, chemicals, labour, disposal costs and product losses, vary between Dfl 1.000,- for old small evaporators and Dfl 10.000,- for modern multi-stage evaporators as illustrated in Table 2. The main differencesare the costs of waste disposal and product losses. Due to the complicated construction of evaporators, the enormous length of the pipe-lines in the pre-heaters and the pasteurising section (4000 m) and the large total area of the tubes of the effects (5000 m^2) it is very difficult to get the installation well cleaned. For all these reasons it is important to make a careful analysis of the complete cleaning procedure in order to get the necessary information for optimising the cleaning process and reducing costs and time of cleaning.

For analysing the cleaning processes the following parameters were continuously measured: temperature, conductivity and flow of the liquid at the entrance and at the end of the installation. During cleaning, once a minute samples were taken from the liquid at the end of the evaporator. In these samples calcium and COD (chemical oxygen demand) were analysed to get

Table 2. Daily costs of cleaning for an old type (A) and a modern evaporator (B).

		plant A		plant B	
capacity	(kg/h)		30 000		38 000
specific energy consumption			0.25		0.11
number of effects			5		7
total area of evaporation (m^2)			1100		5000
electricity		Dfl.	60	Dfl.	110
steam		-	425	-	610
caustic soda		-	165	-	260
acid		-	25	-	160
waste water disposal		-	45	-	1,760
labour		-	95	-	120
product losses		-	200	-	6,000
total costs of cleaning		Dfl.	1,015	Dfl.	9,060

Figure 8. Curves of the calcium content and chemical oxygen demand of the detergent during evaporator cleaning.

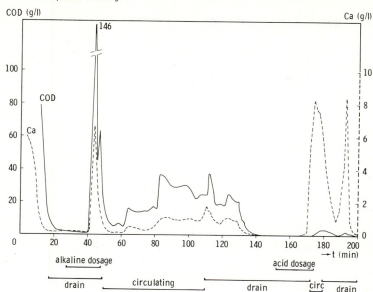

information concerning the mechanism of removal of the deposits during the cleaning process. In Figure 8 the results of such analysis are given. The evaporator was cleaned with alkaline and acid detergents. The calcium curve shows how the mineral deposit (mainly calcium phosphate) is removed. The COD curve indicates the removal of organic compounds (protein, fat, lactose) during the cleaning process. During the first twenty minutes the product is forced out. At forty minutes the caustic soda solution comes out of the plant and at the same time a sharp peak in the calcium and COD curves appears. This peak mostly contains 70 to 90 % of the total fouling matter and should be discharged directly to the drain. After this step an alkaline solution is circulated in the installation during one hour. At 110 minutes from the start this alkaline liquid is drained and the evaporator is rinsed with water. At about 150 minutes the acid wash is started, followed again by a rinsing. The acid cleaning solution again contains much calcium but hardly any organic compounds.

From these results it was concluded that the time of circulation with alkaline solution and the time of rinsing between the alkaline and acid wash could be decreased, resulting in a réduction of the cleaning time of one hour. For a complete analysis of the cleaning procedure a visual inspection before and after cleaning is very helpful to detect where the fouling occurs. Experience in dairy factories has shown that extreme fouling can be caused by faults in the construction of the distribution device or blocked holes in the distribution plate. By improving the construction of an evaporator in one case the product losses could be decreased from 6000 to 2000 kg milk.

RECOMMENDATIONS

To minimize the costs of evaporation the following recommendations should be followed:

1. Start with a clean evaporator.

This condition ensures a good distribution of the product right from the beginning and the scaling and fouling process will be delayed.

2. Provide constant operating conditions.

Abrupt changes during the operation period will lead not only to unstable operation and fluctuations in the final concentration but also to an increase of deposit formation.

3. Reduce mixing of product with rinsing-water.

In order to keep the rinsing losses as low as possible the water supply to the feed tank should be opened when the milk in it is at the lowest level. It is recommended to apply conductivity meters which give a good indication for switching over from the concentrate tank to the sewage system.

4. Improve distribution system.

A uniform distribution of the product is of vital importance to achieve atrouble-free operation and to prevent differences in concentration from tube to tube from occurring.

5. Optimize the cleaning process.

By analysing the cleaning process as described in section 5 it becomes apparent what really happens during cleaning and how the process can be improved with respect to cleaning time and consumption of energy, detergents and water.

6. Avoid shortcomings in the construction.

Visual inspections after a production run and after the cleaning process are very helpful to detect shortcomings in the operation of the distribution devices, sprayballs etc.

REFERENCES
1. Jansen, L.A. et al., Energy conservation in the dairy industry, 244 pp. (NIZO-communication M17), Netherlands Institute for Dairy Research, Ede, The Netherlands (1983).
2. R. Hansen (Ed); Evaporation, membrane filtration and spray-drying in milk powder and cheese production. North European Dairy Journal, Copenhagen (1985).
3. Kessler H.G., Food Engineering and Dairy Technology. Verlag A. Kessler, Germany, 1981.

Preconcentration and Drying of Food Materials, edited by S. Bruin
Elsevier Science Publishers B.V., Amsterdam, 1988 — Printed in The Netherlands

APPLE JUICE CONCENTRATION BY REVERSE OSMOSIS

AND FALLING-FILM EVAPORATION

M. MORESI

I.M.T.A.F. - University of Basilicata - POTENZA (Italy)

SUMMARY

In this work, a design strategy for combined reverse osmosis (RO) and falling-film evaporation (FFE) units was established so as to choose the solute concentration (x_I) in the effluent from the RO unit and number of FFE effects (n) associated with minimum water removal costs.

Within the accuracy of this preliminary study-grade cost estimates, processing costs of concentrated apple juices appear to be greatly reduced by introducing a RO preconcentration step with an input to output ratio increasing with plant capacity. Nevertheless, within the range of variation of solute concentration examined, the overall operating costs of the concentration unit are still more sensitive to live steam specific cost than to either membrane specific cost or progressive reduction of mean permeate flux after a series of cleaning operation.

NOMENCLATURE

A	heat transfer surface (m^2)
A_M	overall membrane area of the hyperfiltration unit (m^2)
A_m	membrane area of the generic RO element (m^2)
A_v	water permeability constant of membrane (m)
C_E	f.o.b. cost of each falling-film evaporator (MLit)
C_e	operating costs of the concentration unit due to electric power consumption (Lit/h)
C_{FFE}	investment costs of the FFE subunit (MLit)
C_H	investment costs of the RO hardware system (MLit)
C_I	investment costs of the concentration unit (MLit)
C_{Io}	investment-related costs of the concentration unit (MLit/h)
C_o	overall operating costs of the concentration unit (MLit/h)
C_P	f.o.b. cost of a generic pump (MLit)
C_{RO}	investment costs of the RO subunit (MLit)
C_s	f.o.b. cost of a generic liquid-vapour separator (MLit)
C_s	operating costs of the concentration unit due to live steam consumption (Lit/h)
C_{Uo}	overall utility costs of the evaporation unit (MLit/h)

C_V installed costs of the vacuum system (MLit)

C_w operating costs of the evaporation unit due to cooling water consumption (Lit/h)

c_e electric power specific cost (Lit/kWh)

c_m RO membrane specific cost (Lit/m^2)

c_{pS} specific heat of solute (J kg^{-1} K^{-1})

c_s steam specific cost (Lit/kg)

c_T specific cost of tube support for RO membranes (Lit/m^2)

c_w cooling water specific cost (Lit m^{-3})

d_i inside diameter of the RO tubular membranes and FFE tubes (m)

d_o outside diameter of the FFE tubes (m)

D_S diffusivity of solute in the liquid phase (m^2/s)

d_e equivalent diameter of RO module (m)

E recirculation ratio (dimensionless)

F flow rate of the solution entering each effect (kg/s)

f Fanning friction factor (dimensionless)

H specific enthalpy of vapour phase (J/kg)

h specific enthalpy of liquid phase from each effect (J/kg)

$\bar{h}$ specific enthalpy of liquid entering each effect (J/kg)

h^* specific enthalpy of condensed steam or cooling water (J/kg)

J_w volumetric permeate flux (m/s or L/(m^2 h))

j_H heat Colburn factor (dimensionless)

K consistency index (Pas)

k thermal conductivity of liquor (W m^{-1} K^{-1})

k_S mass transfer coefficient of solute (m/s)

L overall length of RO membranes or FFE tubes (m)

N_P electric power consumption of a generic pump (kW)

n number of effects (dimensionless)

n_d depreciation time (year)

n_P number of RO modules in parallel per stage (dimensionless)

n_S overall number of stages (dimensionless)

P overall pressure in each stage (Pa)

P_T closeness of tubes (m)

R_d combined inside and outside fouling factor (m^2 K W^{-1})

Re generalised Reynolds number, $= \rho u\, d_e/\mu$ (dimensionless)

r interest rate (dimensionless)

S flow rate of the liquid phase leaving each effect (kg/s)

Sc Schmidt number, $= \mu/(\rho D_S)$ (dimensionless)

T condensation temperature of the vapour phase (K)

t temperature of the vapour and liquid phases leaving each effect and liquor undergoing RO concentration (K)

$\bar{t}$ temperature of liquid entering each effect (K)

t_w boiling temperature of pure water (K)

U_D design overall heat transfer coefficient (W m^{-2} K^{-1})

u_D fluid superficial velocity (m/s)

V flow rate of vapour leaving each effect (kg/s)

V_E motive steam flow rate operating a generic two-stage ejector system (kg/s)

W volumetric flow rate of cooling water (m^3/h)

x solute mass fraction (dimensionless)

Y solute to water mass fraction ratio (dimensionless)

y	weight fraction of solute in the solution entering each effect (dimensionless)
β	thermal loss of each evaporator (dimensionless)
ΔP	pressure difference across the membrane (MPa)
$\Delta \P$	osmotic pressure difference across membrane (MPa)
ΔP_T	overall pressure drop (MPa)
ΔT_b	boiling point rise (BPR) (K)
$\Delta \tau$	annual working period of the concentration unit (h)
ζ_i	totale module factor of a generic element of the concentration unit (dimensionless)
μ, μ_e	dynamic and effective viscosities (Pas)
ν	flow behaviour index (dimensionless)
$\P$	osmotic pressure (MPa)
ρ, ρ_s, ρ_w	liquor, solute and water densities (kg/m^3)
σ	surface tension (N/m)

Subscripts

b	referred to the bulk solution
f	output
i	referred to a generic RO stage
j	referred to a generic FFE effect
m	referred to the membrane surface
O	input

INTRODUCTION

For decades the production of concentrated fruit and vegetable juices has been carried out by evaporation. Nowadays, there is a wide interest in the application of Reverse Osmosis (RO) for the pre-concentration of such juices, mainly because RO uses approximately one-tenth of the amount of energy used by evaporation (ref. 1). However, the actual costs of RO plants, and RO membranes as well, makes the convenience of such a concentration process highly critical, especially when their overall processing costs per unit of water removed are compared with those of other concentration systems, as multiple effect evaporation or mechanical vapour recompression (refs. 2-3).

In order to assess the economic feasibility of using hyperfiltration with different types of RO membranes for the concentration of sugar solutions, a general, simplified model was previously developed to simulate the permeate flux in plate-and-frame, spiral-wound and tubular RO systems operating either batchwise or continuously and then its prediction capability was tested either under laminar flow with clarified tomato and apple juices or turbulent flow with sweet cheese whey (ref. 4). Subsequently, a design strategy based upon such a model was established so as to choose the more appropriate configuration (i.e. plate-and-frame, spiral-wound and tubular systems) and the corresponding operating variables associated with the minimum overall operating costs (refs. 5-6).

Parallel to this, a mathematical model of multiple-effect falling-film (MEFFE) evaporators operating in backward or forward flow was developed by combining the general structure of classic multiple-effect evaporators models with an accurate estimation of the overall heat transfer coefficient in each effect, then tested to simulate the operation of several industrial orange and lemon juice double-effect FFE plants (ref. 7) and finally used to establish a design strategy aimed at minimising water removal costs without affecting product quality (ref. 8).

The main aim of this communication was to check the economic feasibility of replacing a conventional steam-driven multiple-effect FFE unit with a mixed system incorporating RO to pre-concentrate the juice prior to evaporation. To this end, a design procedure was established to determine the optimal operating condition for the production of concentrated apple juices at two different water removal rates (i.e. 3,333 and 33,333 kg/h).

THEORETICAL

Modelling of tubular RO systems

Modelling of a continuous multi-stage hyperfiltration unit was carried out by taking into account the following:

1) the solution undergoing concentration via reverse osmosis was assimilated to a two-component mixture (viz. water and apple sugar), regardless of all the aroma components usually present in fruit and vegetable juices;

2) the solvent flux through RO membranes was described by means of the resulting expression of the solution-diffusion model (ref. 9), as modified by refs. (10-11), to take account of the increase in fluid viscosity with concentration:

$$J_W = A_v (\Delta P - \Delta \pi)/\mu \qquad (1)$$

Since a great number of liquid foods undergoing RO concentration exhibit pseudoplastic behaviour, the above equation was modified (ref. 4) by replacing the dynamic viscosity (μ) of Newtonian fluids with the effective viscosity (μ_e) used to define the generalised Reynolds number in tube flow (ref. 12):

$$\mu_e = K \left(\frac{3\nu+1}{4\nu}\right)^\nu (8 u/d_e)^{\nu-1} \qquad (2)$$

which reduces to the dynamic viscosity of Newtonian fluids when n is equal to 1.

3) as water is removed through the membrane, the rejected solute tends to accumulate at the solution-membrane interface, thus involving the phenomenon of concentration polarization which is counteracted by diffusive flow in the opposite direction (ref. 9). Since the separation effectiveness of the membrane is generally very high (> 92 %), the solute permeability may

be neglected, thus allowing the solute concentration at the membrane surface to be calculated as follows (ref. 9):

$$x_m = x_b \exp(J_W/k_S)$$
(3)

where the mass transfer coefficient (k_S) can be estimated by using Colburn's mass and heat analogy (ref. 13):

$$k_S = j_H D_S \, Re \, Sc^{1/3} /d_e$$
(4)

with

$$j_H = \begin{cases} 1.86 \, Re^{-2/3} \, (d_e/L)^{1/3} & \text{for } Re < 2100 \\ 0.023 \, Re^{-0.2} & \text{for } Re > 10^4 \end{cases}$$
(5)
(6)

where L and d_e are the length and equivalent diameter of each RO tubular
element. However, to take account of the turbulence promoted by flow inversion in multi-tubular elements as those manufactured by Paterson Candy
International Ltd (P.C.I., Whitechurch, GB), eq. (6) referring to fully
turbulent flow (Re > 10⁴) was used as soon as Re was greater than 2100.

4)   As the liquor flows through the tubular membrane, it is possible to eva-
     luate the distributed pressure drop over the element under study (ref. 13):

$$\Delta P_T = 2 \, f \, u^2 \rho L/d_e \qquad \text{(Colburn's)}$$
(7)

with

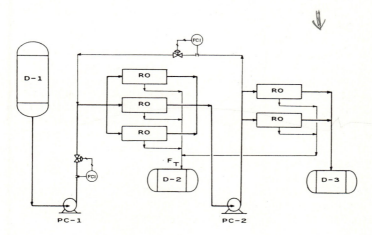

Fig. 1.   Typical flow diagram of a continuous double-stage hyperfiltration
unit.   Equipment and instrument identification items: D-1, feed tank; D-2,
permeate tank ; D-3, concentrate tank ; FCI, feed or recycle flow controller and
indicator; PC-1, high-pressure pump; PC-2, booster pump. (Courtesy of Industrie
Alimentari).

$$
f = \begin{cases} 16/\text{Re} & \text{for Re} < 2100 \\ 0.08\ \text{Re}^{-0.25} & \text{for Re} > 2100 \end{cases} \tag{8}
$$

where f is the Fanning friction factor.

5)   for depectinised and clarified fruit and vegetable juices, the deposit formed on the membrane is negligible; so, the permeate flux is controlled by the osmotic pressure of the fluid only.

With reference to the typical scheme of the continuous hyperfiltration system (FIG. 1), the fluid velocity through the modules was held about constant so that the number of modules in parallel (n_p) per each stage decreases as the net flow of concentrate decreases.

Once estimated n_p, each single stage i can be subdivided into a series of elements, the overall number of which can be assigned by trial and check to make permeate flux evaluation more precise. For more details of the calculation procedure see refs. (5-6).

Modelling of falling-film evaporators

Modelling of multiple-effect FFE operating in forward flow was carried out by taking into account the following:

i)   At the prevailing conditions the solute can be regarded as non-volatile, thus allowing a complete vaporisation of the solvent without removal of the solute.

ii)   The available temperature difference in each effect is reduced by the effect of boiling point rise only.

iii) Incondensable gases (such as, air leakage and air release from the feed liquors) do not affect the overall pressure and the effectiveness of heat transfer in the system, whereas their amount has to be estimated in order to design the vacuum equipment (e.g. ejector or vacuum pump, barometric orsurface condensers, extraction pump or barometric leg), as shown in Section 8 of ref. (8).

With reference to the typical scheme of forward MEFFE systems (Fig. 2), it is possible to describe such a system by imposing the overall and solute mate-rial balances, and the heat balance across each generic effect j:

$$
S_{j-1} = S_j + V_j \tag{9}
$$

$$
S_{j-1}\, x_{j-1} = S_j\, x_j \tag{10}
$$

$$
S_{j-1}\, h_{j-1} + V_{j-1}\, (H_{j-1} - h^*_{j-1})\, (1 - \beta_j) = S_j\, h_j + V_j\, H_j \tag{11}
$$

where all the symbols are reported in the Nomenclature section.

The performance of each FFE is also described by the following heat transfer equation:

$$V_{j-1} (H_{j-1} - h^*_{j-1}) (1- \beta_j) = U_{Dj} A_j (T_{j-1} - t_j) \qquad (12)$$

where T_{j-1} is the condensation temperature of the steam, which comes from the (j-1)th effect and condenses in the shell of the j-th evaporator

$$T_{j-1} = t_{j-1} - \Delta T_{b,j-1} \qquad \text{for } j = 2, 3,... \qquad (13)$$

and T_o is the condensation temperature of live steam.

Provided that the equilibrium conditions are achieved in each effect, the temperature of the boiling liquor and solvent vapourised are equal (t_j). Moreover, owing to the boiling point elevation ($\Delta T_{b,j-1}$) of the liquor, the vapour leaving the j-th effect is superheated, the overall pressure (P_j) in the j-th separator being equal to vapour pressure of the solvent

$$P_j = p_s(T_j) \qquad (14)$$

where p_s is the vapour pressure of solvent.

When the liquor recirculates through the evaporator, the weight flow rate (F_j), composition (y_j) and temperature ($\bar{t}_j$) of the solution entering the j-th evaporator can be easily determined by solving the following overall- and solute-material and heat balances:

$$F_j = S_{j-1} - E_j S_j \qquad (15)$$

$$F_j y_j = S_{j-1} x_{j-1} - E_j S_j x_j \qquad (16)$$

$$F_j \bar{h}_j = S_{j-1} h_{j-1} - E_j S_j h_j \qquad (17)$$

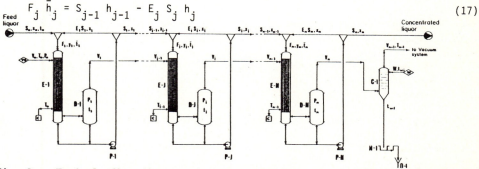

Fig. 2. Typical flow diagram of a forward MEFFE unit. Equipment identification items: C = barometric condenser, D = liquid-vapour separator; E = FFE; H = hydraulic seals; P = centrifugal pump; Q = sewage discarges. Utility identification items: c = condensed steam; VB = low pressure steam; W = cooling water. Stream symbols as in the Nomenclature section. (Courtesy of Journal of Food Technology).

where E_j is the recirculation ratio. When single pass FFE are considered E_j is equal to zero.

The system of non-linear equations (9-17) can be used to design MEFFE according to the calculation procedure outlined in Section 4.2 of a previous paper (ref. 8), provided that the following parameters are specified to make the problem determinate: weight flow rate (S_I), composition (x_I) and temperature (t_I) of the feed liquor; solute composition of the final product (x_n); operating conditions (T_o, P_o, P_n); identical thermal loss (β_j) and heat transfer surfaces ($A_i = A$), overall heat transfer coefficient (U_{D_j}) and recirculation ratio (E_j) for each effect.

OPTIMISATION PROCEDURE

The design of a mixed concentration unit capable of concentrating a given flow rate S_o of a feed liquor at temperature t_o from an initial solute composition (x_o) to an intermediate one (x_I) via reverse osmosis and then to a final one (x_f) via evaporation requires several design parameters(that is, configuration and geometric dimensions of RO modules; number of effects n; size - d_o, d_i, L - and closeness - P_T - of tubes and their type of pitch) and operating variables (temperature, pressure and fluid superficial velocity for the RO unit; live steam condensation temperature T_o; inlet cooling water temperature; and recirculation ratio E_j in each effect) to be defined.

In a series of previous works, a number of the above variables were optimized. In particular, the tubular RO design was found to be more remunerative than the spiral-wound (ref. 5) or plate-and-frame (ref. 6) one, while the optimal design of MEFFE systems was based upon identical heat transfer surfaces in all the effects and live steam condensation temperature able to maintain the maximum wall temperature smaller than 90 $^{\circ}$C. (ref. 8).

So, the unknown variables of the mixed system to be submitted to optimisation are the solute concentration (x_I) in the liquor leaving the RO unit and the optimal number of effects of the FFE unit only.

More specifically, such design may be optimised as follows:

1) Choose an initial set of operating variables (x_I, and n).

2) Design the RO stage as reported previously (ref. 5-6).

3) Design the MEFFE stage as shown before (refs. 7-8).

4) Evaluate the investment costs of the RO subunit (which consists of n_s stages, 1 high-pressure pump with stand-by, and (n_s -1) booster pumps each one with stand-by) and of the MEFFE one (which consists of n FFE, n centrifugal pumps each one with stand-by, n liquid-vapour separators and a vacuum system), by taking into account both the bare equipment costs and auxiliary costs (instruments, piping and valves, insulation, civil work, electrical,

installation, etc.). By using Guthrie's concept (ref. 14) of total module factor (ζ_i), which represents the contribution of all direct and indirect costs in the bare process module plus the contingencies necessary to adjust for unlisted items or insufficient design definition, as well as for con- tractor fees, the total cost of each item of the concentration unit can be roughly evaluated on the basis of free on board (f.o.b.) equipment costs, thus yielding the following overall cost (C_I) of the concentration unit. In particular, the investment costs for the RO system include the costs for the membrane and for their support. More specifically, once sized the stainless steel support of RO membranes, tube cost (c_T) was estimated on the basis of Lit 6000 per kg of material installed and referred to the unit of membrane area (see TABLE 1). Therefore, the investment costs of the unit are:

$$C_I = C_{RO} + C_{FFE} \tag{18}$$

with

$$C_{RO} = c_m A_M + C_H \tag{19}$$

$$C_H = c_T A_M + \sum_{i=0}^{n_s - 1} 2 \zeta_p C_{Pi} \tag{20}$$

and

$$C_{FFE} = \sum_{j=1}^{n} (\zeta_E C_{Ej} + 2 \zeta_p C_{Pj} + \zeta_S C_{Sj}) + C_V \tag{21}$$

where C_H is the investment cost for the RO hardware system; C_{Ej}, C_{Pj} and C_{Sj} are, respectively, the f.o.b. costs of the j-th FFE, centrifugal pump and liquid-vapour separator; C_y is the installed cost of the vacuum system; and c_m and c_T are the specific costs of RO membrane and tube support (see TABLE 1). All the aforementioned costs can be calculated via the correla- tions that were reported in the Appendix of ref. (8).

5) Evaluate the operating costs(C_o) of the concentration unit by taking into account the following items: investment-related (C_{Io}) and utility (C_{Uo}) costs. The first item includes depreciation and maintenance. Whereas the latter includes ordinary maintenance (estimable as a percentage of about 3 % of C_H and C_{FFE}) and membrane replacement (estimable as one-third of the total membrane area per year), the former can be estimated over a 10-year period (n_d) at an interest rate (r) of 15 %. C_{Io} was referred to a working period ($\Delta\tau$) of the plant of 2880 h per year. The utility costs include steam, cooling water and electricity, while the labour costs, being independent of either RO configuration or the number of effects of the FFE unit, were not taken into account. Therefore, the over- all operating costs of the concentration unit are:

$$C_o = C_{Io} + C_{Uo} \tag{22}$$

with

$$C_{Io} = \left(\frac{r\,(1+r)^{n_d}}{(1+r)^{n_d} - 1} \, C_I + 0.03 \, (C_H + C_{FFE}) + c_m \, A_M/3 \right)/\Delta\tau \tag{23}$$

$$C_{Uo} = C_s + C_w + C_e \tag{24}$$

$$C_s = (V_0 + V_E)\, c_s \tag{25}$$

$$C_w = W\, c_w \tag{26}$$

$$C_e = \left(\sum_{j}^{n} N_{Pj} + \sum_{i}^{n_s - 1} N_{Pi} \right) c_e \tag{27}$$

where c_s (=Lit 35/kg), c_w (=Lit 100/m^3), and c_e (=Lit 150/kWh) are, respectively, the specific costs of steam, cooling water and electric power, while the other symbols are reported in the Nomenclature section.

6) Determine the operating conditions associated with the minimum operating costs(C_o) of the concentration unit examined as a function of the intermediate concentration (x_I) and the number of effects (n), by repeating the procedure from step 2.

OPTIMAL DESIGN OF RO-MEFFE UNITS

The optimisation procedure outlined in the previous section has been applied to the production of concentrated apple juices, by assuming as a basis of computation two typical plants of medium and large size with working capacities of about 4,000 and 40,000 kg of depectinised, clarified apple juice per hour in the overall range 11.9 - 71 $^\circ$Brix.

All the input data required for this study are summarised in TABLE 1. More specifically, the main design parameters of the tubular RO modules and FFEs coincide with those of the systems manufactured by P.C.I. Ltd (ref. 15) and by Officine Metalmeccaniche Santoro (Messina, I), respectively.

As far as the tubular RO configuration is concerned, minimum permeate costs were obtained by assembling in series 2 basic tubular elements, each one is composed of 18 tubes 3.6 m long connected in series, thus involving an overall membrane tube length of about 132 m per stage (refs. 5-6).

TABLE 1
Input data required for apple juice RO and FFE concentration system design.

PARAMETER		VALUE	UNIT
FEED			
- Flow Rate	(Q_0)	4,000 - 40,000	kg/h
- Temperature	(T)	318	K
- Concentration	(x_0)	11.9	°Brix
OUTPUT CONCENTRATION (x_f)		71	°Brix
RO UNIT			
- Working Pressure	(P)	7	MPa
- Feed Superficial Velocity	(u_0)	1	m/s
- RO module type		B1(18 tubes in series)	
- Membrane type		ZF99	
- Membrane Area	(A_m)	3.66	m^2
- A		2.5×10^{-15}	m
- T^v		318	K
- P^{max}		7	MPa
- Geometric	(d_i)	12.5	mm
Dimensions	(L)	3.66	m
- Specific costs			
c_T		38,000	Lit/m^2
c_m		260,000	Lit/m^2
FFE UNIT			
- Live Steam Temperature	(T_0)	363 - 373	K
- Cooling Water Temperature Range		294 - 306	K
- Thermal loss	(β_j)	0.03	-
- Recirculation Ratio	(E_j)	0 - 5	-
- Tube inside/outside diameter	(d_i /d_o)	39 / 42.5	mm
- Tube length	(L)	10	m
- Tube closeness	(P_T)	47	mm
- Type of Pitch		Δ	-
- Fouling Factor	(R_d)	4×10^{-4}	m^2 K W^{-1}
- Operation		Co-current	-
- Design Strategy		A = const	-

A synopsis of the regression equations used to predict the physical properties of depectinised, clarified apple juices necessary for this study (e.g. osmotic pressure, solute diffusivity, rheological behaviour, density, boiling point rise, specific heat, thermal conductivity, and surface tension) is shown in TABLE 2 (refs. 16-18).

It is worth noting that apple juice was assimilated to a binary mixture consisting of water and a pseudo-component (i.e. apple sugar), the concentration

TABLE 2
Regressions used to predit the physical properties of clarified apple juices.

PARAMETER		REGRESSION	REF.
Osmotic Pressure	(MPa)	$\P = \dfrac{24.217}{(2.657/x_m -3.94)}$	16
Boiling Point Rise	(K)	$\Delta T_b = (A-B\ t_w)\ t_w/(B_0+B\ t_w)$	17
	(K)	$A = 14.85\ x$	
	(K)	$B = 5234$	
	(-)	$B_0 = 0.383\ x-1.122\ x^2+1.871\ x^3$	
$(D_s \times \mu_e)$	(N)	2.092×10^{-15}	18
Rheological	(Pas)	$K = \exp(C + D/t)$	17
Behaviour	(-)	$C = -13.4+4.88\ Y-2.38\ Y^2$	
	(K)	$D = 1926.48+588\ Y -873\ Y^2 -106.7\ Y^3$	
	(-)	$\nu = 1-0.186\ Y+0.047\ Y^2$	
	(-)	$Y = x/(1-x)$	
Thermal Conductivity	$(W\ m^{-1}\ K^{-1})$	$k = 0.123+1.316 \times 10^{-3}\ t -0.339\ x$	17
Surface Tension	(N/m)	$\sigma = 0.0727+1.1 \times 10^{-4}\ x$	17
Specific Heat	$(J\ g^{-1}\ K^{-1})$	$c_{ps} = 1.1$	17
Density	(kg/m^3)	$\rho_s = 1619$	17

of which was determined by refractometer and expressed as degrees Brix. Over the ranges of temperature and concentration examined, the rheological behaviour of apple juice was classified as non-Newtonian fluids of the pseudo-plastic type according to the power-law model (ref. 17).

Moreover, since the diffusivity of the above pseudo-component is unknown, D_S was assumed as equal to the diffusivity of glucose in water and its variation with temperature and solute concentration was expressed by means of Wilke and

Chang's classic correlation (ref. 13):

$$D_S\ \mu_e/t = const \tag{28}$$

though it should be applied to very diluted solutions only.

Finally, the cost correlations used to estimate the f.o.b. costs of FFEs, centrifugal pumps, liquid-vapour separators and the vacuum system, as extracted from Mulet _et al_. (ref. 19), Corripio _et al_. (ref. 20) and Ryans and Croll (ref. 21) and reported in the Appendix of ref. (8), were updated by introducing the most recent values actually available of the <u>Chemical Engineering Plant Cost Index</u>es (July 87) (ref. 22).

<u>Optimal number of effects</u> vs. <u>intermediate solute concentration</u>

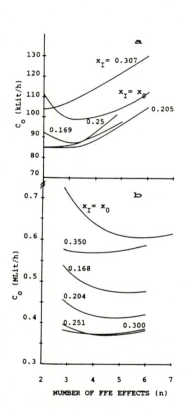

In order to minimise the investment costs of the concentration unit to be realized and its water removal costs, several calculations based on the afore-mentioned design strategy were carried out by varying either the intermediate solute concentration (x_I) and the number of effects of the FFE unit.

FIG. 3 shows the overall operating costs (C_o) of the mixed concentration plants examined as a function of the number of FFE effects for a series of x_I values, while TABLE 3 reports more details of each subunit of the above plants, as well as the corresponding utility consumption and investment and operating costs.

Whatever the water removal rate, processing costs of concentrated apple juices appear to be greatly reduced by introducing a RO preconcentration step. However, the amount of solvent to be removed by RO tends to increase with plant capacity. In fact, the optimal values of the solute concentration (x_I) in the effluent from the RO subunit vary in the ranges of 20-25 $^{\circ}$Brix and 25-30 $^{\circ}$Brix for the smaller and greater plants examined, respectively. For such ranges of x_I values, the variation in the overall processing costs of the RO-MEFFE plant is however insignificant within the precision of this study-grade cost estimates. It would therefore appear that the best configuration for the combined concentration system is that consisting of the minimum number of stages (n_s) and/or effects (n), as underlined in TABLE 3.

Fig. 3 Effect of the number of FFE effects (n) on the overall operating costs of the medium (a) and large (b) size RO-MEFFE units examined at several values of the intermediate solute concentration (x_I).

TABLE 3
Main design and operating parameters of RO and FFE subunits and overall operating costs (C_o, in * = kLit/h) of the RO-MEFFE unit.

x_I	RO					FFE							RO-FFE
	A_M	n_s	ΣN_{Pi}	C_{RO}	C_o	n	ΣA_j	ΣN_{Pj}	Steam	W	C_{FFE}	C_o	C_o
	m^2	-	kW	MLit	*	-	m^2	kW	kg/h	m^3/h	MLit	*	*
					FEED : S_o = 4,000 kg/h								
0.119	-	-	-	-	-	3	193	4	1456	62	514	98.68	98.7
0.169	47	1	31	62	10.82	3	132	3	966	43	468	75.89	86.7
0.205	78	2	32	122	16.57	2	75	2	1017	47	350	68.37	84.9
0.251	124	4	34	242	27.69	2	60	2	766	36	333	57.20	84.9
0.307	212	9	41	545	55.36	2	46	2	567	28	320	48.36	103.7
					FEED : S_o = 40,000 kg/h								
0.119	-	-	-	-	-	6	3542	41	8366	281	3498	605.4	605.4
0.168	450	1	134	241	51.65	5	2127	29	6235	223	2220	421.5	473.2
0.204	766	2	137	371	71.08	5	1743	26	4845	176	1890	341.5	412.6
0.251	1242	4	142	587	102.05	4	1118	19	4215	162	1310	270.9	373.0
0.300	1982	8	153	955	153.26	4	908	18	3203	126	1133	217.6	370.8
0.350	5195	30	214	2731	391.71	4	747	17	2460	99	1000	178.1	569.7

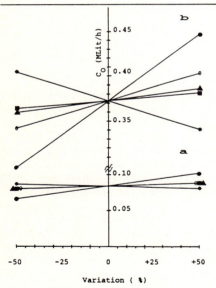

Sensitivity analysis

To verify the stability of C_o with respect to several parameters, such as membrane (c_m) and utility (c_w, c_e, and c_s) specific costs, as well as mean permeate flux , a sensitivity analysis was carried out by assuming a $\pm$ 50 % variation for each parameter mentioned above. Its main results are shown in Fig. 4 for both plants examined.

For both plants, the overall operating costs increase less than 3.2 % provided that c_e and c_w rise by 50 %, or 20-21 % for a similar variation in c_s, thus showing how sensitive are process-

Fig. 4   Effect of membrane and utility specific costs, as well as mean permeate flux, on the overall operating costs (C_o) of the optimal large (a) and medium (b) size RO-MEFFE plants shown in Table 3: ▲, c_e ; ■, c_w ; ●, c_s ; o, c_m ; *, mean J_w value.

ing costs to live steam consumption in spite of the RO preconcentration step. In fact, a 50 % variation in membrane specific cost would respectively involve a 2.2 % or 8 % increase in the processing costs of the smaller and larger plants considered. Finally, in order to take account of the progressive reduction in the mean permeate flux through the membrane that is usually observed after a series of cleaning operations, it was found that a 50 % reduction of such a parameter with respect to the basic case would result in 8.5 % or 2.2 % increase in C_o for the larger and smaller plants.

DISCUSSION OF RESULTS AND CONCLUSIONS

Following a series of previous works (refs. 4-8) on modelling of sugar solution concentration by reverse osmosis and falling-film evaporation, a design strategy for mixed concentration units was established so as to choose the solute concentration (x_I) in the liquor leaving the RO unit and the number of effects of the FFE unit associated with minimum water removal costs.

With specific reference to large scale production of concentrated apple juices, the minimum value of the overall operating costs was associated with the operation of a RO-MEFFE unit consisting of a four-stage RO subunit operating at 318 K and 7 MPa so as to preconcentrate the juice up to 25 $^\circ$ Brix and a four-effect FFE subunit designed on the basis of identical heat transfer surfaces (to save engineering costs as suggested by ref. 8) and operating in forward flow (to minimise thermal damage of product).

As far as the medium scale production of concentrated apple juice is concerned, the optimal operation of a RO-MEFFE unit was obtained when the apple juice was preconcentrated up to 20 $^\circ$ Brix by a two-stage RO subunit and finally concentrated to 71 $^\circ$ Brix by a two-effect FFE one.

Whatever the plant size, processing costs of concentrated apple juices appear to be greatly reduced by introducing a RO preconcentration step with an input to output ratio increasing with plant capacity.

Nevertheless, within the solute concentrations examined the overall operating costs of the concentration unit are more affected by live steam specific cost than by either membrane specific cost or the progressive reduction of the mean permeate flux after sequential cleaning operations.

In conclusion, it is worthwhile pointing out that the mathematical model here described can be used not only to design and optimise a new concentration unit, but also to calculate the suitability of an existing concentration unit for new process conditions.

REFERENCES

1   H.G. Schwartzberg, Energy requirements for liquid food concentration, Food Tecnol., 31(3) (1977) 67 - 71

2 T.A. Renshaw, S.F. Sapakie and M.C. Hanson, Concentration Economics in the Food Industry, Chem. Engng. Prog. 78 (5) (1982) 33-40

3 S.F. Sapakie and T.A. Renshaw, in: B.M. McKenna (Ed.), Engineering and Food. Processing Applications, Vol. 2, Elsevier Applied Science Publishers, London, 1984, pp. 927 - 937

4 G. Lombardi and M. Moresi, Modelling of sugar solution concentration by reverse osmosis, Industrie Alimentari, 26 (1987) 205 -215

5. G. Lombardi and M. Moresi, Optimal design of multi-stage Hyperfiltration units for semi-concentrated apple juices, Proc. ACOFoP, Paris, 5-6 November 1986, in press

6 G. Lombardi and M. Moresi, Dimensionamento ottimale di impianti di iperfiltrazione in continuo, Industrie Alimentari, 27 (1988) in press

7 S. Angeletti and M. Moresi, Modelling of Multiple-Effect Falling-Film Evaporators, J. Food Technol., 18 (1983) 539 - 563

8 M. Moresi, Design and optimisation of falling-film evaporators. In: S. Thorne (Ed.) Developments in Food Preservation, Vol. 3, Elsevier Applied Science Publishers, London, 1985, pp. 183 - 244

9. H.K. Lonsdale, Theory and practice of reverse osmosis and ultrafiltration. In: R.E. Lacey and S. Loeb (Eds.) Industrial Processing with Membranes, Wiley Interscience, New York, 1972, pp. 123 - 178

10. M. Dale, M.R. Okos and P. Nelson, Concentration of tomato products: Analysis of energy saving process alternatives, J. Food Sci., 47 (1982) 1853 - 58

11. M. Cheryan and D.J. Nichols, Optimisation of flux in laminar flow ultrafiltration. In: P. Linko, Y. Malkki, J. Olkku and J. Larinkari (Ed.s) Food Process Engineering. Food Processing Systems, Vol. 1, Applied Science Publishers, London, 1980, pp. 572 - 577

12. A.H.P. Skelland, Non-Newtonian Flow and Heat Transfer, John Wiley & Sons, Inc., New York, 1967

13. R.B. Bird, W.E. Stewart and E.N. Lightfoot, Transport Phenomena, John Wiley & Sons, New York, 1960

14. K. Guthrie, Data and techniques for preliminary capital cost estimating, Chem. Eng., 76 (1969) 114 - 42

15. R.L. Hedges (Paterson Candy International Ltd, Whitechurch, GB) personal communication (1986)

16. T. Matsuura, A.G. Baxter and S. Sourirajan, Studies on reverse osmosis for concentration of fruit juices, J. Food Sci. 39 (1974) 704 - 711

17. M. Moresi and M. Spinosi, Physical properties of concentrated apple juices, in: B.M. McKenna (Ed.) Engineering and Food. Engineering Sciences in the Food Industry, Vol. 1, Elsevier Applied Science Publishers, London, 1984, pp. 475 - 487

18. R.H. Perry, C.H. Chilton and S.D. Kirkpatrick, Chemical Engineers' Handbook, 4th Ed. McGraw-Hill Book Co., New York (1963)

19. A. Mulet, A.B. Corripio and L.B. Evans, Estimate costs of pressure vessels via correlations, Chem. Eng., 88 (1981) 145 - 150

20. A.B. Corripio, K.S. Chrien and L.B. Evans, Estimate costs of centrifugal pumps and electric motors, Chem. Eng., 89 (1982) 115 - 118

21. J.L. Ryans and S. Croll, Selecting vacuum systems, Chem. Eng., 88 (1981) 72 - 90

22. Anon., Economic Indicators, Chem. Eng., 94 (1987) 7

FREEZE CONCENTRATION ECONOMICS AND APPLICATIONS

W.H.J.M. van Pelt   and   H.A. Jansen

Grenco Process Technology B.V., P.O. Box 253, 5201 AG

's-Hertogenbosch (The Netherlands)

1. INTRODUCTION

Freeze concentration in the food industry has been investigated and tried intensively in the sixties. Freeze concentration never found a commercial application due mainly to three disadvantages:
- Losses of solids in the discharged water
- High energy consumption
- High capital investment

At the University of Technology in Eindhoven, Prof. Thijsssen developed a process which overcame the first drawback. Though even with successful operation, the single stage freeze concentration equipment still had the last two disadvantages.

New developments, into multistage plants and upscaling the size of individual components, resulted in considerable reduction of energy consumption and· capital costs.

In this paper we will describe the Grenco freeze concentration process and examine the effects of multistage and larger components on the water removal costs and energy use in four typical plant configurations.

2. PRINCIPLE

In freeze concentration water is first partly segregated from the aqueous solution by crystallization and then the ice crystals are separated from the concentrated liquid phase. This is shown in Figure 1.

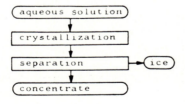

Fig. 1: Basic operation in freeze concentration.

The process as such is based on the physical phenomena of freezing point depression of which the results are depicted in Figure 2 for two different types of citrus juices, orange juice and lemon juice.

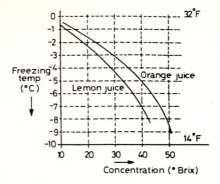

Fig. 2: Freezing point as function of dissolved solids concentration

As shown in Figure 2 pure water freezes at a temperature of 0°C and in the case that dry solid is dissolved this temperature is lower. For example, if orange juice with a dry solid content of 11% is cooled, the first pure water freezes at a temperature of about -2°C, leaving a liquid with a higher concentration. Orange juice of 50% dry solids will have a freezing temperature of -9°C.

3.   FUNDAMENTALS

3.1. Concentration

The amount of water to be removed from a solution to achieve a certain concentration level is shown in Figure 3, starting from a feed solution of 10% D.S.

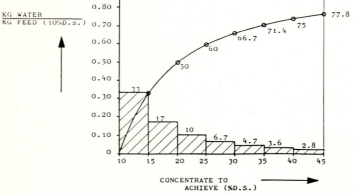

Fig. 3: The percentage of feed to be removed from the feed in the form of pure water to achieve a certain concentration level.

The amount of water to be removed to achieve a certain concentration factor is given by equation (1)

$$X_{feed} = 1 - (Co/Cb) \qquad (1)$$

in which

X_feed = weight percentage of water to be removed from the feed

X_{feed} = weight percentage of water to be removed from the feed
Co = dry solid content of the feed
Cb = dry solid content of the concentrate in the slurry

It is clear that most of the water has to be removed in the initial stage of the concentration process.

3.2. Crystallization

During the crystallization step two kinetic processes take place:
- formation of nuclei
- growth of crystals

In general the nucleation is a quadratic function of the bulk supercooling and the growth is a linear function of the bulk supercooling. Because the bulk supercooling is influenced by the crystal mass concentration and the hydrodynamic behaviour of the suspension the interaction of nucleation and growth is rather complicated. The question is how to increase the growth rate of the crystals and how to decrease the nucleation rate.

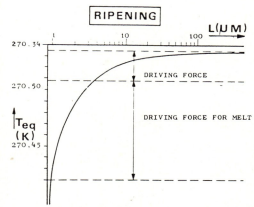

Fig. 4: Relation between melt temperature and size of the crystals for ice – 30Wt% sucrose.

In an adiabatic growth zone the mean bulk temperature of the liquid attains a value between the extreme values of the various melting temperatures of the crystals and nuclei. This results in a driving force for growth of the large crystals and a driving force for melt of the small crystals (nuclei).

In the Grenco process externally cooled ripening crystallizers are used where nucleation takes place in the heat withdrawal section and the crystals grow adiabatically, at the expense of the newly generated nuclei, by ripening in a separate recrystallizer vessel.

Ripening is based on the thermodynamic phenomenon that the melt temperature depends slightly on the size of the crystals which means that the nuclei have a lower melt temperature than the larger crystals in the growth section. The relation between melt temperature and size of the crystals for ice (-30Wt% sucrose) is given in figure 4.

80

In other freeze concentration processes, nucleation and growth take place in the same apparatus, i.e. normally being some form of scraped surface heat exchanger.

The disadvantages of this process versus the Grenco process are:
- considerably lower heat transfer coefficient in the scraped surface heat exchanger.
- The average size of the ice crystals formed is a factor 3 to 6 smaller. The advantage of this process is that continuous filtration of ice crystals in the crystallization stage can be avoided. In the Grenco freeze concentration process the ice nuclei are formed in a scraped surface heat exchanger. Heat is withdrawn only in the nucleation zone (see Figure 5). By applying a large heat flux in the nucleation zone there will be high degree of supercooling. This causes a high nucleation rate so that very small ice crystals are formed. An extremely small residence time of the crystals in the heat exchanger is chosen, so consequently the crystals formed do not get the opportunity to grow. The small crystals produced in the scraped surface heat exchanger are fed continuously to the growth zone, called the recrystallizer. The small crystals are intensively mixed with the suspension of large crystals that are present in the adiabatic recrystallizer. At every point in this recrystallizer the solution temperature will adjust itself to a value between the equilibrium temperature of the small crystals and that of the larger ones. In this way the larger crystals will grow at the expense of the smaller ones, which melt. In this way almost spherical pure ice crystals without inclusions of product are formed.

3.3. Separation

The separation of ice crystals from the concentrated liquid can be performed in washcolumns the superficial velocity of a liquid through a packed bed is given by equation (2).

$$V = \frac{E^3 \times d_p^2 \times \emptyset^2}{180 \ (1-E)^2} \times \frac{1}{\eta} \times \frac{dP}{dz} \tag{2}$$

in which V = Superficial liquid velocity   (m/s)

    E = Volume fraction of liquid   (1)

    d_p = Particle diameter of the crystals   (m)

    $\emptyset$ = Shape factor of the crystals   (1)

    η = Dynamic viscosity (Ns/m^2)

    $\frac{dP}{dz}$ = Pressure drop along the packed bed (N/m^3)

In the Grenco process the separation section is a washcolumn (see Fig. 6). The washcolumn consists of a vertical cylinder, a piston mounted in the bottom portion of it, and a scraping device at the top. The piston has a central inlet hole and a perforated surface. The piston can move from position S_1 to position S3 and back.

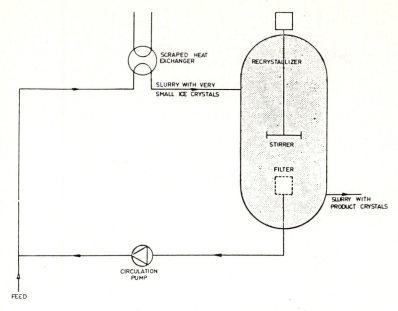

Fig. 5: Externally cooled ripening vessel.

Suppose the space between S_1 and the scraping device is filled with a compacted porous ice bed. When the piston is in position S_1 and we close valve B and valve C while we open valve A, then due to the overpressure in the recrystallizer, the piston will move downward and the space formed will become filled with concentrate and ice crystals.

When the piston reaches position S_3, valve A is closed and valve B is opened. The hydraulic (or pneumatic) cylinder E forces the piston to move upwards. Concentrate filter through the perforated surface of the piston and leaves the washcolumn through valve B, while the crystals remain.

When the piston reaches position S_2, it builds up an ice bed. The top of the bed is forced against the scraping device. Ice flakes that are scraped off are recirculated together with their melt over a heat exchanger. A small part of the melt is used to wash down the concentrate that is held between crystals in the ice bed.

Washing the ice bed is achieved by simply closing drain valve C for the melted ice. A photo-electric cell controls the position of the wash-front by opening or closing valve C. The temperature of the washwater is adjustable by a temperature controller which opens or closes steam inlet valve D. The concentration of dissolved solids in the water removed from the system is usually less than 100 p.p.m.

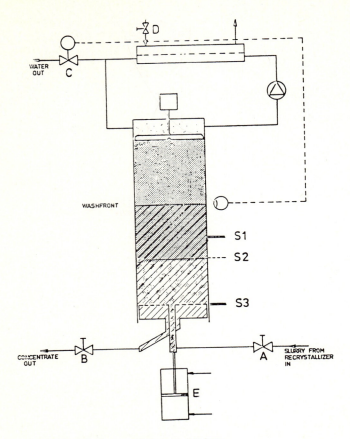

WATER OUT

WASHFRONT

S1

S2

S3

CONCENTRATE OUT

B

A

SLURRY FROM RECRYSTALLIZER IN

E

Fig. 6: Grenco piston washcolumn

4. THE MULTISTAGE COUNTER CURRENT PROCESS

To introduce the multistage operation, it is helpful to discuss first the one stage operation and to pay attention, on that basis, to the multistage counter current operation.

4.1. One stage operation

In one stage operation the freeze concentration process consists of one crystallization step and one separation step, as is shown in Fig. 7.

This means that in starting up the equipment to come to a continuous operation one can distinguish four time intervals, as is shown in Fig. 8. First a period of pre-cooling has to take place, followed by a period of crystallization to form the first ice slurry, next a period of crystallization and separation, in which the bulk dry solid concentration increases to end level, and finally the steady state operation.

In cooling temperature this means that in one stage continuous operation the heat has to be withdrawn at one temperature level.

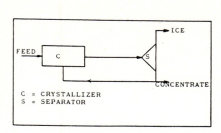

Fig. 7: One stage freeze concentration operation.

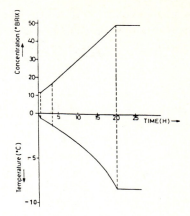

Fig. 8: Single stage operation
Concentration of orange juice up to 50°Brix.

Summarizing the characteristics of one stage freeze concentration level:
- All heat has to be removed at the lowest temperature level.
- All crystals have to grow under the most infavourable conditions (high concentration and high viscosity, the latter caused by dry solid content and by the low temperature, which results in longer residence times for the crystals, which means bigger crystallizers).
- All crystals have to be separated at the most infavourable condition: high viscosity and consequently smaller crystals which have to be separated.
- Pumping and mixing have to be done at a high viscosity resulting in a high energy requirement and also high energy input, which has to be removed.

4.2. Multistage counter current operation

The multistage counter current operation is represented in Figure 9.

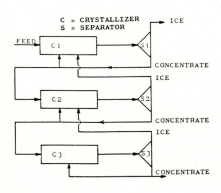

Fig. 9: Schematic representation of multi stage counter current operation.

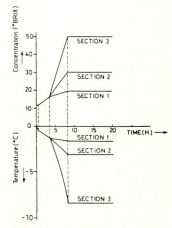

Fig. 10: Three stage counter current operation.
Three-fold concentration of orange juice.

From an energy saving point of view there is a direct application for counter current operation because of the fact that the bulk of the heat can be removed in section 1 and 2 at much higher freezing temperature (see Figure 10).

From a process point of view there are reasons for choosing a counter current performance (see Figure 10).

1) All ice has to be separated at the lowest dry solid concentration, this means the lowest viscosity, which results in the highest separating velocity (dry solid content and temperature).

2) The formed ice crystals can grow under increasing better conditions caused by the lower dry solid content, resulting in a bigger crystal size, which influences to a great extent the separating velocity.

3) The better growing conditions can also be translated to shorter residence times, which means smaller apparatus, or, with same apparatus higher capacities can be achieved.

Some indication in this field is given in Figure 11.

SYSTEM	RESIDENCE TIME
ONE STAGE	4
FIVE STAGE COUNTER CURRENT	1.0

Fig. 11: Necessary residence time to obtain separable ice crystals.
Model solution 10% d.s. ——> 50% d.s. (sugar solution).

5.   CONTINUOUS PACKED BED WASHCOLUMN (See Figure 12).

An important factor in view of higher capacities and consequently reduction of dewatering costs is the development of the continuous packed bed washcolumn. In fact this is the first flooded washcolumn, which is fully continuous, which operates with a flat washfront and of which the design is insensitive to upscaling.

The column consists of an annular space of which the axle rotates. On the axle vanes are mounted, which have a double function: scraping the bottom filter and transportation of ice crystals. Above these vanes a homogeneous bed of ice crystals is packed, in which the concentrated liquid

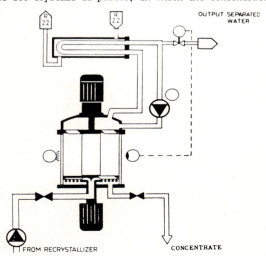

Fig. 12: Grenco continuous washcolumn.

is pushed out of the interstices in the packed bed of ice crystals by means of a plug flow of washwater, gained from separated and subsequently melted ice crystals.

This displacement of concentrate by less viscous washwater is stable because of a decrease of permeability mainly caused by the dendritic recrystallization of washwater on the colder ice crystals.

The column has a capacity of 10-20 ton/m^2 hour and has all the advantages of the already mentioned Grenco piston washcolumn, such as:
- no losses of dry solids or aromas with the separated ice
- no freezing of filter screens
- a perfect separation over 1 cm of bed length.

6. ECONOMICS OF FREEZE CONCENTRATION PLANTS

Here we will investigate the influence of applying freeze concentration units in multistage counter current configuration on the energy consumption and water removal costs of these plants. Also the effect of upscaling in size of the various components of a freeze concentration unit on energy consumption and water removal costs will be examined.

The first single stage GFC-W33 was installed in 1975 with a water removal capacity of 250 kg/h. Then in 1980 the multistage counter current process was introduced with the three stage GFC-W33 with a water removal capacity of 1600 kg/h. Multistage operation reduced the water removal costs from US$ 390/ton water to US$ 172/ton water and energy consumption was reduced from 244 kW/ton water to 142 KW/ton water.

The effect of upscaling can be seen by the introduction of larger components in 1984, with the five stage counter current GFC-W60. Water removal capacity was increased to 12 ton water/hour, water removal costs were decreased from US$ 172/ton water to US$ 70/ton water and energy use dropped from 142 kW/ton water to 91 kW/ton water.

New developments with even larger components in the six stage GFC-W100, water removal capacity at 24.5 ton/hour, show a reduction in water removal costs by a factor 2.3 and energy use reduction by a factor of 1.4. The reduction in water removal costs is depicted in Figure 13 and energy consumption in Figure 14 as a function of plant size.

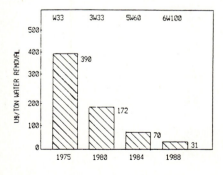

Fig.13.   Investment cost (US $/ TWR) as function of plant size.

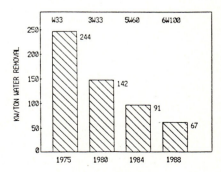

Fig.14.   Energy use (kW/TWR) as function of plant size.

7.   APPLICATIONS

The Grenco freeze concentration process has been industrially applied
to many food products including:

citrus juices   - orange, grapefruit, mandarin

coffee extracts   - as preconcentration before drying

vinegar

beer

other fruit juices - strawberry, blackberry, rasberry, black currant,
                            peach

Successful pilot scale tests on:

dairy products   - whole, skim milk, whey

tea extracts

waste water

and presently testing with industrial scale purification of organic
chemicals.

8.   LITERATURE

1   Chen, S.S. (1982)   American Institute of Chemical Engineers,
                                  Orlando, Fla. 1982.

2   Malen, B.G.M. van der   Multistage Freeze Concentration

3   Pelt, W.H.J.M. van (1981)   Economics and Potentials, Milan 3-5 June,
                                  1981. Symposium Progress in Food
                                  Engineering.

4   Pelt, W.H.J.M. van,)
     Roodenrijs, J.P.   )   USP 4,316,368

5   Thijssen, H.A.C. (1974)   In Advance in Preconcentration and
                                  Dehydration of Foods (Spicer A.), pp
                                  115-149 Applies Science Publishers Ltd.,
                                  London.

6   Thijssen, H.A.C.,)
     Oyen, N.S.M. van) (1977)   in 7th European Symposium - Food Product
                                  and Process Selection in the Food
                                  Industry, Preprints. Eindhoven September
                                  1977, pp 231-252.

Preconcentration and Drying of Food Materials, edited by S. Bruin
Elsevier Science Publishers B.V., Amsterdam, 1988 — Printed in The Netherlands

MEMBRANE PROCESSING OF INDUSTRIAL ENZYMES

P.J.A.M. Kerkhof & G.H. Schoutens

Dept. of Process Development & Engineering, R&D, Gist-brocades, P.O.Box 1, 2600 MA Delft, the Netherlands

SUMMARY

For the processing of enzymes at present ultrafiltration (UF) is an industrial operation; cross-flow microfiltration (MF) is a rather new development. Experiments on the influence of transmembrane pressure on flux in MF are presented for microbial cell suspension, protein solution and for a mixture of both. After a description of the data with resistance models an analysis is made based on a molecular friction model; it is shown that most probably flux in MF is limited by pore-blocking due to cell debris. For UF an analysis is made of flux vs. pressure; the cake-filtration model is seen to give a reasonable description. A new model is presented for the retention of colour components, based on a molecular friction taking place in a packed bed of protein spheres. This model gives promising results.

I. INTRODUCTION

In recent years the application of membrane processing in separating food components and especially in dewatering has grown substantially. Both the field of application and the capacities installed are still increasing. For reviews the reader is referred to Gekas and Hallström (1). Fundamental considerations of transport phenomena involved in membrane processing have been presented in the literature over the last four decades, ranging from coupled transport equations (Spiegler and Kedem,2) to hydrodynamical considerations of particle motion in cross-flow microfiltration (Belfort and Nagata,3). It appears that on the user side of membrane processes one still mostly works from qualitative and semi-phenomenological experience in the use and design of modules.

Also in the biotechnological industries membrane processing is an area of interest. In the present paper we will discuss cross-flow microfiltration (MF) of enzyme-containing fermentation broth, and ultrafiltration (UF) of aqueous enzyme solutions. In the former the aim is to separate the enzyme from the cell suspension, in the latter the enzyme solution is concentrated. Important in the MF process is then to obtain a maximum yield; in the UF - example we also treat a purification in which small colour components are to be removed through the membrane. In both processes two aspects are of great importance :
 - minimization of the membrane area used
 - optimization of the conditions for both product yield and transport rate of the desired components through the membrane.

These systems and the associated problems have parallels also in food processing, e.g. separation of lactic acid or aroma components from producing cell suspensions by MF, concentration of dairy products containing proteins and small components like sugars with UF. We therefore feel that results as obtained from our investigations reported here, may also be of interest in the food processing area.

Following from the industrial interest in optimization, our aims were to gain insight into the phenomena governing the membrane processes in our field of (potential) application. As follows from studying the relevant literature several models exist for the description of the flux in MF of cell suspensions and of that in UF of protein solutions, and so our first target was to find out which models were most relevant for our experiments. Previously we presented experimental results on the retention of "small components" in UF (van der Zee & Webbers,4); also for other systems experiments have been reported recently (Papamichael and Kula,5). Models for this however were lacking. Thus as a second target we set the development and testing of a first model for these phenomena.

II. CROSS-FLOW MICROFILTRATION OF FERMENTATION BROTH

II.1. Experiments and interpretation through resistance models

Generally cross-flow microfiltration (CFMF or for short MF) is studied with respect to concentration of particulate suspensions. In biotechnological applications, MF is considered to be an alternative for dead-end cake filtration e.g. in harvesting and or concentrating microbial cells from fermentation broths. When a specific product e.g. a protein has to be recovered from a fermentation broth via MF, description of the flux behaviour becomes particularly tedious. This study was set up to assess the usefulness of mathematical models, described in the literature, for predicting and describing the flux behaviour in MF.

The model system chosen consisted of a mixture of microbial cells (5 µm diameter) and proteins (30000 - 50000 D). The cross-flow microfiltration experiments were set up according to the scheme in Fig.1. The membrane used was a 1.2 m Carbosep membrane (nominal pore size 0.14 µm) with an internal diameter of 0.006 m. Cross-flow velocities were varied between 2.1 and 3.7 m/s, transmembrane pressure was varied between 0.6 and 3 bar. The permeate was returned to the feed tank to obtain constant feed conditions.

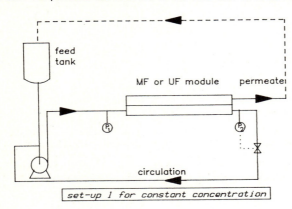

Fig.1. Experimental set-up for micro- and ultrafiltration

The temperature was kept at 18 °C. The microbial cells were suspended in water (containing salts) as a 6% suspension on dry basis. We used three feed compositions :
    A : microbial cell suspension
    B : protein solution
    C : microbial cells + protein
The protein solution was obtained as permeate from MF of a fermentation broth.

In order to interpret the experimental data resistance models of the form :

$$J= \Delta p/R \qquad (1)$$

were used, in which J = transmembrane flux
                    ΔP = transmembrane pressure
                    R = resistance
Although the notation for J as the volumetric flux is well adopted in the field of membrane literature, in order to avoid confusion with the chemical engineering notation we will use here the symbol v_0 for the transmembrane velocity, and which will be expressed in m/s. Resistances are in kg/m^2s, and pressure is expressed in Pa. As is usual in literature, the resistance is considered to be built up from a series of resistances :

$$R = R_m + R_{foul} + R_{film} \qquad (2)$$

The first term is R_m, the membrane resistance, which is determined from measurement of the water flux through the clean membrane, the "clean water flux". R_{foul} is the resistance formed by a fouling layer; it can be determined by measuring the water flux straight after a microfiltration experiment. The fouling layer is assumed to be irreversibly present. R_{film} is the resistance formed by a film of (polarized) protein/microbial cells and is considered to be reversible. It is determined from the overall resistance during a microfiltration experiment.

For the variations mentioned above the values of the resistance terms were determined. Next it was considered whether these terms could be described by relationships known from literature.

As may be expected for ceramic membranes, R_m proved to be a constant independent of pressure. For R_{foul}, which is very much dependent on the feed used, an empirical relationship has to be established. In R_{film} two contributions can be discerned; one resulting from the microbial cells and one for protein effects. An approach to calculate R_{film} for microbial cells is to use ultrafiltration theory in the film control region :

$$R_{film} = \frac{\Delta p}{k \ln \left(C_w / C_b \right)} \qquad (3)$$

This assumes the microbial cells to be polarized towards the membrane surface (C_{bulk} and C_{wall} respectively); the mass transfer coefficient k depends on the bulk or circulation velocity u_b (6) :

$$k \cong U_b^{0.33} \qquad \text{laminar} \qquad (4a)$$

$$k \cong U_b^{0.8} \qquad \text{turbulent} \qquad (4b)$$

In many publications on micro- and ultrafiltration (6-11) of particulate suspensions, it is acknowledged that these polarization models cannot describe and predict flux behaviour with sufficient accuracy. For these particulate suspensions the cross-flow velocity dependence of J is more pronounced than mentioned above. Zydney and Coulton (7) use a correction of k by introducing a shear enhanced diffusivity effect (D $= f(d_p^2, \gamma)$ for large particles, thus boosting the effect of k (and of u_b) in the polarization term. Porter (8) accounts for the strong dependence of flux on velocity via an augmented back migration of particles from the film on the membrane. The contribution of this particle migration velocity, u_r, increases with increasing particle diameter and also depends on the tube Reynolds number. Belfort (9) and Green (10) basically use the same principle but a slightly different way to calculate u_r, based on inertia induced lift velocities of these particles.
For the film controlled flux region this results in :

$$R_{film} = \frac{\Delta p}{k \ln \left(C_w / C_b \right) + U_r} \qquad (5a)$$

with :

$$k = 0.023 \left(\frac{\rho}{\mu} \right)^{0.47} D^{0.67} U_b^{0.8} d_h^{-0.2} \qquad (5b)$$

$$U_r = \alpha \ \kappa^2 \ \frac{d_p}{\nu} \left(1 - \frac{r^\star}{d_h} \right) U_b^2 \qquad (5c)$$

$$D = \frac{k_B . T}{3 \pi \mu d_p} \qquad (5d)$$

90

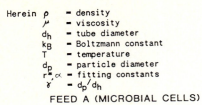

Herein ρ = density
      μ = viscosity
      d_h = tube diameter
      k_B = Boltzmann constant
      T = temperature
      d_p = particle diameter
      r^*, α = fitting constants
      γ = d_p/d_h

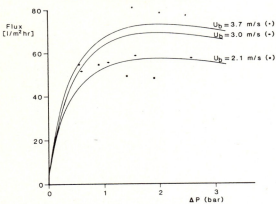

FEED A (MICROBIAL CELLS)

Flux [l/m²hr]

U_b = 3.7 m/s (·)
U_b = 3.0 m/s (-)
U_b = 2.1 m/s (•)

ΔP (bar)

Fig.2. Flux vs. transmembrane pressure in MF. Drawn lines represent model calculations

Figure 2 shows the results of flux vs. ΔP and bulk velocity for feed A (microbial cells, protein free). The drawn lines in the figure represent the model calculations; parameter values are given in the table. It can be concluded that the trends in flux behaviour as a function of ΔP and u_b for the protein free cell suspension can be described by the above-mentioned approach. The fouling term was found to be pressure-dependent. This may be caused by compacting of cells or cell debris irreversibly blocking pores.

Data used in MF – calculations			
	Feed A microbial cells	Feed B protein	Feed C microbial cells + protein
density (kg/m³)	1020	1015	1025
viscosity (Pa.s)	0.01	0.001	0.01
d_p (m)	5×10^{-6}		
D (m²/s)		5.55×10^{-9}	
d_h = 0.006 m T = 18 °C			
α = 85 (Eq.5c) R_{foul} = 230 $\Delta P^{1.4}$			

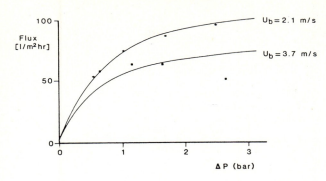

FEED B (PROTEIN SOLUTION)

Flux [l/m²hr]

$U_b = 2.1$ m/s

$U_b = 3.7$ m/s

ΔP (bar)

Fig.3. Flux vs. transmembrane pressure in MF. Drawn lines represent model calculations.

In Figure 3 the results of feed B (cell-free protein solution) are presented. It is clear that the protein solution itself, although the protein size is much smaller than that of the pores, causes flux decline too. Again this effect can be sufficiently described by (again) an empirically determined fouling term and a polarization term (classical), as indicated by the drawn lines. Ultimately the results obtained from modelling microfiltration of feed A and B were combined, to form a model describing the flux behaviour of feed C, cells + protein. In separate experiments the fouling term R_{foul} was found to be the same for feed C and feed A, so the empirically established relation for feed A was used. Both film resistances due to particle effects and due to protein polarization were used. The comparison between model prediction (drawn lines) and experimentally determined flux values is given in Fig. 4. At a high cross flow velocity the approach seems valid. At a low value the discrepancy between measured and calculated values is larger. This might be caused by a less severe influence of protein polarization at low flux values. Particle effects may diminish protein polarization effects to some extent.

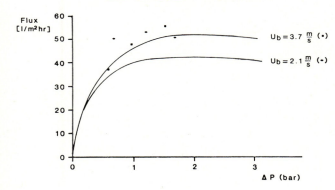

FEED C (CELLS+PROTEIN)

Flux [l/m²hr]

$U_b = 3.7 \frac{m}{s}$ (•)

$U_b = 2.1 \frac{m}{s}$ (•)

ΔP (bar)

Fig.4. Flux vs. transmembrane pressure for a mixture of cell suspension and protein solution. Drawn lines are model calculations.

Although the description presented may reasonably suffice for practical purposes, the question why a protein solution (as shown in Fig. 3) causes such a large flux decline in a microporous membrane remains unresolved. This was the reason that in the next section some theoretical modelling is presented on the motion of protein molecules through porous systems.

II.2. Theoretical considerations of protein transport in MF

Transport model

For the effects of protein on the flux in MF possible explanations can be found in adsorption in pores, and in friction between protein and membrane material combined with polarization effects. The specified pore size from the supplier, 0.14 µm, is about 30 times larger than the molecular diameter of the protein. Also for smaller pores still a multilayer adsorption would be necessary to effectively block the pores; in view of the low concentration levels used, < 1 kg/m^3, this seems doubtful. In order to elucidate the effect of friction, we developed a model attack more or less along the same lines as Jonsson (12). We consider the system schematically as indicated in Fig.5.

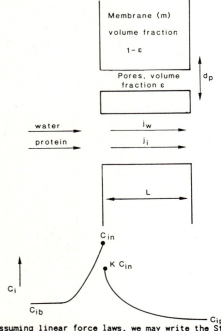

Fig.5. Schematic representation of flow through porous membrane and associated concentration profile of protein.

Assuming linear force laws, we may write the Stefan—Maxwell equation for transport of a component i :

$$\rho_i \nabla \ln a_i = \frac{1}{\rho D_{iw}} \{\rho_i j_w - \rho_w j_i\} + \frac{1}{\rho D_{im}} \{\rho_i j_m - \rho_m j_i\} \qquad (6)$$

with ρ_i = mass concentration of i, based on total volume
$\quad$ a_i = thermodynamic activity
$\quad$ ρ = density of the system
$\quad$ j_i = mass flux of i
$\quad$ D_{iw} = molecular diffusion coefficient of i in water
$\quad$ D_{im} = diffusion coefficient of i with respect to the membrane

Assuming ideal behaviour of the solute i, we have $a_i = x_i$. Assuming dilute solutions we may write :

$$\rho_m = (1-\varepsilon)\ d_m \tag{7a}$$

$$\rho_w = \varepsilon\ d_w \tag{7b}$$

$$v_o = j_w/d_w \tag{8}$$

in which ε is the porosity of the membrane and d_m and d_w are the true densities of the membrane material and water respectively. Taking the membrane as the reference coordinate we have $j_m = 0$, and after some rearrangement we obtain :

$$\nabla\rho_i = \frac{1}{D_{iw}}\ \rho_i v_o - j_i\ \left\{\ \frac{\varepsilon}{D_{iw}}\ +\ \frac{1-\varepsilon}{D_{im}}\ \right\} \tag{9}$$

which in the limit for $\varepsilon \to 1$ becomes the well known transport equation :

$$\lim_{\varepsilon \to 1}\ \nabla\rho_i = \frac{1}{D_{iw}}\ \left(\rho_i v_o - j_i\right) \tag{10}$$

Writing $C_i = \rho_i/\varepsilon$, the true concentration in the liquid, we obtain after some manipulation :

$$j_i = f_1\ C_i v_o - f_1\ D_{iw}\ \nabla\ C_i \tag{11}$$

in which :

$$f_1 = \frac{\varepsilon\ D_{im}}{\varepsilon\ D_{im} + (1-\varepsilon)\ D_{iw}} \tag{12}$$

Integration over the membrane thickness L, and assuming a distribution coefficient K between pore and bulk liquid, gives for the concentration ratio over the membrane :

$$\frac{C_{iw}}{C_{ip}} = \frac{1}{1-R_t} = \frac{1}{Kf_1} + \left(1 - \frac{1}{Kf_1}\right)\ \exp\ \left(-\ \frac{v_o L}{D_{iw}}\right) \tag{13}$$

with C_{iw} and C_{ip} as the wall and permeate concentration respectively.

For a quantification of the diffusion parameter f_1, and for the distribution coefficient K, the Stefan-Maxwell equation itself does not give information. Based on a model for the friction of a spherical particle with a cylindrical wall, Jonson obtained a result identical to Eq. (13), with

$$f_1 = 1/b \tag{14}$$

in which b is a friction coefficient. From the Ferry-Faxen equation he derived the following relationships :

$$K = \frac{(A_i/A_p)\text{ steric}}{(A_w/A_p)\text{ steric}} \tag{15}$$

and

$$b = \frac{(A_w/A_p)\text{ friction}}{(A_i/A_p)\text{ friction}} \tag{16}$$

in which

$$(A_i/A_p)\text{ steric} = 2(1-\alpha)^2 - (1-\alpha)^4 \tag{17}$$

$$(A_i/A_p)\text{ friction} = 1-2.104\alpha + 2.09\alpha^3 - 0.95\alpha^5 \tag{18}$$

with $\alpha = (r_i/r_p)$, the ratio of particle to pore radius. Instead of the constant 0.95 we employed 0.9836 in order to obtain a value of 0 for the limit $\alpha = 1$.
Using Eq (10) for the transport in the film we obtain :

$$\frac{C_{ib}}{C_{ip}} = \frac{1}{1 - R_{app}} = \frac{R_t}{1 - R_t} \exp(-v_o/k_m) + 1 \tag{19}$$

in which C_{ib} = protein bulk concentration
R_{ib} = apparent retention
R_t^{app} = true retention
k_m = mass transfer coefficient in film.

For the radius of a water molecule $r_w = 2.15 \times 10^{-10}$ m was used, for that of protein a fit was made to results as given by Bailey (13) :

$$r_i = 7.93 \times 10^{-11} (M_i)^{0.339} \tag{20}$$

For the molecular diffusion coefficient we again made a fit to Bailey's data :

$$D_{iw} = 2.56 \times 10^{-9} (M_i)^{-0.33} \tag{21}$$

For the protein used we have a molecular mass of 36000 D, from which follows : $r_i = 2.78 \times 10^{-9}$ m, $D_{iw} = 7.8 \times 10^{-11}$ m²/s.
For the diffusive transport inside the membrane however a correction should be made for the tortuosity κ of the pores; the porosity effect was already included in the transport equation. We have then :

$$D'_{iw} = D_{iw}/\kappa_1 \tag{22}$$

From an extensive theoretical effort by Bahtia (14) follows that for a system with a large standard deviation in pore size and a large number of pores meeting at intersections, we may expect κ to reach high values, as high as 50.
For the pressure drop across the membrane the relationship of Jonsson & Boesen may be rewritten as :

$$\Delta p_m = \Delta p_o \left\{ 1 + \frac{r^2}{8\mu} (b-1) \frac{C_{ip}}{M_i} \frac{RT}{D'_{iw}} \right\} \tag{23}$$

Herein Δp_0 is the pressure drop in the absence of solute; the second term within brackets reflects the effect of friction between solute and the wall, which necessitates extra pressure drop in order to keep the flux at the same value. For Δp_0 we have :

$$\Delta p_o = \frac{8 \mu L v_o \kappa_2}{\epsilon r_p^2} \tag{24}$$

Herein κ_2 is the tortuosity to be used for the correction of the pressure drop; as is seen from data of Beek & Mutzall (15) on resistance of packed beds this may be expected to be in the order of 2-3. As specifications from the supplier we had $d_p = 0.14 \mu m$, and $L = 10 - 1000$ (10^{-10}) m. In order to stay within reasonable limits for the ratio of pore size to membrane thickness we applied for L the latter value.

II.2.2. Calculation results

It is clear that the sintered membranes may have a rather broad pore size distribution, as was found in studies of Katz and Baruch (16). In order to obtain insight into the model performance we varied a number of parameters, such as pore diameter and tortuosity. A typical result is shown in Fig. 6. We see that for the small pore size used indeed the friction leads to a levelling off of the flux–pressure curve.

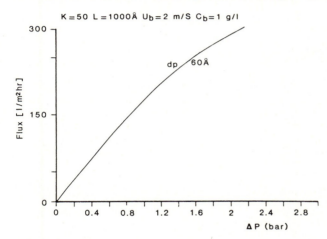

K = 50 L = 1000Å U_b = 2 m/S C_b = 1 g/l

Fig.6. Theoretically calculated relationship between flux and transmembrane pressure in MF

However if we look at the range of both flux and pressure, we find ourselves in a different region than that of our experimental observations. Changing parameters within reasonable ranges does not lead to improvement of this situation : increasing the pore size, lowering of the tortuosity and of the flux for a given pore all lead to a shift towards the more linear part of the curve.

Interesting is also to investigate the concentration near the membrane wall which follows from the calculations. For the low bulk concentrations employed in this study we may see quite some concentration near the membrane wall, as high as 20 times C_{bulk}, but still the values do not come into the range where formation of a gel layer may be expected.

Thus we must conclude that even for very small pores we can not explain the flux behaviour by means of the friction transport model.

We may add a fouling resistance to the film and membrane resistance :

$$\Delta p_m = \Delta p_o \left\{ 1 + \frac{r^2}{8\mu} (b-1) \frac{C_{ip}}{M_i} \frac{RT}{D'_{iw}} \right\} + \Delta p_{foul} \tag{25}$$

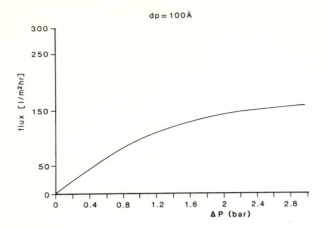

dp = 100Å

Fig.7. Theoretically
calculated flux -
pressure relationship
including experimen-
tally determined
fouling resistance

A typical example of such a calculation is given in Fig. 7. We see that now the
influence of Δ P on the flux v_0 is now much more pronounced, also at much higher pore
sizes.

In Fig. 8 we have presented some typical data on enzyme retention in relation to
the flux as follows from the model. Only for very small pores we calculate considerable
retention, while for pores of 500 Å and larger we have an apparent retention of a few
percent. This coincides with our experimental findings.

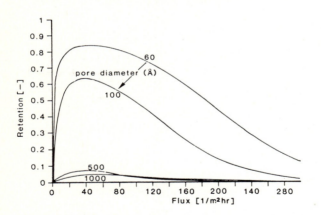

Fig. 8. Theoretically
calculated protein
retention in MF

II.3. Concluding remarks on MF : the pore blocking hypothesis

From the above it was shown that the fouling of the membrane in MF of the protein
solution cannot be caused by local gellayer formation. Reconsidering of our
experimental findings : pressure-dependent fouling for both microbial cells and for the
protein solution, about similar fouling resistances for microbial cell suspension,
protein solutions and combinations of the two excludes in our view also the phenomenon
of adsorption, but leaves as a working hypothesis that in both cases pore blocking by
cell debris must cause the fouling. Since the protein solution was obtained as permeate

from a MF separation, cell fragments may have been transported through the larger pores, leading to blocking of smaller pores in the experimental runs we made with it. Subsequent microscopic investigation indicated that indeed in the permeate small particles are present, which may well be cell debris. A rough calculation of the amount necessary to block the wall of the module indicates that a few mg/l would suffice. Also the decrease of R_{foul} with increasing bulk velocity seems to support the pore blocking idea. In future research we will try to test this hypothesis further.

III. ULTRAFILTRATION

III.1. General aspects

In previous work in our laboratory a comparison was made of the behaviour of several membranes with regard to the performance in the ultrafiltration of enzymes (van der Zee & Webbers, 4). Studied were the effects of pressure drop on the flux, enzyme retention and the retention of colour components. The latter may be present due to for instance Maillard reactions upon medium sterilization before fermentation, or may stem directly from the raw materials. For several product applications the removal of these components is required. In Fig. 9 a typical example of these data is shown. We see the well-known limiting flux at higher pressures, the value of which increases with increasing circulation velocity. Both enzyme retention and colour retention are seen to increase with increasing pressure. The explanation for the flux behaviour is the concentration polarization and gel layer formation; the increase in protein retention with increasing pressure is a consequence of increasing flux and consequently increasing membrane Peclet number $v_0 L/D_{iw}$. The increase in retention of colour components was considered to be caused by the formation of a secondary membrane which retained these components.

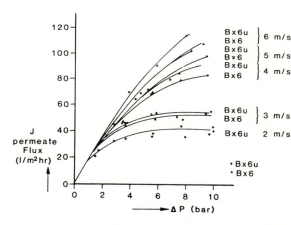

Fig. 9a. Experimentally observed relationship between flux and transmembrane pressure in UF of enzyme solution. Tube length 1.2 m; tube diameter 1.25 mm supplier PCI. Numbers at curves represent membrane types.

In the following a model is presented for the case of a membrane which retains 100% of the enzyme, and which has virtually zero rejection for colour components. The results of this model are compared with the results obtained for the BX-6U membrane (supplier PCI).

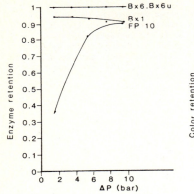

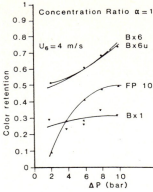

Fig. 9b. Experimen-
tally observed
retention of enzyme
and of colour
components in UF of
enzyme solution for
different membranes.

III.2. Modelling the flux vs pressure

In Fig. 9a the flux is given vs. the transmembrane pressure for different
circulation velocities. For the velocities of 2,3 and 4 m/s a maximum level may be
estimated from the graphs. In a separate concentration run the dependence of flux vs.
concentration ratio was determined. The plot was found to be linear, and from it the
value of C_{gel} was estimated. This corresponded to C_{gel} = 600 kg/m^3. In this value not
only enzyme, but also other proteins and high-molecular components contribute. Using
this value for the runs at constant concentration at C_{bulk} = 84 kg/m^3 for the three
velocities mentioned above, the mass transfer coefficients were calculated from :

$$v_o^\infty = k_m \ln (C_g/C_b) \qquad (26)$$

These values were plotted vs. the circulation velocity u_b. A fit gave then the
following relation for the mass transfer coefficient k_m :

$$k_m = 2.67 \times 10^{-6} u \qquad (27)$$

indicating a virtually linear dependence on this velocity.
From the slope at low transmembrane pressures in Fig. 9a we can estimate the membrane
resistance R_m, which for the BX-6U membrane was about 1.8×10^{10} kg/m^{2}s. With this
information we can cover the extreme ends of the flux-pressure curves. For the
intermediate region we assume that concentration polarization takes place, and that the
concentration profile in the film is given by :

$$\frac{C_w - C_p}{C_b - C_p} = \exp \left\{ \frac{v_o z}{k_m \delta} \right\} \qquad (28)$$

This equation is based on the diffusion-convection model in which in principle the
molecules are mobile. In order to be able to calculate the pressure drop over this
layer we view the force field as being dominated by the friction forces between protein
molecules and water on the one hand, and the force exerted by the membrane in rejecting
the bouncing protein molecules. Assuming a linear relationship between force and
relative velocity, we then have in the absence of overall acceleration phenomena the
same pressure drop over the film as would be found in a packed bed with the same
porosity gradient. For a small slice in such a bed we write Darcy's law :

$$\frac{dp_f}{dz} = \frac{\mu v_o}{P} \tag{29}$$

in which P is the permeability. Considering the protein molecules as spherical we write for P :

$$P = \frac{\varepsilon^3 d_p^2}{170 \ (1-\varepsilon)^2} \tag{30}$$

For the porosity we can write :

$$\varepsilon = 1 - c/d_s \tag{31}$$

in which C is the protein concentration and d_s the density in the hydrated form. Thus we may write for the pressure drop over the film :

$$\Delta p_f = \mu v_o \int_o^\delta \frac{1}{P} \ dz \tag{32}$$

With $dz = dC/(dC/dz)$ we can rearrange this to :

$$\Delta p_f = \frac{170 \ \mu \ k_m \delta}{d_p^2} \int_{\varepsilon_w}^{\varepsilon_b} \frac{(1-\varepsilon)}{\varepsilon^3} \ d\varepsilon \tag{33}$$

resulting in :

$$\Delta p_f = \frac{170 \ \mu \ k_m \delta}{d_p^2} \ \{ \ \frac{1}{2} \ (\frac{1}{\varepsilon_w^2} - \frac{1}{\varepsilon_b^2} \ ) - (\frac{1}{\varepsilon_w} - \frac{1}{\varepsilon_b}) \} \tag{34}$$

This holds for the case of full retention. Analogously for a gel layer of constant porosity ε_g holds :

$$\Delta p_{gl} = \frac{170 \ (1-\varepsilon_g)^2 \ \mu \ v_o \ \delta_{gl}}{\varepsilon_g^3 \ d_p^2} \tag{35}$$

Calculation results

In the calculations we used the following scheme. We first made steps in C_w for the protein concentration, up to C_{gel}. For each C_w follows the flux v_0 according to Eq.(25). From Eq.(33) follows then Δp_f, and from R_m follows Δp_m, thus giving Δp_{tot}. This curve goes up to the limiting flux and a corresponding critical transmembrane pressure Δp_g. For transmembrane pressures higher than Δp_g we keep the flux at v_0. The results are shown in Fig. 10, together with the data points. As can be seen, we have a reasonable coverage of the experimental data. This confirms the results which were obtained for dextran in stirred cells by Reihanian et al (17).
It is interesting to note that also for values of v_0 well below the gellayer value the pressure drop over the film is already in the same order as that over the membrane. In the foregoing we neglected the effect of osmotic pressure; from van 't Hoffs Law we estimate this at maximum 0.1 bar, which is low enough in comparison with the actual pressure drops.

FLUX IN UF OF PROTEASE

BX—6U membrane

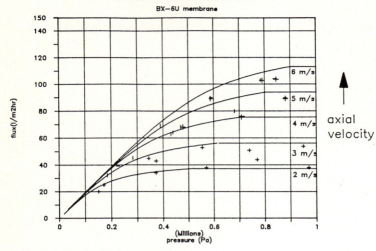

Fig.10. Comparison between theoretically calculated and experimentally observed flux in UF of enzyme solution. Parameter is the circulation velocity.

III.3. Colour retention

As found in experiments, the colour retention of the membrane is negligible. We now propose the following view of the transport of colour components, as depicted in Fig. 11. The small colour components are transported by convection and diffusion in between the large protein spheres, and experience friction with those spheres.

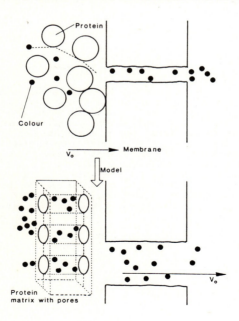

Fig. 11. Schematic view of the motion of colour molecules between large protein molecules, depicted in the lower half as motion in a protein matrix with cylindrical pores.

For the description of this process we can thus employ a similar description as used for the MF-system. In this model of section II.2 a pore radius has to be introduced. For this we take an effective pore radius, which in first approximation is taken equal to that of a cylindrical pore in a regular array of those pores at the same specific area and porosity as the array of spheres. This would give :

$$r_{cyl} = \frac{2\varepsilon}{3(1-\varepsilon)} \, r_{sphere} \tag{36}$$

Since it is imagined that some geometric correction should be made, we allow for a geometry correction a, and thus define :

$$r_{cyl} = a \cdot \frac{2\varepsilon}{3(1-\varepsilon)} \, r_{sphere} \tag{37}$$

Calculation results

For the transport in the film we divide this film in a number of small steps (20). Over each step the concentration is calculated with the average porosity as determined from the protein profile in the previous section. The thickness of the film was estimate from the mass transfer coefficient by :

$$\delta = \frac{D_{pw}}{k_m} \tag{38}$$

with D_{pw} following from Eq.(21) with $M_p = 26000$, and k_m from Eq.(27). By calculating the concentration ratio C_{cb}/C_{cm} over each step, and subsequently over the whole film, the color retention is found. For the region in which the gel layer is present the retention caused by the gel layer can be described by :

$$\frac{C_{cw}}{C_{cm}} = \left(\frac{1}{Kf_1}\right)_g + \left(1 - \frac{1}{(Kf_1)_g}\right) \exp\left(-\frac{v_o \delta_{gl}}{D'_{cw}}\right) \tag{39}$$

in which δ_{gl} follows from Eq.(35).

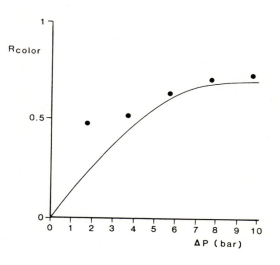

Fig.12. Comparison between theoretically calculated and experimentally observed colour retention in UF of enzyme solution Membrane type BX-6U, ciculation velocity 4 m/s.

Since we had no accurate information on the molecular mass of the colour component we have used M_{colour} as a variable. From the calculations emerged that a good fit was obtained for $M_{colour} = 300$. For the geometric correction on r_{cyl} a value of 3 was used. The tortuosity effect on D_{cw} was found to be about equal to 2. This is consistent with Bahtia's considerations for nearly uniform spheres. The results are shown in Fig. 12 and may be seen to be in good agreement with the experimental data; only at low pressure the model predicts a too low retention.

IV CONCLUDING REMARKS

We have presented some experimental work on microfiltration of protein-containing broth, and of UF of colour-containing enzyme solutions. By means of comparison of resistances and by considerations of the ternary transport it was shown, that the most probable factors affecting flux in cross-flow microfiltration are cells and cell debris. The retention of enzymes for the membrane in question is very low, unless very small pore sizes are considered. For the UF of enzyme solutions the pressure drop vs. flux relationship can be reasonably approximated with the hydrodynamic cake model, in which the protein molecules are viewed as hydrated spheres. The new friction model for small colour components moving through the protein layer gives a good fit with the experimental data on retention as a function of pressure. It would be interesting to further explore the possibilities of this model in more fundamental studies.

LITERATURE

1. V.Gekas, B.Hallström and G.Trägård, Food and dairy applications : the state of the art, Desalination, 53(1-3),(1985),95-128
2. K.S.Spiegler and O.Kedem, Thermodynamics of hyperfiltration (reverse osmosis) : criteria for efficient membranes, Desalination, 1,(1966), 311-326
3. G.Belfort and N.Nagata,Fluid mechanics and cross-flow filtration : some thoughts, Desalination,53(1-3),(1985),57-80
4. R.J.E.M. van der Zee and J.J.P. Webbers, The ultrafiltration of enzymes, lecture held at the Symposium on "Membranes in Biotechnology", Hilversum, (1985),available through Gist-brocades
5. N.Papamichael and M.-R.Kula, Abtrennung von Polyethylenglykol aus proteinhaltigen Lösungen mit Cellulose-Acetat-Membranen, in M.R.Kula, K.Schugerl and Ch.Wandrey (Eds) "Technische Membranen in der Biotechnologie", GBF-Monographien,9,(1987),140-150
6. A.G.Fane, Factors affecting flux and rejection in ultrafiltration, J.Sep.Proc.Technol.,4,(1983),15-23
7. A.L.Zydney and C.K.Colton, A concentration polarization model for the filtrate flux in cross-flow microfiltration of particulate suspensions, Chem.Engng.Commun.,47,(1986),1-21
8. M.C.Porter, Concentration polarization with membrane ultrafiltration, Ind.Eng.Chem.Prod.Res.Develop.,11,(1972),234-248
9. G.Belfort,P.Chin and A.Dziewulski,A new gel-polarization model incorporating lateral migration for membrane fouling, in "World Filtration Congress III : Harnessing Theory for Practical Applications",2,(1982)
10. G.Green and G.Belfort, Fouling of ultrafiltration membranes, Desalination,35,(1980),129-147
11. P.N.Patel,M.A.Mehaia and M.Cheryan,Cross-flow membrane filtration of yeast suspensions, J. of Biotechnol,5,(1987),1-16
12. G.Jonsson, Molecular weight cut-off curves for ultrafiltration membranes of varying pore sizes, Desalination,53(1-3),(1985),3-10
13. J.E.Bailey and D.F.Ollis, Biochemical and Engineering Fundamentals, McGraw Hill, New York, (1977)
14. S.K. Bahtia, Stochastic theory of transport in inhomogeneous media, Chem.Engng.Sci.,41(5),(1986),1137-1153
15. W.J.Beek and K.M.K. Mutzall, Transport Phenomena, J.Wiley and Sons,(1983)
16. M.G.Katz and G.Baruch,New insights into the structure of microporous membranes obtained using a new pore size evaluation method, Desalination,58,(1986),199-211

17. H.Reihanian,C.R.Robertson and A.S.Michaels, Mechanisms of polarization and fouling of ultrafiltration membranes by proteins,J.Membr.Sci,16,(1983),237-258

Preconcentration and Drying of Food Materials, edited by S. Bruin
Elsevier Science Publishers B.V., Amsterdam, 1988 — Printed in The Netherlands

AN EXERGETIC ANALYSIS OF TOMATO JUICE CONCENTRATION BY MEMBRANE
PROCESSES

E. DRIOLI[1], V. CALABRO'[1], R. MOLINARI[1], B. DE CINDIO[2]
[1]Chemistry Department, Chemical Engineering Section, University
of Calabria (Italy)
[2]Chemical Engineering Department, University of Naples (Italy)

SUMMARY
The exergetic analysis has been developed for typical membrane
processes namely microfiltration and reverse osmosis, and applied
to the concentration of a tomato juice. A comparison with the
traditional evaporating plant is done in terms of substitution
coefficient. From the obtained results it clearly appears the net
advantage in using these new techniques and indicates the need for
a deeper development of the practical aspects involved in their
application to food industries.

INTRODUCTION
   The industrial development urges today the use of processes with
low energy consumption, a more rational use of available raw
materials, non-destructive separation techniques permitting the
recovery and re-use of the chemical species. Membrane technology
offers positive answer to most of the problems indicated and in
particular pressure driven membrane separation processes, such as
cross flow microfiltration, ultrafiltration and reverse osmosis.
These processes considered already as basic unit operations, are
athermal, gentle and non-destructive; they do not require chemical
additives. Those properties appear to be of particular interest
for the rationalization of food processes. The advantages in
concentrating,for example,liquid food or beverages with an energy
efficient process combined with a minimum heat damage to the colour,
aroma and viscosity characteristics of the product, are evident.
   Some limits exist to the maximum obtainable concentration level
when high osmotic pressure values or solutes solubility are reached.
   The use of integrated membrane systems and of new membrane
technologies such as membrane distillation might contribute to a
further development of these processes for solving in particular
concentration problems.
   The possibilities of combining various membrane separation steps
and membrane reactors in the same industrial production is also
particularly attractive. Integrated membrane processes are
considered a rational and innovative solution in the future
industries (ref. 1). Some limits exist to the use of membrane
technology wich might be at least partially overcome today. The
high osmotic pressure of various solution of interest, limits the
applications of R.O. to their pre-concentration; membrane
distillation (refs. 2-3) might however operate at much higher
concentration than R.O.. New R.O. membranes are becoming available

with interesting selectivities which might also solve the problem
of aroma and nutrient retention. Fouling, module sanitation, etc.
are other aspects of membrane technology easier to control and
solve than in the past (ref. 4).

Food industry traditionally requires large amounts of thermal
energy particularly in the sterilization, concentration and drying
of the products. Reverse osmosis is the membrane technology which
is substituting in various industrial plants evaporation processes
(e.g. brackish water and sea water desalination);its growing in
the food industries is also significant. Electricity is the energy
generally used in R.O. and in all membrane processes with an
evident advantage respect to the use of thermal energy. Exergetic
analysis might contribute therefore (ref. 5) to a correct
evaluation of the potentialities of its introduction in the
industrial cycles. In this paper a study on the exergetic analysis
in concentrate tomato juice production based on combined membrane
processes is reported. A comparison with traditional evaporating
technique has been carried out in terms of substitution coefficients
for the innovative cycle proposed.

EXERGETIC ANALYSIS APPROACH

The exergetic analysis has been recognized to be an helpful
technique for judging the economic advantages of proposed cycles
(ref. 5) in particular in the case of food production plants
(refs. 6-7) and its use has become a well accepted rule. In the
following the main features of this analysis are summarised. The
definition of the exergy for a fluid stream is given by:

$$Ex = G \cdot ((h - h_o) - T_o \cdot (s - s_o)) \tag{1}$$

where Ex is the exergy, G is the mass flow rate, h is the specific
enthalphy, T_o is the reference temperature and s is the specific
entropy. Subscript o stands for reference status. This latter is
often taken at the surrounding conditions. For multicomponent
systems the previous equation is transformed to:

$$Ex = G \cdot \{C_p \cdot [(T-T_o) - T_o \cdot \ln(T/T_o)] + (R \cdot T_o/MW) \cdot [\Sigma_j (x_j \cdot \ln(a_j))] +$$
$$+ [(P-P_o)/\rho]\} \tag{2}$$

where the sum is extended to all the j components, MW and ρ are
respectively the mean molecular weight and the mean density of the
liquid solution, x_j is the molar fraction and a_j the activity of
the jth component, C_p is the specific heat of the solution and P
the total pressure. During a process there will be a change in the
exergetic content;therefore the corresponding variation may be
formally written as:

$$\Delta Ex = - T_o \cdot \dot{R}_S + \dot{W}_u + \dot{W}'_u \tag{3}$$

according to the second thermodinamic principle. In eqn.(3) $\dot{W}_u$ and
$\dot{W}'_u$ are respectively the electric energy and the thermal exergy
supplied to the system. $\dot{R}_S$ is the rate of entropy production.
From eqn.(3) it is then possible to compute the term $T_o \cdot \dot{R}_S$ that

represents the total entropic loss:

$$T_o \cdot \dot{R}_S = \dot{W}_u + \dot{W}'_u - \Delta Ex \tag{4}$$

Let us consider a typical thermal evaporation process (see Fig.1). A mass rate G_1 comes into the evaporator where the product losses a certain amount of water at mass rate G_d. Then the product leaves the evaporator with a mass rate G_2. Fresh water is supplied to the condenser with a mass rate G_w. To achieve this separation it is necessary to supply some electric and thermal energy. Very often this latter is done by means of condensing steam at mass rate G_V.

To compute the total exergetic variation of this step, one needs to take into account also the exergetic variation involved in the thermal energy supply sistem. Refering to the steam inlet and the condensed and cooled liquid outlet and by making use of eqn.(4), the total entropic loss may be written as the sum of the exergetic variation of the product and of the condensed water and the sum of the useful thermal work of the steam and electrical:

$$T_o \cdot \dot{R}_S = \dot{W}_u + \dot{W}'_u - (\Delta Ex_p + \Delta Ex_w) \tag{5}$$

where:

$$\Delta Ex_p = Ex_{G_d} + Ex_{G_2} - Ex_{G_1} \tag{6}$$

$$\Delta Ex_w = Ex_{Gw_{out}} - Ex_{Gw_{in}} \tag{7}$$

$$\dot{W}'_u = - \Delta Ex_{G_V} \tag{8}$$

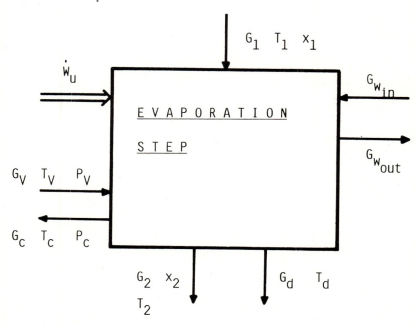

Fig. 1. Evaporation step with flow streams description.

For a membrane separation process (see Fig.2), assuming that the whole process is reasonably isothermal, the exergetic analysis leads to:

$$T_o \cdot \dot{R}_S = \dot{W}_u - \Delta Ex \tag{9}$$

$$\Delta Ex = \Delta Ex_{pump} + \Delta Ex_{valve} + \Delta Ex_{module} \tag{10}$$

where:

$$\Delta Ex_{pump} = G_1 \cdot ((P' - P)/\rho_1) \tag{11}$$

$$\Delta Ex_{valve} = G_3 \cdot ((P - P'')/\rho_3) \tag{12}$$

$$\Delta Ex_{module} = [(G_3 \cdot Cp_3 + G_2 \cdot Cp_2 - G_1 \cdot Cp_1) \cdot (T - T_o - T_o \cdot \ln(T/T_o)] +$$
$$+ [G_3 \cdot (P'' - P_o)/\rho_3 + G_2 \cdot (P - P_o)/\rho_2 - G_1 \cdot (P' - P_o)/\rho_1] +$$
$$+ (R \cdot T_o) \cdot \{(G_3/MW_3) \cdot [\Sigma_j(x_j \cdot \ln(a_j))_3] +$$
$$- (G_1/MW_1) \cdot [\Sigma_j(x_j \cdot \ln(a_j))_1]\} \tag{13}$$

Thus it is possible to define an exergetic substitution coefficient in order to compare different cycles. The following expression can be used for an economic evaluation of the substitution of a given cycle A with an alternative cycle B:

$$\eta_{Ex} = \frac{\dot{W'}_{u_A} - \dot{W'}_{u_B}}{\dot{W}_{u_B} - \dot{W}_{u_A}} \tag{14}$$

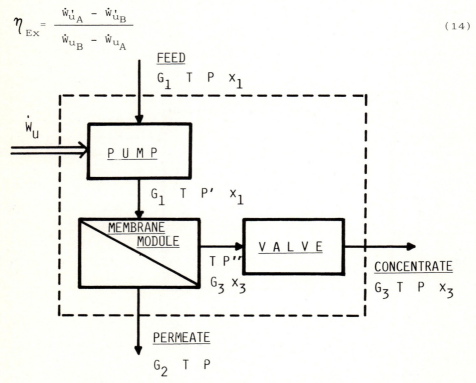

Fig. 2. Membrane Process step with flow streams description.

The terms on the right side of eqn.(14) can be evaluated according to the effective operative conditions. When η_{Ex} is more than one it means that the substitution is favorable, whereas less than one corresponds to a not favorable substitution. It is wortwhile to remark that the given definition is somewhat different from the usual energetic definition (ref.8) because it takes implicity into account also the entropic losses that are hidden in $\dot{W}'_u$.

THE CASE OF TOMATO JUICE CONCENTRATION

In Fig. 3 a general scheme of the concentration process of a tomato paste from 5.5 Brix to 29 Brix is shown.

The tomatoes are firstly sorted, washed and crushed, then a hot break process allows the enzyme inactivation and the thermal elimination of the peels that are eliminated in the pulper and refiner together with the seeds. After a holding tank the concentration process occurs. Then another holding tank is generally used and thereafter the sterilization and the canning process are usually done. Also if there are some peculiarities, the previous general scheme may be applied both to "traditional" and "alternative with membrane processes", the only thing that will change is the concentration block and eventually some heat recovery.

In the following the exergetic analysis has been applied to those schemes with the values that refer to an usual production (refs. 9-10). When considering a traditional evaporating scheme, with reference to a three effect evaporator, the results listed in Table 1 are obtained.

TABLE 1
Traditional Cycle for Tomato Juice Production

Single Block	ΔEx MJ/hr	$\dot{W}_u$ MJ/hr	$\dot{W}'_u$ MJ/hr	$T_O \cdot \dot{R}_S$ MJ/hr	$T_O \dot{R}_S$ %
SORTER WASHER CRUSHER	0.0	123.5	0.0	123.5	1.60
HOT BREAK	622.8	0.0	2197.3	1574.5	20.64
PULPER & FINISHER	- 168.3	201.4	0.0	369.7	4.82
HOLDING TANK	- 137.1	0.0	0.0	137.1	1.79
EVAPORATOR	230.3	504.0	4838.8	5112.5	66.68
HOLDING TANK	- 7.5	0.0	0.0	7.5	0.10
PASTORIZATION	59.4	72.0	131.1	143.7	1.87
CANNING PROCESSES	- 62.5	41.6	94.2	198.3	2.59
TOTAL	537.1	942.5	7261.4	7666.8	100.00

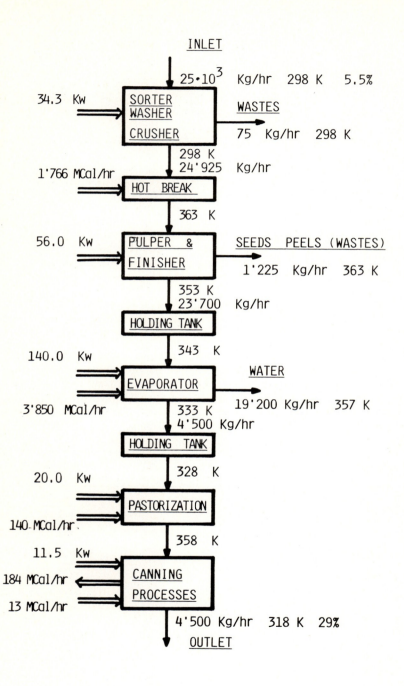

Fig. 3. Traditional Cycle for Tomato Juice Production

Some of these results have been computed using industrial performance data. It clearly appears that the evaporation step requires the largest amount of thermal energy when compared to the other steps. As a consequence the entropic losses are also the largest ones. This can be easily understood by considering that in this process it is necessary first warming up the fluid stream to a certain temperature level and then cooling it down. Also the hot break process results to be a high consuming step of the whole cycle. Some improvements could be obtained recovering part of the heat by putting heat exchangers in some strategic positions (ref.6)

The concentration step may be performed by means of R.O. modules (ref. 10). Of course in this case the inlet temperature may be rather low and in the considered case has been assumed to be 300 K°. Therefore a heat recovery can be introduced and in Fig. 4 the proposed cycle is sketched. Also the overall heat need is decreased due to the possibility of a heat recycle according to the fact the R.O. unit is feed at much lower temperature. The electrical energy is about doubled. The proposed solution has some practical operative difficulties, the biggest one beeing the high osmotic pressure driving from the desired high concentration level of the treated juice. Other technological difficulties arise from the fouling of the membranes, the concentration polarization and the increased viscosity during the process wich limit the life time and the efficiency of the proposed plant.

An answer to the outlined problems may be found in integrated membrane processes. As an example in Fig. 5 it is reported a possible combination of microfiltration and R.O. processes.

In principle it is possible to make a first gross separation between the pulp and an aqueous solution containing low molecular weight compounds such as mineral salts, vitamins etc.. This can be achieved by means of an appropriate choice of a microfiltration membrane unit positioned after the pulper and finisher. The solution is then concentrated in a typical R.O. unit that operates in much better conditions than in the previous proposed cycle. The two outcoming fluid currents are then mixed together in order to reconstituite the product. The exergetic analysis has been performed also for this cycle to investigate the eventual gains in terms of substitution.

The results are listed in Table 2 for the concentrator step and in Table 3 for the alternative cycle.

As it was expected there is a great decrease in the entropic losses and in the thermal heat supplied to the evaporator in the concentrator step. The membrane process does not require any thermal energy input, therefore there is a net advantage respect to the evaporator process. The entropic loss of the combined processes is much lower than in the evaporator cycle.

A detailed comparison of the two cycles is reported in Table 4 in terms of electric energy, thermal exergy and total exergetic variation respect to the total entropic loss.

It appears that in the case of M.F./R.O. cycle there is a better ripartition of the energetic and exergetic inputs.

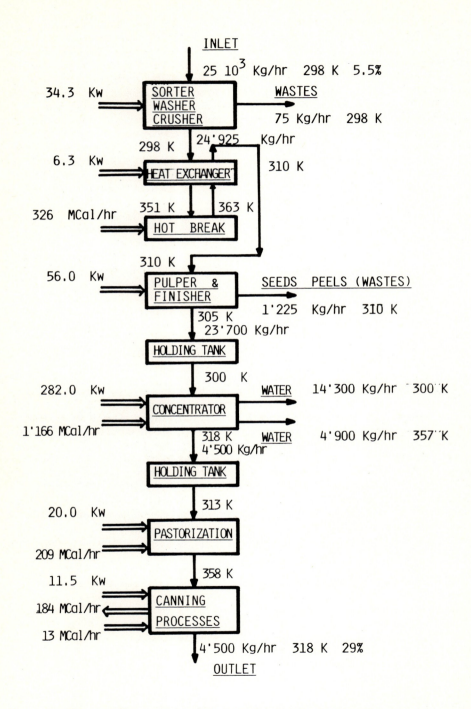

Fig. 4. Alternative Cycle for Tomato Juice Production

On the basis of the eqn. (14) assuming as reference the evaporator cycle, the exergetic substitution coefficient was found equal to 9.5 MJ/MJ. If the energetic coefficient is computed, it was found   equal to 40 MCal/Kwh.

It clearly appears also with this partial criterium the net advantage of M.F./R.O. cycle. Again the integrated cycle is convenient for some extent.

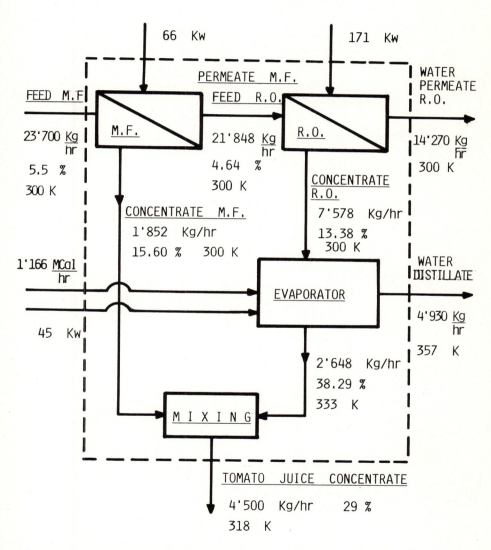

Fig. 5.   Concentrator step in the alternative cycle with integrated membrane processes.

TABLE   2

Concentrator Step in the Alternative Cycle with Integrated Membrane Processes.

Single Process	ΔEx MJ/hr	$\dot{W}_u$ MJ/hr	$\dot{W}_u'$ MJ/hr	$T_O \cdot \dot{R}_S$ MJ/hr	$T_O \dot{R}_S$ %
MICROFILTRATION (PUMP–MODULE–VALVE)	0.00	237.60	0.00	237.60	10.3
REVERSE OSMOSIS (PUMP–MODULE–VALVE)	22.25	615.60	0.00	593.35	25.6
EVAPORATOR	159.05	162.00	1466.07	1469.07	63.5
MIXING	− 14.42	0.00	0.00	14.42	0.6
TOTAL	166.88	1015.20	1466.07	2314.39	100.0

TABLE   3

Alternative Cycle for Tomato Juice Production

Single Block	ΔEx MJ/hr	$\dot{W}_u$ MJ/hr	$\dot{W}_u'$ MJ/hr	$T_O \cdot \dot{R}_S$ MJ/hr	$T_O \dot{R}_S$ %
SORTER WASHER CRUSHER	0.0	123.5	0.0	123.5	3.57
HEAT EXCHANGER	− 175.4	22.8	0.0	198.2	5.72
HOT BREAK	199.1	0.0	405.6	206.5	5.96
PULPER & FINISHER	− 15.5	201.4	0.0	216.9	6.27
HOLDING TANK	− 7.1	0.0	0.0	7.1	0.21
CONCENTRATOR STEP	166.9	1015.2	1466.1	2314.4	66.84
HOLDING TANK	− 4.2	0.0	0.0	4.2	0.12
PASTORIZATION	75.3	72.0	196.5	193.2	5.58
CANNING PROCESSES	− 62.5	41.6	94.2	198.3	5.73
TOTAL	176.6	1476.5	2162.4	3462.3	100.00

TABLE 4

Comparison between the two cycles

CYCLE	$\dot{W}_u'/T_o \cdot \dot{R}_s$ (%)	$\dot{W}_u/T_o \cdot \dot{R}_s$ (%)	$\Delta Ex/T_o \cdot \dot{R}_s$ (%)
TRADITIONAL CYCLE	94.71	12.29	− 7.00
ALTERNATIVE CYCLE	62.46	42.64	− 5.10

CONCLUSIONS

This work has shown on one hand the extent for wich membrane processes may be advantageous in the concentration of a tomato paste from an exergetic point of view. On the other hand, from a more general point of view, the application of the exergetic approach to the specific case here treated, has once more demonstrated the validity and the usefulness of the method when comparing different cycles.

The results show a net advantage when using M.F./R.O. respect only evaporator. In fact from the reported table it clearly appears that M.F./R.O. shows the better ripartition of all the entropic losses, the worst beeing the evaporator cycle.

Also in this case some practical difficulties are found, among then mainly the reconstitution of the fluid product texture.

It should be recognized that in the light of the exergetic advantages shown, further researches have to be done to obtain R.O. membranes able to reach higher level of juice concentration. Solutions as those presented with coupled M.F./R.O. processes also require a deeper study focused on the rheological reconstitution aspects of the texture of the obtained juice. At the moment what is already possible to propose are combinations of traditional evaporators with membrane processes.

Nevertheless it is possible to conclude that the proposed cycles, also with their actual limits, represent a real innovation in the field of food processing because on one side they are not based on an industrial reproduction of housewife of craftsman operations, and, on the other hand they process all the characteristics of the new trend of using mild technologies in food production with the aim to reduce thermal, mechanical and biological damages.

REFERENCES

1 E. Drioli, Integrated membrane processes, in: The 1987 ICOM, Tokio, Japan, June 8-12,1987.
2 E. Drioli, V. Calabrò, Y. Wu, Membrane distillation, J. of Memb. Science, in printing.
3 E. Drioli and M. Nakagaki, Scientific and industrial membrane development, in: P.F. Chimica Fine Rept.,CNR, Rome, Italy, 1985.
4 B. Hallstrom and G. Tragardh, Membrane processes in food industry: hopes and realities, in: Ystad Symposium, Proc. Eur. Symp. Food

114

Work, Party E.F.C.E., C.Cantarelli and C. Peri Eds., Forster-Verlag, 1983, pp. 281-288.

5   J.E. Ahern, The Exergy Method of Energy System Analysis, John Wiley & Sons Inc., 1984.

6   E. Rotstein, The exergy balance: a diagnostic tool for Energy optimization, J. Food Sci., 48 (1983) 945-950.

7   G. Tragardh, Energy and exergy analysis in some food processing industries, Lebsem Wiss Techn., 14 (1981) 213-217

8   Electricitè de France - SEPAC, Parigi, Le coefficient de substitution, le gain net de petrole, 1981

9   L. Palmieri, A. Porretta, G. Dall'Aglio e M. Baccarini, Analisi energetica di un impianto per la produzione di concentrato di pomodoro mediante il bilancio exergetico, Ind. Conserve, 61 (1986) 240-245.

10 V. Calabrò, R. Molinari, B. de Cindio and E. Drioli, I processi a membrana nella produzione dei succhi alimentari: analisi exergetica della produzione di concentrati di pomodoro, Chim. Oggi, 12 (1986) 15-18.

Preconcentration and Drying of Food Materials, edited by S. Bruin
Elsevier Science Publishers B.V., Amsterdam, 1988 — Printed in The Netherlands

THE CONCENTRATION OF SOLUTIONS OF HIGH OSMOTIC PRESSURE BY REVERSE OSMOSIS

H.F. van Wijk, R.J.M. Creusen and A.E. Jansen
MT-TNO Zeist, the Netherlands

ABSTRACT

In reverse osmosis the osmotic pressure of the retentate limits the attainable concentration of the solute. This problem can be solved by increasing the solute concentration of the permeate.
Two methods are considered:
A. Reflux Reverse osmosis (REFRO)
B. The Low Retention method (LRM)
It is shown that REFRO is only effective when very thin hollow fiber membranes are used. The axial pressure losses in these fibers are considerable and reduce the effect of the reflux.
Moreover thin hollow fibers are not very suitable to handle fouling solutions.
LRM can be used with tubular, flat and spiral wound membrane configurations.
It is shown that the optimal retention depends on the feed concentration and the concentrationfactor.
The additional membrane capacity needed for the reflux is very low.
A loss of solute via the permeate can be prevented either by coupling the reverse osmosis process to a reactor or fermentor or by coupling the low retention modules to one or more high retention modules.
When hollow fibers are used in LRM it is favourable to use hollow fibers with a gradually decreasing retention in the direction of the flow of the retentate.

INTRODUCTION

In conventional reverse osmosis the increasing osmotic pressure of the solution to be concentrated reduces the flux through the membrane. The applied hydraulic pressure must exceed the osmotic pressure otherwise there is no flux at all.
This well known fact limits the concentration that can be obtained in particular of solutes of low molecular mass. In practice the effect of the osmotic pressure on the flux is even higher than predicted on the basis of the osmotic value of the solution.

Fouling increases the concentrationpolarization by an increase of the stationary layer on the membrane surface.

Restoring the flux by the application of a higher hydraulic pressure is not feasible in most cases. Asymmetrical and composite membranes can not withstand higher pressures than 40-80 bar without compaction or collaps of the membrane structure.

However, the _effective_ osmotic pressure in a membrane process is determined by the difference of the osmotic pressure across the membrane. The disadvantageous effect of increasing osmotic pressure can be reduced by increasing the concentration of the solutes at the permeate side of the membrane.

Methods to reduce the effective osmotic pressure in this way are:

A. Reflux Reverse Osmosis (REFRO)

B. The application of low retention membranes: The Low Retention Method (LRM)

In REFRO a part of the concentrate is returned to the permeate side of the membrane.

In LRM a part of the solutes passes the membrane. The reduction of the osmotic pressure is an intrinsic property of the membrane itself. Theoretically both methods have the possibility to reduce the counteracting effect of the osmotic pressure to any desired level: In REFRO by a proper choice of the amount of reflux and in LRM by a proper choice of the membrane retention. In practice there are several limitations for the application of both methods which will be considered in this paper for the concentration of glucose solutions.

REFLUX REVERSE OSMOSIS (REFRO)

When REFRO is applied a part of the concentrate is recycled to the permeate side of the membrane as is shown in fig. 1.

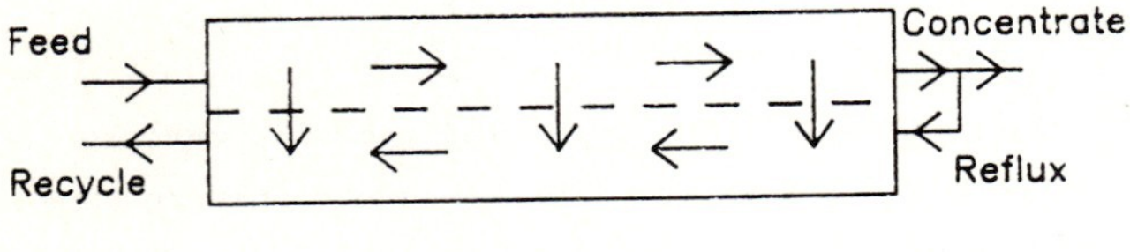

Figure 1 REFLUX REVERSE OSMOSIS

The process is preferably carried out as a counter current process in order to minimize the concentration differences across the membrane.

The effective concentration of the solutes at the permeate side of membrane is determined by the diffusion of the solutes in the supporting layers of the membrane against the waterflux through the membrane. As a result of these opposing effects a "reverse" concentrationpolarization will occur. The concentration of the solutes near the separating part of the membrane will be lower than in the bulk of the permeate.

The reverse concentrationpolarization of a flat membrane is determined by

$$c_w/c_b = e^{-Fd/D} \qquad (1)$$

cw: the concentration of the solute near the membrane surface at the permeate side, determining the effective osmotic value of the permeate (kg/m^3).

cb: the concentration of the bulk of the permeate (kg/m^3).

F : the flux through the membrane (m/s).

d : the thickness of the supporting layers of the membrane (m).

D : the diffusioncoefficcent of the solute (m^2/s).

The thickness of the supporting layers in flat, tubular and spiral wound membrane modules is at least 10^{-3}m. Assuming a diffusioncoefficcent of 6×10^{-10} m^2/s (glucose in water) and a flux of 6×10^{-6} $m\,s^{-1}$ the calculated cw/cb value amounts only 4.5×10^{-5}. This means that there is no effect of the reflux of solutes.

It can be computed that in order to obtain a reasonable effect of the reflux, the thickness of the supporting layer must be less than 25×10^{-6}m.

Such thin supporting layers can only be realized with asymmetrical or composite hollow fibers. The thin wall thickness of the fibers requires an inner diameter of the fibers of about the same size in order to withstand pressures in the range of 40-80 bar.

The pressure drop in the axial direction of the hollow fibers may largely compensate the effect of the reduced effective osmotic pressure. Assuming an inner diameter of the fibers of 25×10^{-6}m, the pressure loss in axial direction amounts about 30 bar over only 0.50 m at a pressure of 40 bar. The flux efficiency is only 47%.

Hollow fiber membrane modules are not very suitable for handling fouling solutions like fruitjuices, hydrolysates, etc.

This is another serious disadvantage for the application of REFRO.

THE USE OF LOW RETENTION MEMBRANES (LRM)

A reverse concentrationpolarization can be avoided by using membranes with a low retention.

This method permits using tubular, flat and spiral wound membrane modules and can be applied on fouling solutions.

Membranes with a low retention can be obtained by a controlled curing of asymmetrical cellulose acetate membranes or by special preparation methods of composite membranes.

Both types of membranes have in common that their flux is much higher than the flux of high retention membranes. The flux of a cellulose acetate membrane with a retention of 0.7 is 2 times higher and with a retention of 0.55 even 4-5 times higher than the flux of a membrane with a retention of 0.99. These high fluxes compensate the fact that the reflux in case of LRM must pass the membrane.

Solute losses via the membrane can be prevented either by returning the permeate stream to the reactor or fermentor in which the solute is produced or by recycling the permeate to a membrane module with a high retention. Both possibilities are considered in the next section for glucose solutions.

RECYCLING OF THE SOLUTE TO THE PRODUCTSOURCE

This method is suitable when the concentration of the product limits its own production (product inhibition).

In fig. 2, a membrane module is continuously fed by a reactor. Clean up steps between the reactor and membrane module may be necessary but are left out. Total mixing of the retentate in the membrane module is assumed.

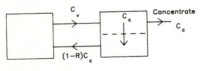

Figure 2

The concentration range for the configuration of figure 2 is determined by the mass balance and the effective osmotic pressure across the membrane.

The mass balance gives: $\dfrac{Cc}{Cv} \leq \dfrac{1}{1-R}$ (2)

$$R = 1 - \frac{Cr}{Cf}.$$

or $R \geq 1 - \dfrac{Cv}{Cc}$ (2a)

The applied pressure P must be higher than the osmotic pressure difference $\Delta \pi$ across the membrane

$$P > \Delta \pi \quad (3)$$

$$\Delta \pi = R \pi$$

$$R < \frac{P}{\pi} \quad (3a)$$

Cc and Cv are the concentrate and feedconcentrations of the solute and R the retention of the membrane.

The maximum productionrate is inbetween the retention values $(1-\frac{Cv}{Cc})$ a

In order to find the minimal productions costs the energy costs of the reflux must be taken into account.

In fig. 3 the reciprocal production costs are computed as a function of the retention of a cellulose acetate membrane for concentrating glucose solutions of 8-13% wt to 25% wt.

Every line in fig. 3 represents a different start concentration, starting at at 8% glucose (the lower curve) in steps of 0.5% up to 13% glucose. The maximum in fig. 3 represent minimal production costs. In the concentration ranges mentioned above the optimum retention is always lower than 1.

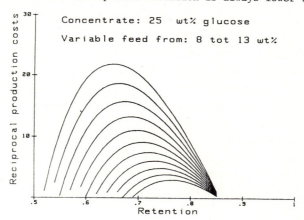

Figure 3

COMBINATION OF LOW RETENTION MEMBRANES (LR)
WITH HIGH RETENTION MEMBRANES (HR)

In order to prevent losses of solute via the permeate it also is possible to recycle the permeate stream to one or more high retention modules. (fig. 4 & 5)

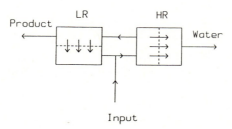

Figure 4: PROCESS WITH ONE LOW RETENTION MODULE (LR) AND ONE HIGH RETENTION
          MODULE (HR)

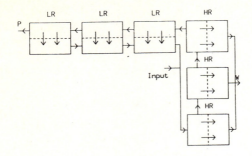

Figure 5: PROCESS WITH THREE LOW RETENTION MODULES (LR) AND THREE HIGH
          RETENTION MODULES (HR)

The water is removed via the permeate of the high retention module which
operates at a favourable osmotic pressure.

As has been shown in previous papers (5,6), it is favourable to use a set of
HR and LR modules for a stepwise increase of the concentration.

In table 1 the results are presented for concentrating a 5% wt glucose
solution to 30% wt at a hydraulic pressure of 40 bar.

Table 1 shows that the combination of 3 low retention modules (R=0.55) and
three high retention modules (R=0.99) gives the highest production rate per
m² membrane area. The combination of one low retention module and 3 high
retention modules gives the lowest reflux (lowest energy costs).

It is worthwhile to mention that in the latter case only 25% of the feed-
stream has to be recycled.

As has been shown earlier the costs of concentrating by reverse osmosis are
lower than a 6 step multi-effect evaporation, even at the very high osmotic
value of the concentrate (30% wt).

This osmotic value is even higher than the applied hydraulic pressure of 40
bar.

The results mentioned in table 1 are confirmed experimentally with solutions
of hydrolyzed starch and cellulose.

However, it appears that a production loss of 20-60% may occur by fouling of
the membranes after several days of operation.

The low retention membranes are more susceptable for fouling than high
retention membrane.

HOLLOW FIBER MEMBRANES WITH A LOW RETENTION

The results mentioned in this paper concern the concentration of glucose
solutions with a number coupled but separately stirred

tube shaped membrane modules.

The low retention method can also be applied with hollow fibers. As the low retention method allows the application of fibers of larger wall thickness and larger inner diameter the axial pressure losses can be reduced to an acceptable level.

If plug flow in and outside the fibers can be realized the number of modules in a low retention-high retention combination can be restricted to 2.

It is obvious that fibers with a gradually decreasing retention along the axial direction of the fiber will give the best results in obtaining high concentrations.

It seems possible to produce fibers with such properties. However, such fibers are not yet commercially available.

CONCENTRATING: 5 TO 30 WT% GLUCOSE (40BAR)

N	LR membrane-area [m2]			HR membrane-area [m2]			Production [l/m2.h]	Reflux ratio
	1	2	3	1	2	3		
2	1	–	–	1.6	–	–	1.1	0.48
3	1	–	–	0.9	1.2	–	1.6	0.30
3	1	1.0	–	3.4	–	–	2.0	0.85
4	1	–	–	0.6	0.7	0.9	1.9	0.25
4	1	0.9	–	1.9	2.6	–	2.3	0.50
4	1	1.0	1.3	5.6	–	–	2.4	1.04
5	1	0.9	–	1.3	1.6	2.1	2.5	0.39
5	1	1.0	1.1	3.0	4.0	–	2.7	0.64
6	1	1.0	1.0	2.1	2.5	3.3	2.8	0.50

Table 1

REFERENCES

1. S. Loeb and M.R. Block;
   Countercurrent flow osmotic processes for the production of solutions
   having a high osmotic pressure.
   Desalination 13 (1973) 207-213

2. G.D. Metha;
   Comparison of membrane processes with destillation for alcohol-water
   separation.
   J. Membr. Sc. 17 12 (1982) 1-26

3. G.D. Metha;
   Survey and evaluation of different membrane processes for purification of
   fermentation ethanol: Final Report to the Solar Institute under contract-
   nr. XK1-9417 July 1, 1981

4. Ch Elata U.S. Patent 3.617.550 April 1969

5. H.F. van Wijk, A.E. Jansen and R.J.M. Creusen;
   An optimized Hyperfiltration Process for Concentrating Aqueous Solutions
   of high osmotic Pressure, Desalination 51 (1984) 103-112

6. H.F. van Wijk, A.E. Jansen and R.J.M. Creusen;
   The concentration of aqueous solutions of high osmotic pressure by
   hyperfiltration.
   Proceedings of the 4th World Filtration Congres Part 2 volume 8 (1986)
   11.95-11.98

Preconcentration and Drying of Food Materials, edited by S. Bruin
Elsevier Science Publishers B.V., Amsterdam, 1988 — Printed in The Netherlands

OSMOTIC CONCENTRATION IN FOOD PROCESSING

C.R. LERICI[1], D. MASTROCOLA[2], A. SENSIDONI[1] and M. DALLA ROSA[1].
[1]Istituto di Tecnologie Alimentari, Università degli Studi,
Piazzale Kolbe, 4, 33100 Udine (Italy).

[2]Dipartimento di Protezione e Valorizzazione Agro-Alimentare,
Università degli Studi, Via San Giacomo, 7, 40126 Bologna
(Italy).

SUMMARY

Osmotic concentration is a water removal process which is
based on placing foods, such as pieces of fruit or vegetables, in
a hypertonic solution. Because of the higher osmotic pressure of
the solution a driving force for water removal arises between
solution and food, while the natural cells acts as a "semi-
permeable" membrane (refs. 1-2). For substitution in Van't Hoff'
law, it is possible to relate the osmotic pressure with the water
activity (a_w) as follow (ref. 3): $\pi = -(RT \ln a_w)/V_w$, where V_w is
the partial molar volume of water. Thus the osmotic solution used
must have a low a_w, the solute must be harmless and have a good
taste, such as concentrated sucrose solution and commercial
syrups (HFCS).

INTRODUCTION

"Direct" osmosis, so called in opposition to "reverse"
osmosis, at present is the only practical, and practiced, system
for the concentration of pieces of solid food. From the
conceptual point of view direct osmosis is a very simple process
as it is based on placing foods, such as pieces of fruit or
vegetables in a hypertonic solution. Because of the higher
osmotic pressure of the solution, a driving force for water
removal arises between solution and food, while the natural cells
act as "semipermeable" membrane (refs. 1,2,3,4,5,6).

Osmotic concentration can be considered a simultaneous water
and solute diffusion process. In fact, as the membrane is only
partially selective there is always some leakage of solute from
the solution into the food and from the food into the solution.

By means of a suitable choice of osmotic solution and of the
processing conditions, the solute diffusion can be minimized or
enhanced depending on the desired characteristics of the osmosed
food (refs. 7-8).

It is this duplicity of action in respect to the food (partial dehydration and controlled changes of chemical composition) which makes direct osmosis so interesting in food processing.

The aim of this paper is to give a concise overall view of the existing or potential applications of osmotic dehydration.

PROCESSING ASPECTS OF OSMOTIC DEHYDRATION.

A great amount of recently reviewed researches has made it possible to identify the factors which have the greatest influence on the exchange processes in osmotic dehydration, largely confirming the forecast made on the basis of theory.

Thus, for the same food material the mass transfer rate is conditioned by the following variables:

- osmotic pressure of the solution given by the solute osmosity
  and concentration;
- temperature;
- food/solution weight ratio.

Furthermore, the process rate is accelerated when the mass transfer resistances are reduced and the driving forces are enhanced (e.g. stirring of solutions; use of vacuum; continuous re-concentration of the solution)(refs. 5,9).

As far as the food material is concerned the principal characteristics affecting osmosis rate are chemical composition, physical structure and specific surface area of each piece. For a given fruit or vegetable, the ripening stage, the cultivar etc. are very important.

Considering that the diffusion of the solutes initially present in a food into the concentrated osmotic solution, is small as compared to the solute uptake from the solution, direct osmosis can be defined by the following variables (refs.7,10):

W.R.= weight reduction, % by wt
W.C.= water content, % by wt
T.S.= total solid, % by wt
W.L.= water loss, g/100g raw food
S.G.= solid gain, g/100g raw food.

Moreover, as the osmotic pressure is thermodynamically related to water activity, according to:

$$\pi = - RT(\ln A\omega / V\omega) \qquad (1)$$

Where:

π = osmotic pressure
R = gas law constant
T = absolute temperature
Aω = water activity
Vω = partial molar volume of water

the process can be described in terms of changes in water activity. Figure 1 show the influence of two different osmotic solutions (1: glucose solution 51°Bx ; 2: HFCS solution 72°Bx) on the Aω, W.C., W.L., W.R. and S.G. changes of apple pieces during direct osmosis at room temperature (ref. 2).

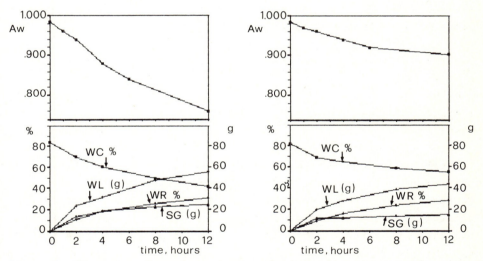

Fig. 1. Changes of apple pieces during direct osmosis in a glucose solution (51°Bx) (right) and in a HFCS (72°Bx) (left); aw= Water activity, WC= water content in grams, WL= water loss in grams, WR= weight reduction %, SG= solid gain in grams (ref. 2).

Obviously, the selection of osmotic agent cannot only be made on the basis of its osmosity, but other factors must be considered. It can be said that the principal qualities of an osmotic solute should be: absolute wholesomeness, high solubility, high Aω lowering capacity and good organoleptic characteristics depending on the osmosed product (e.g. sweetness, saltiness, etc.). Thus, for every food product it's possible to select the most suitable solutes or combination of these, in order to obtain the best levels of water removal and of solid gain, and the desired changes in sensorial characteristics. So it is possible to obtain osmosed products which are different as regards final water content, solid gain, Aw and sweetness level, by using hydrolized starch syrups with different chemical composition for the osmotic solution (2,11). For example, for the osmosed apple, a fructose-rich syrup resulted as more suitable whereas for the osmosed carrot a maltose-rich syrup was better (see table 1).

TABLE 1
  Characteristics of 6 hrs osmosed carrot cubes treated with two different corn syrups. A= fructose; B= dextrose; C= maltose; D=polysaccharydes).

Syrups	Syrups Composition				Osmosed Carrot Characteristics				
	A	B	C	D	WR	WC	WL	SG	Aw
	(% on dry matter)				%	%	g	g	
FRUDEX	42	52	3	3	56	45	69	11.3	.855
GLICOSA	0	50	46	24	66	54	72	5.2	.915

Another variable which affects process rate and the final quality of the osmosed product is the temperature. Fig. 2 reports the curves representing time-temperature combinations required to obtain the same reduction in Aw. In this example, referring to direct osmosis of apple cubes in HFCS, we can see that to obtain the same Aw reduction, the time tends to decrease exponentially as the temperature increases (refs. 11,12).

High-temperature short-time osmosis can be used successfully to combine the drying effect of the osmosis with the inactivating effect on enzymatic activity of high temperatures. (tab. 2).

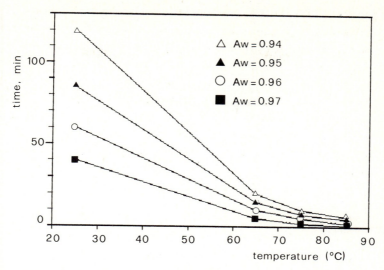

Fig. 2. Time to realize a prefixed weight reduction % as a function of temperature of osmotic solution in apple cubes (ref. 11).

TABLE 2

Percentual of the initial enzymatic activity of fruit after osmotic concentration carried out at different temperature.

Product	Treatment		% Enzymatic activity
	Temp. (°C)	Time (min)	
Apple	65	5	21
	" "	10	16
	" "	20	10
	75	2	10
	" "	3	5
	" "	5	3
	" "	10	0
	85	2	3
	" "	3	0
Carrot	70	3	37
	" "	5	16
	" "	10	9
	80	1	8
	" "	2	0
	90	.5	4
	" "	1	0

128

DIRECT OSMOSIS APPLICATION IN FOOD PROCESSING TECHNOLOGY.

The principal possibilities of direct osmosis in food processing are expressed in schematic form in fig. 3.

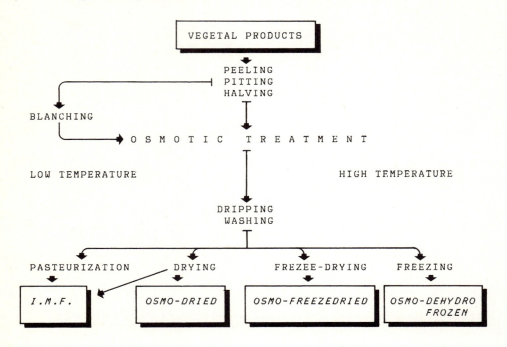

Fig. 3. Flow diagram of process operations combining the osmotic concentration with the thermal treatment at high temperature to disactive enzymatic activity.

Fig. 4 shows the curves which describe the water content vs time changes in osmosed and non-osmosed carrot cubes during air drying (refs.13,14,15). Compared to untreated sample, the osmosed one shows a lower drying rate. Nevertheless, the difference in W.C. change among osmosed and non-osmosed samples is maintained up to very low W.C. values (about 10%); this means that the drying time necessary to obtain IMF, when other condition are the same, is considerably lower for osmosed sample.

This is even clearer if the curves showing Aw vs time changes, reported in fig. 5, and the desorption isotherms, reported in fig. 6, are observed.

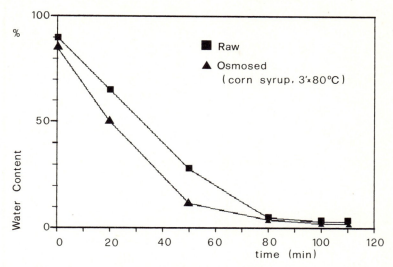

Fig. 4. Behaviour of water content % versus drying time during the air drying of raw and osmosed carrots.

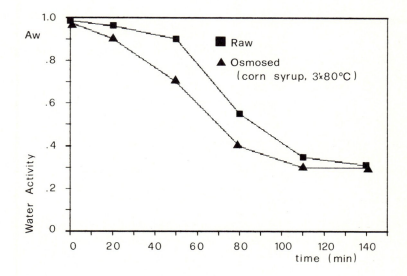

Fig. 5. Evolution of a$_w$'s values of raw and osmosed carrot cubes during air drying process.

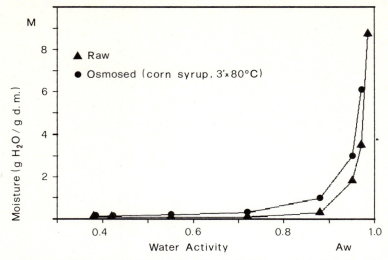

Fig. 6. Desorption isotherms of raw and osmosed carrot cubes. Dried materials evaluated at 20°C.

The advantages of osmotic treatment, in terms of reducing processing time, are particularly interesting in freeze-drying, where, as is known, the removal of water is a very long and expensive process (refs. 5,10).

Osmotic concentration can be used as a preparative step prior to freezing (refs. 16,17). In fact, the gain of solute and the water removal give rise to a product with low free-water content.

During the freezing phase the osmosed product shows a shorter freezing time and an evident depression of the freezing point (fig. 7).

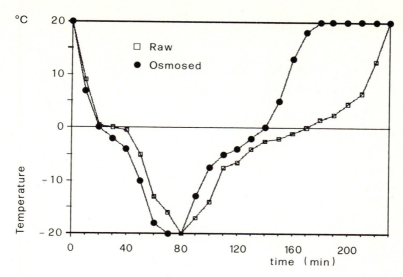

Fig. 7. Freezing-thawing thermal diagram of fresh and osmosed strawberries.

In the frozen state osmo-dehydro-frozen fruit in general shows a pleasant, firm texture and after thawing, reduced drip loss and often better firmness than the non-osmosed fruit.

The low energy demand during freezing (less water to freeze, lesser volume and weight of the product to store and to transport), make the osmo-dehydro-freezing an interesting process to reduce energy consumption in food freezing and to improve product quality. In order to further improve the mass transfer processes in direct osmosis a proposal has been made to blanch the raw material prior to osmosis. In figs. 8 and 9 the water loss and solid gain respectively vs time observed in apricot halves, blanched (3' at 90°C), and not blanched, during osmosis in HFCS at room temperature are reported. The blanching seems to provoke a partial collapse with great absorption of syrup by the fruit.

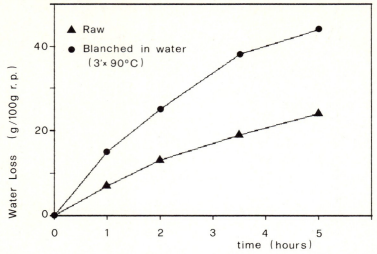

Fig. 8. Water loss (g per 100 g of raw product) versus osmosis time of raw and blanched apricot halves (6 hours at 25°C in HFCS).

It is probable that in the case of "blanching-osmosis" too it will be possible to determine the blanching conditions which would enhance the water removal process, while keeping the solid gain within acceptable limits.

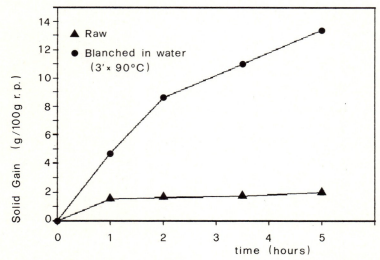

Fig. 9. Solid gain (g per 100 g of raw material) increase versus osmosis time during osmosis concentration of raw and blanched apricot halves. (6 hours at 25°C in HFCS).

CONCLUSIONS

Direct osmosis appears to be a successful method of concentrating fruit and vegetables. The osmosed product shows with the reduction of Aw values, very good texture and high aroma and color retention.

As a treatment prior to drying, freezing or freeze-drying, direct osmosis appears particularly useful as a means of limiting energy consumption. In addition, the use of osmotic solutions which are suitable both as regards composition and concentration, makes it possible to control water content and chemical changes in osmosed food, and thus to improve its sensorial characteristics.

Finally, concentration effect can be combined with enzymatic inactivation by blanching prior to osmosis or in one operation, by HTST-osmosis.

REFERENCES

1   J.D. Ponting, G.G. Waters, R.R. Forrey, R. Jackson and W.L. Stanley, Osmotic dehydration of fruits, Food Technology, 20 (1966) 125.
2   C.R. Lerici, G. Pinnavaia, M. Dalla Rosa and L. Bartolucci, Osmotic Dehydration of Fruit: Influence of Osmotic Agents on Drying Behavior and Product Quality, J.of Food Science, 50 (1985) 1217.
3   C.R. Lerici, M. Riva, E. Maltini and D. Torreggiani, La disidratazione osmotica, in "Progress in dehydration of fruit and vegetables", C.R.Lerici and C.Peri editors, CNR-IPRA, Rome Monograph n.4 (1985) 130.
4   D.F. Farkas and M.E. Lazar, Osmotic dehydration of apple pieces: effect of temperature and syrup concentration on rates, Food Technol., 23 (1969) 688.
5   C.R. Lerici, M. Pepe and G. Pinnavaia, La disidratazione della frutta mediante osmosi diretta. I. Risultati di esperienze effettuate in laboratorio, Industria Conserve 52 (1977) 125.
6   R. Andreotti, M. Tomasicchio and L. Macchiavelli, Disidratazione parziale della frutta per osmosi, Industria Conserve 58 (1983) 90.
7   A. Lenart and J.M. Flink, Osmotic concentration of potato. 1: Criteria for the end-point of the osmosis process, J. Fd. Techn. 19 (1984) 45.
8   J. Conway, F. Castaigne, G. Picard and X. Vovan, Mass transfert consideration in the osmotic dehydration of apples. Can. Inst. Food Sci. Techn. 16 (1983) 25.
9   M. Dalla Rosa, G. Pinnavaia and C.R. Lerici, La disidratazione della frutta mediante osmosi diretta. II. Esperienze di laboratorio su alcuni generi di frutta. Industrie Conserve 57 (1982) 3.

134

10   J. Hawkes and J.M. Flink, Osmotic concentration of fruit slices prior to freeze dehydration, J. Food Proc. and Pres. 2 (1978) 265.

11   D. Mastrocola, C. Severini, C.R. Lerici and A. Sensidoni, Disidratazione per via osmotica della carota, Industrie Alimentari 26 (1987) 133.

12   C.R. Lerici, D. Mastrocola and G. Pinnavaia, Esperienze di osmosi diretta ad alta temperatura per tempi brevi, Industrie Conserve 61 (1986) 223.

13   C.R. Lerici, G. Pinnavaia, M. Dalla Rosa and D. Mastrocola, Applicazione dell'osmosi diretta nella disidratazione della frutta, Industrie Alimentari 22 (1983) 184.

14   G.M. Dixon, J.J. Jen and V.A. Paynter, Tasty apples slices results from combined osmotic dehydration and vacuum drying process, Food Prod. Dev. 10 (1976) 60.

15   M.M. Islam and J.M. Flink, Dehydration of potato. II: Osmotic concentration and its effect on air drying behaviour, J.Fd.Technol. 17 (1984) 387.

16   M. Dalla Rosa, C.R. Lerici and G. Dall'Aglio, Pretrattamento osmotico nella congelazione della frutta, in: P. De Leo, P. Ghezzi and A. Monzini (Eds.), Atti 1°Convegno per l'Area Mediterranea, Vol.1, Bari, Italy, January 28-30, 1985, CLUP, Milano.

17   G. Pinnavaia, M. Dalla Rosa and C.R. Lerici, Dehydrofreezing of fruit using direct osmosis as concentration process, Acta Alimentaria Polonica, in press.

Preconcentration and Drying of Food Materials, edited by S. Bruin
Elsevier Science Publishers B.V., Amsterdam, 1988 — Printed in The Netherlands

SUPERCRITICAL EXTRACTION OF FERMENTATION PRODUCTS

A.M.M. VAN EIJS, J.M.P. WOKKE and B. TEN BRINK

TNO—CIVO Institutes, P.O. Box 360, 3700 AJ Zeist (The Netherlands)

ABSTRACT
   Supercritical extraction with carbon dioxide can be applied for downstream
processing of fermentation media.
   From a synthetic medium simulating a Clostridium acetobutylicum
fermentation broth acetone, butanol and ethanol are extracted.
   The behaviour of different sorts of biocatalysts, when exposed to
supercritical carbon dioxide, is described. Important parameters which are
related to the survival of biocatalysts are pH and the compression rate.

INTRODUCTION

   Supercritical extraction is nowadays a well known unit—operation, with some
industrial and many lab— and pilot—scale applications (ref. 1). The most
important supercritical solvent, especially for food and pharmaceutical
applications, is carbon dioxide. The advantages of supercritical carbon
dioxide extraction fit well to those of biotechnological production processes:
the mild processing temperature, the absence of toxic chemical solvents and
the selectivity of the processes are the most important features they have in
common.

   Product recovery from a fermentation broth needs other procedures than the
downstream processing methods applied in chemical industry, with respect to
product concentration, broth viscosity and (bio—)catalyst properties (ref. 2).
Supercritical extraction may provide solutions to these special problems. The
low product concentrations make distillation expensive, due to the energy
needed to heat the bulk water. Extraction with supercritical carbon dioxide
can be carried out at fermentation temperature, thus avoiding possible thermal
damage of the product and saving energy costs.

   Supercritical carbon dioxide introduced in a liquid decreases the overall
viscosity (ref. 1), and thus facilitates the handling of the broth and
enhances mass transfer from the liquid to the supercritical phase.

   Some examples of extracting fermentation products with supercritical (or
near critical) carbon dioxide are reported in literature (refs. 3,4,5).

   De Philippi and Moses describe the extraction of ethanol from aqueous
solutions, e.g. a yeast fermentation broth (ref. 3). They report lower energy
costs as compared to distillation. The whole fermentation broth, including

yeast cells and other solids, could be handled without problems in their pilot-plant.

Shimshick reports the extraction of carboxylic acids from dilute aqueous media with supercritical carbon dioxide (refs. 4,5). The specific advantage of supercritical carbon dioxide extraction in this application is the pH decrease of the aqueous phase, which results in a shift of the ratio undissociated acid/dissociated acid and a higher concentration of the free acids. This shift is necessary for effective extraction of the carboxylic acids.

However, none of these authors has studied the effect of supercritical carbon dioxide on the biocatalyst. Resistance of the biocatalyst to the preconcentration conditions implies that it can be re-used, reducing overall fermentation costs. Furthermore, if micro-organisms (or plant or animal cells) would survive, they might also produce under these conditions.

A Japanese patent describes an alcohol fermentation using immobilized yeast cells (ref. 6). The researchers claim that the fermentation can be carried out under conditions in which carbon dioxide is in the liquid or supercritical state. On the other hand Kamihira et al. report the sterilization of yeasts, bacteria and fungi with supercritical carbon dioxide (ref. 7). They ascribe the sterilizing effect of carbon dioxide to acidification of the medium and extraction of cellular compounds such as phospholipids.

In this paper we report on the extraction of acetone, butanol and ethanol from synthetic media, simulating the downstream processing of a Clostridium acetobutylicum fermentation broth. Clostridium acetobutylicum is inhibited by high product concentrations, which makes it important to remove the product in situ (ref. 8).

As a first step towards an integrated production/extraction unit, the influence of the supercritical carbon dioxide procedure on the viability of the biocatalysts is determined.

MATERIAL

Chemicals

Carbon dioxide was supplied by Rommenhöller Koolzuur B.V., Rotterdam, the Netherlands.

Acetone, butanol and ethanol were purchased from Merck GMBH, Darmstadt, FRG. All chemicals were p.a. grade.

High pressure extraction pilot plant

The TNO pilot plant we used for supercritical extraction consists of four extraction vessels, with a capacity of 1.8 l each, and one separation vessel, with a capacity of 3.8 l. The compressor capacity is 11 kg CO_2/h.

METHODS

Extraction procedure

The extraction vessels were filled with 200–500 ml aqueous medium. The vessels were connected in series. The separation vessel was partially filled with water to assure effective product separation.

The system was pressurized with carbon dioxide by a compressor. After attaining the desired pressure the system was heated to 35 °C and carbon dioxide was pumped through the extraction vessels at a rate of 5–10 kg/h.

Exposure of biocatalysts to supercritical carbon dioxide

Aqueous growth media were inoculated with fresh plant cells, yeast cells or bacteria and contacted with supercritical carbon dioxide. The four extraction vessels were connected in a parallel way to avoid contact between the broths. In the case of plant cells the system was filled with 6–7 bar air, before supplying the carbon dioxide.

After attaining the desired pressure the compressor was shut off and the system was left at that pressure during the incubation time.

Pressurization and expansion conditions were controlled to avoid pressure changes faster than 60 bar/h.

Testing of cell viability

After contact with carbon dioxide the microbial viability was tested by counting the number of colony forming units (cfu) after overnight incubation on trypticase soy broth agar at 37 °C.

Determination of cell density

Growth of bacterial cells was monitored by measuring the optical density (OD) of the broth at 666 nm, before and after the experiments.

RESULTS

1. Extractions

A synthetic solution of acetone, butanol and ethanol in water was extracted with supercritical carbon dioxide. Concentrations were chosen to fit those of fermentation broths of Clostridium acetobutylicum cells (ref. 8). Figures 1 and 2 show the partition of the compounds extracted and those remaining in the raffinate after half an hour extraction with supercritical carbon dioxide.

FIGURE 1

AMOUNTS OF ACETONE/BUTANOL/ETHANOL IN THE EXTRACT
AND RAFFINATE AFTER 0.5 HOUR EXTRACTION WITH
SUPERCRITICAL CARBON DIOXIDE

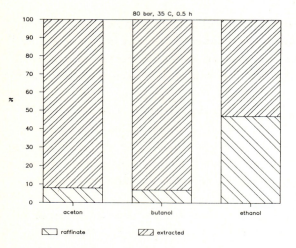

FIGURE 2

AMOUNTS OF ACETONE/BUTANOL/ETHANOL IN THE EXTRACT
AND RAFFINATE AFTER 0.5 HOUR EXTRACTION WITH
SUPERCRITICAL CARBON DIOXIDE

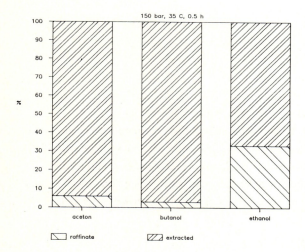

Butanol and acetone were extracted faster and to a higher degree than ethanol. At 150 bar more than 95 % of the acetone and butanol were extracted in 0.5 h. At that time 33 % of the ethanol was left in the broth. After 0.5 h extraction with supercritical carbon dioxide at 80 bar the broth contained only 8 and 7 % of the initial amount of acetone and butanol respectively and 47 % of the initial amount of ethanol.

These results prove that acetone, butanol and ethanol can be extracted with supercritical carbon dioxide. Acetone and butanol can be easily separated from ethanol by fractionated extraction or expansion. Under the applied conditions it was not possible to separate acetone from butanol, but other methods based on supercritical fluid processing may be successful (ref. 9).

Fractionation of the products of a hetero-fermentative process will lead to higher value products.

2. Survival of the biocatalysts

From the experiments described above it is evident that supercritical extraction has great potential as an extracting agent for fermentation products from dilute, aqueous broths. Fig. 3 represents an extraction process to remove product from fermentation broth in situ, feasible with the present state of the art. Before entering the extraction unit the biocatalyst has to be removed from the broth and recycled to the fermenter by a separate route.

Research at our laboratory concentrates on the possibilities to make cells survive during the supercritical extraction process. This would lead to an in situ extraction process without broth clearing, as illustrated in figure 4.

The effects of introduction and release of high pressure carbon dioxide in and from aqueous fermentation media can be numerous. Possible complications are:
- extraction of essential components form the cells
- acidification of the medium
- cell cracking (bursting)
- carbon dioxide poisoning

In view of these complications we screened a variety of cells for their resistance to supercritical carbon dioxide. The only precaution taken was a restriction of the compression and expansion rates of the system.

Aqueous buffer media were inoculated with plant cells, yeasts and bacteria and contacted with supercritical carbon dioxide at 150 bar, 35 °C. To avoid starvation of the strictly aerobic plant cells, air (6 bar) was supplied before filling the system with carbon dioxide. After reaching 150 bar pressure, carbon dioxide and air circulated through the system for 3 hours.

FIGURE 3

FERMENTATION AND PRODUCT RECOVERY FROM THE CLEARED

BROTH

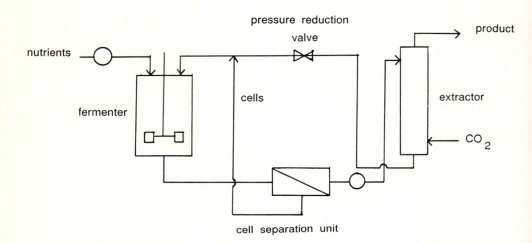

FIGURE 4

FERMENTATION AND PRODUCT RECOVERY FROM THE WHOLE

BROTH

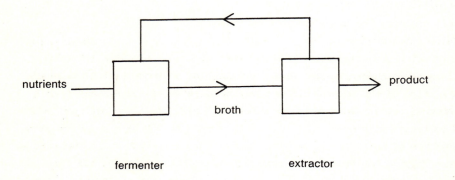

During this experiment the plant cells were disrupted, but the bacterial and yeast cells showed no visible damage under the light-microscope. Table 1 shows the survival of the micro-organisms.

During contact with the carbon dioxide, cell density of the Lactobacillus culture increased about three fold. The density of a reference culture at ambient pressure increased by a factor 9 during the same time.

Comparison of the cell concentration estimated by optical density, with cell viability shows 100 % survival of the cells. In contrast E.coli and C.albicans did not grow during the incubation with supercritical carbon dioxide (whereas the controls did grow) and in addition the viability decreased dramatically.

Repeating the experiment with only Lactobacillus cells did not produce the same, encouraging survival number. The speed of compression of the carbon dioxide was found to be a critical parameter for the survival of micro-organisms.

These results do not permit to conclude which of the above mentioned factors causes cell death. The fact that only Lactobacillus cells were able to survive in the first experiment implies that the low pH in the presence of supercritical carbon dioxide is the main problem. Lactobacilli are known to be resistant to relatively low pH.

In another series of experiments we tried to elucidate the effect of pressurized carbon dioxide on the survival of Lactobacillus cells. Table 2 represents viability of cells brought in contact with carbon dioxide at different pressures, and the effect of supplied air on this viability.

Raising the pressure had a strong, negative effect on the survival of cells brought into contact with carbon dioxide. At supercritical conditions, less than 1 % of the cells in the fermentation medium survived the treatment. However, if the same broth was buffered, 60 % of the cells survived the carbon dioxide treatment. The broths with and without buffer were exposed to carbon dioxide with equal compression and expansion rates.

These results give an indication of the most important conditions that must be fulfilled for cell-survival. Kamihira et al. obtained effective sterilization of wet, microbial cells by treatment with carbon dioxide at 200 bar, 35 °C (ref. 7). Cells with a water content of 2-10 % could not be sterilized in the same way. The authors concluded that sterilization is caused by a complex mechanism, involving a pH decrease and extraction of essential matter from the cells. In some cases they found bursted E. coli cells whereas bakers yeast cells were found to be intact after sterilization by super-critical carbon dioxide treatment. We too found a sterilizing effect of pH

TABLE 1
Viability of cells after treatment of broth with supercritical carbon dioxide.

Biocatalyst	cell viability					
	start		end		control	
	OD_{666}	cfu/ml	OD_{666}	cfu/ml	OD_{666}	cfu/ml
L. plantarum	0.19	1×10^8	0.52	3.0×10^8	1.3	9.1×10^8
E. coli	0.15	1×10^8	0.19	$<10^5$	0.84	1.3×10^9
C. albicans	0.18	?	0.17	$<10^5$	0.60	1.3×10^7

Conditions: – pressure: air 6 bar, CO_2 150 bar
– temperature: 35 °C
– contact time: 3 h

TABLE 2
Viability of Lactobacillus broths after treatment with high pressure carbon dioxide

pressure [bar]	gas	survival [%]
1	CO_2	100
7	CO_2	100
60	CO_2	40
100	CO_2	<1
100*	CO_2	60
6	air	100
6+50	air+CO_2	10

conditions: temperature : 35 °C
$\frac{dP}{dt}$: 50 –100 bar/h
contact time : 4 h

* = buffered

decrease after introduction of carbon dioxide in aqueous media. Even in cases were the survival is very low (0.1–2 %, results not included) we found a positive effect of buffering the medium on survival of Lactobacillus cells. This supports the finding of Kamihira et al. on the survival of dry cells (ref. 7).

A second important parameter of survival during contact with supercritical carbon dioxide is the compression rate. The expansion procedure applied in these experiments seems gentle enough to make cells survive.

CONCLUSIONS

1 Supercritical extraction can be used in downstream processing of fermentation broths. Acetone, butanol and ethanol can be extracted from dilute broths with supercritical carbon dioxide at 80–150 bar, 35 °C. Ethanol can be separated from the mixture with butanol and acetone in water.
2 Lactobacillus cells can survive being in contact with supercritical carbon dioxide.
3 Survival during contact with supercritical carbon dioxide depends at least partly on pH, and partly on the compression rate.

REFERENCE

1   G.G. Hoyer, Chemtech July 1985, 440–448.
2   B. Atkinson and P. Sainter, J. Chem. Tech. Biotechnol. 32 (1983) 100–108
3   R.P. De Filippi and J.M. Moses, Biotechnol. Bioeng. Symp. 12 (1982) 205–219
4   E.J. Shimshick, United States Patent 4 (1981) 250, 331
5   E.J. Shimshick, Chemtech June 1983, 374–375
6   Hitachi, Ltd, Jpn Kokai Tokkyo Koho J.P. 60 94 089
7   M. Kamihira, M. Taniguchi and T. Kobayashi, Agric. Biol. Chem. 51 (1987), 407–412.
8   T.G. Lenz and R. Moreira, Ind. Eng. Chem. Prod. Res. Dev. 19 (1980), 478–483.
9   Octrooi 143430, Studiengesellschaft Kohle M.B.H., Mülheim FRG.

DRYING OF FOOD MATERIALS:
PRINCIPLES AND MODELLING

Preconcentration and Drying of Food Materials, edited by S. Bruin   147
Elsevier Science Publishers B.V., Amsterdam, 1988 — Printed in The Netherlands

SPRAY DRYING OF FOOD LIQUIDS, AND VOLATILES RETENTION

C. J. KING

Department of Chemical Engineering, University of California,
Berkeley CA 94720 (U. S. A.)

ABSTRACT
   The selective-diffusion concept of Thijssen and co-workers has
been seminal for understanding the factors governing losses of
volatile flavor and aroma substances during spray drying. This
understanding has led to important avenues for improving retention
of these substances.
   Under common spray-drying conditions losses of volatile
substances are determined by the combined effects of mass transfer
during the atomization process and from drops, once they are
formed. Several processing factors, such as feed concentration and
degrees of foaming and/or emulsification, have opposing effects
upon these two loss mechanisms. It is probable that there are
substantial additional losses due to morphological changes, but
these are poorly characterized.
   Measurement and modeling of flow and temperature fields during
spray drying with pressure atomization reveal that air pumping by
the spray is a dominant factor. As atomizer pressure increases,
the lifetime of the contiguous pre-atomization liquid sheet
decreases, the rate at which hot air is entrained into the spray
increases, and recirculation of air within the spray dryer
increases. There should therefore be an optimum atomizer pressure
for maximum volatiles retention. Another interesting prediction
from modeling is that sprays tend to dry radially inward from the
outer edge of the spray cone, because of much higher temperatures
at the edge of the spray.

THEME

   The goal of this presentation is to demonstrate the major

progress in spray drying that has stemmed from Hans Thijssen's

seminal concept of "selective diffusion". This unobvious, but very

simple, concept brought about a powerful understanding of the

factors governing the loss of volatile flavor and aroma substances

during all sorts of drying and concentration processes. It enabled

insight which has led, and will continue to lead, to very

considerable improvements in dried and concentrated foods.

INTRODUCTION

   Most drying and evaporative concentration processes for liquid

foods have been plagued by reduced product quality resulting from

large losses of volatile flavor and aroma substances. The
resulting "flat" product has less appeal to the consumer. The
volatile flavor and aroma substances are lost because they have
very high relative volatilities with respect to water (ref. 1).

Selective Diffusion

In the mid 1960's Hans Thijssen proposed a <u>selective diffusion</u>
mechanism which could lead to much greater retention of volatile
flavor and aroma substances (refs. 2-4). This concept is built
upon recognition of the fact that the diffusion coefficient of
water in concentrated solutions behaves in a different fashion from
the diffusion coefficients of other substances. Figs. 1 and 2
(refs. 3,4) demonstrate this phenomenon. Diffusion coefficients of
water and of other solutes decrease substantially as water
concentration decreases in aqueous solutions of carbohydrates and
other food-related substances (Fig. 1). However, the essential
point is that the diffusion coefficient of water decreases by a

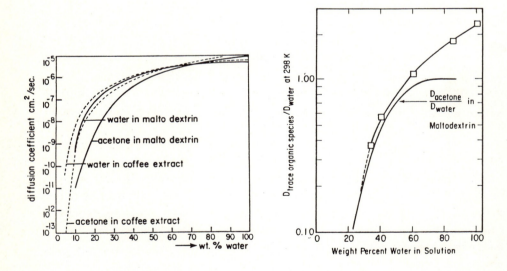

Fig. 1 (Left). Effect of Water Concentration on the Diffusion
Coefficients of Water and Acetone in Coffee Extract and
Maltodextrin at 25 C (ref. 4).

Fig. 2 (Right). Effect of Water Concentration in Coffee Extract
(squares) and in Maltodextrin Solution on the Ratio of the
Diffusion Coefficients of Acetone and Water at 25 C (ref. 4).

much lesser factor than do the diffusion coefficients of other substances. This behavior is general, applying to numerous different organic solutes and mixtures of dissolved solids (ref. 1). Even the diffusion coefficient of oxygen in sucrose solution decreases much more rapidly with increasing sucrose concentration than does the diffusion coefficient of water (refs. 5,6).

The result of this general phenomenon is that above some dissolved solids content the diffusion coefficients of other substances become much less than that of water (Fig. 2). Therefore, if it is possible to reach a high enough concentration of dissolved solids at the surface of material being dried before there has been massive loss of volatile flavor and aroma, the rest of the volatiles should become imprisoned because the surface becomes effectively impermeable to them.

Thus there is often good retention of volatiles in freeze drying because of the concentrating effect caused by the prior freezing step. And the retention of volatiles in spray drying can be improved if a high concentration of dissolved solids is built up on the surfaces of drops early enough in the drying process. This goal can be accomplished by rapid initial drying, since high rates of water evaporation and transport create substantial concentration gradients within the drops. Build-up of high surface concentrations of dissolved solids can be assisted considerably by supplying a more concentrated liquid feed to a spray dryer, because there will be lower diffusion coefficients and less of a gradient is needed to yield the critical surface concentration.

The existence of selective diffusion has been verified in a number of different ways:

1. Measurements of diffusion coefficients under carefully controlled conditions have demonstrated that the trend in the ratio of diffusion coefficients shown in Figure 2 does indeed occur (refs. 7,8).

2. It has been found that volatiles retentions in spray drying (refs. 3,9) and freeze drying (ref. 10) vary with changing operating conditions in the directions that are predicted by selective diffusion.

3. It was possible to model losses from suspended drops under controlled conditions on the basis of measured diffusion coefficients (refs. 11,12).

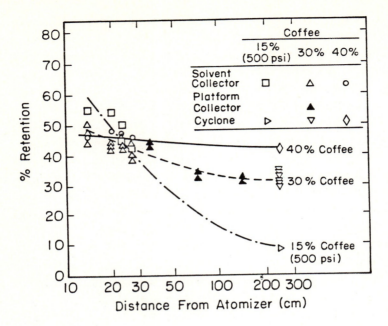

Fig. 3. Retention of n-Propyl Acetate as a Function of Axial Distance from the Atomizer during Laboratory Spray Drying of Coffee Extract. (500 ppm (w/w) Initial Acetate Concentration; 200 C Air Inlet Temperature; 7.0 MPa Atomizer Pressure; 49.5 C Liquid Feed Temperature) (ref. 13).

4. In our group at Berkeley we have taken samples at various axial and radial positions within a laboratory spray dryer. As shown in Figure 3, we have found that, for high enough feed concentrations, volatiles retention does indeed approach a non-zero asymptotic value at large distances from the atomizer, as the surface becomes impermeable to the volatile substances through the development of high surface concentrations (ref. 13). Notice that the horizontal coordinate in Fig. 3 is logarithmic. On a linear plot the approach to the asymptote is still more pronounced.

5. It has been found that the order of retentions of substances with different volatilities during spray drying is consistent with liquid-phase, rather than gas-phase, mass-transfer control. This is true for both retentions in the dry products (refs. 3,4) and retentions at various axial locations near the atomizer (ref. 14). Also, the changes in volatiles retention as a function of axial distance from the atomizer caused by changes in air temperature and

liquid feed temperature are consistent with the predictions of selective-diffusion theory (ref. 14).

Other aspects of mass transfer within drops during spray drying have been reviewed recently (ref. 15).

Mechanisms of Volatiles Loss in Spray Drying

Kerkhof and Thijssen (ref. 9) observed that retentions of three different volatile alcohols during spray drying of maltodextrin solutions could be interpreted in terms of diffusional losses from droplets plus additional losses. Possible sources of additional loss include the drop-formation process at the atomizer and morphological changes to drops and particles (frothing, expansion, cratering) during the drying process.

Kieckbusch and King (ref. 14) used special samplers to probe within the region close to a pressure atomizer and found large losses of volatiles there. These losses result from diffusion within the very thin and fast-moving film or sheet of liquid that issues from the atomizer. There may also be contributions from mass transfer within the ligaments formed upon break-up of the sheet and from circulation and oscillation of drops as they are initially formed. Under many conditions, most of the volatiles loss occurs in a large spray dryer takes place in the region within 50 cm of the atomizer.

Other than the rather scattered results obtained by Furuta, et al (ref. 16) in a difficult experiment, there have not yet been direct measurements of the effects of morphological changes upon volatiles losses during spray drying. However, video recordings made by El-Sayed (ref. 17) reveal a tortured history for drying of drops of coffee extract and maltodextrin solutions, with much frothing and bursting of bubbles repeatedly through the drop surface. From these observations, there should be ample opportunity for additional losses of volatiles from interior liquid thrust out through the drop surfaces.

These observations and others lead to a relatively simple picture of successive stages of volatiles loss and the dominant factors controlling them:

1. For a pressure atomizer, initial losses occur by diffusion from the expanding liquid sheet issuing from the atomizer. The model of Simpson and Lynn (ref. 18), based upon the equivalent heat-transfer solution of Hasson, et al (ref. 19), describes this

loss in terms of molecular diffusion within a laminar sheet. There is probably enhanced transport due to turbulence within the liquid, as well as additional resistance in the gas phase. It appears that these two additional effects may roughly offset one another. These "sheet" losses are primarily determined by the length of the liquid sheet, with greater sheet lengths giving greater loss.

For pneumatic atomizers and centrifugal atomizers there should be similar losses from fast-moving contiguous liquid before break-up. For all atomizers, there may be additional losses during atomization due to droplet oscillation and circulation.

2. Once drops are formed and oscillation and circulation cease or are absent, the loss can be described by a model of diffusion within a stagnant sphere. The phenomenon is actually one of ternary diffusion with highly variable diffusion coefficients (ref. 20), but the amount of volatiles loss is primarily determined by the diffusion of water and the resultant concentration profile for dissolved solids, with there being a rough coincidence between the beginning of the falling-rate period of drying and the cessation of substantial losses of volatiles (ref. 21).

Schoeber and Thijssen (ref. 22) introduced a powerful approximation based upon a penetration period followed by a regular regime of drying. This approach provides a simple method for predicting the transition from the constant-activity to the falling-rate period in cases of highly variable diffusion coefficient. The technique has been further developed (ref. 23) and extended to allow for non-isothermal conditions, particle shrinkage, and internal voids (ref. 24).

3. There are probably additional losses in cases where frothing, expansion and cratering of drops occur. The amounts of these losses are relatively unknown and uncharacterized.

In many cases, effects on volatiles losses from changes in operating parameters can be analyzed in terms of the competing effects of sheet loss and droplet diffusion.

AVENUES TOWARD PROCESS IMPROVEMENT

Feed Concentration. As already noted, increasing feed concentration markedly improves volatiles retention, as a result of lower diffusion coefficients of dissolved solids and a lesser internal concentration gradient needed to reach the critical surface concentration for selective diffusion.

A striking example of the effect of feed concentration is shown
in Fig. 3, where for 30% and 40% coffee-extract solutions most of
the loss occurs from the expanding sheet, whereas for 15%
coffee-extract solutions the loss through droplet diffusion is
greater than that from the sheet. There is almost total loss of
volatiles from 15% solutions because of the delayed onset of
selective diffusion. As can also be seen in Fig. 3, higher feed
concentration for some substances gives the unwanted effect of
greater sheet losses, since more viscous liquids can form longer
sheets before break-up.

Of course, if the original material is not sufficiently
concentrated, the only way to achieve a higher feed concentration
of dissolved solids is by means of a preconcentration process that
is itself volatiles-retentive. Candidates include freeze
concentration and, in some cases, reverse osmosis. Another
possibility is removal and sequestering of volatiles and then
adding them back to the spray dryer feed.

Inlet Air Temperature. Since faster drying imposes steeper
internal water concentration gradients, hotter feed air to a spray
dryer will, in general, give better volatiles retention. As was
pointed out by Thijssen (ref. 26), this factor must be balanced
against the possibility of greater thermal degradation of the
product.

Improved Mixing in the Atomizer Zone. It is important for hot
air to be drawn into the atomizer zone sufficiently to give high
temperature and humidity driving forces for drying. This turns out
to be a dominant effect, and is discussed in more detail in the
next section.

Atomizer Pressure (for Pressure Atomizers). As atomizer
pressure increases, the liquid sheet becomes shorter, and losses
from the sheet become less. This effect is shown in Fig. 4, where
it can be seem that retention profiles in the droplet-diffusion
zone parallel one another for different atomizer pressures, with
the differences coming from changes in the sheet losses at very
short distances from the atomizer.

Changes in atomizer pressure also strongly affect entrainment of
air into the spray and overall flow and mixing patterns within the
dryer, and thereby have additional effects upon volatiles
retention. These factors are discussed in more detail later.

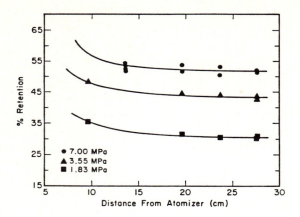

Fig. 4. Retention on n-Propyl Acetate as a Function of Axial Distance from the Atomizer during Laboratory Spray Drying of 60% (w/w) Aqueous Sucrose Solution at Various Atomizer Pressures. (650 ppm (w/w) Initial Acetate Concentration; 200 C Air Inlet Temperature; 49.5 C Liquid Feed Temperature) (ref. 25).

Foaming of the Feed. For products where a certain product bulk density must be achieved, foaming the feed provides a means of enabling the use of a higher feed concentration while not exceeding that bulk density. Foaming the feed can also lead to more ready redissolution of the product.

Frey and King have examined the effects of foaming of the feed upon volatiles retention, both theoretically (ref. 27) and experimentally (ref. 25). Foaming by mechanical admixing of a gas introduces a perforation mechanism which causes the liquid sheet to break up sooner, thereby reducing volatiles loss. On the other hand, foaming gives a more open drop structure and thereby gives greater losses by drop diffusion. Fig. 5 (ref. 13) shows axial profiles of volatiles concentration measured for an unfoamed feed and for a feed foamed by mechanical admixing of gas. For this particular case the greater droplet diffusion losses almost exactly offset the lower sheet losses.

Foaming can also be accomplished by desorption of a soluble gas, such as carbon dioxide, from a supersaturated feed. In this case, foam bubbles cannot grow rapidly enough to affect sheet break-up, and the only effect is one of greater diffusional loss from drops, as is shown in Fig. 6 (ref. 25).

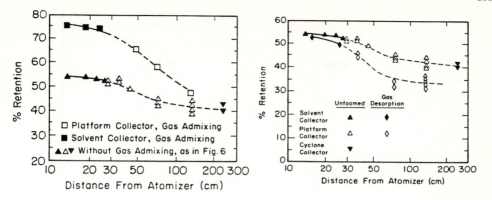

Fig. 5 (Left). Retention of n-Propyl Acetate as a Function of Axial Distance from the Atomizer during Laboratory Spray Drying of 60% (w/w) Aqueous Sucrose Solution, with and without Foaming by Admixing of Nitrogen Gas. (500 ppm (w/w) Initial Acetate Concentration; 200 C Air Inlet Temperature; 7.0 MPa Atomizer Pressure; 49.5 C Liquid Feed Temperature) (ref. 13).

Fig. 6 (Right). Retention of n-Propyl Acetate as a Function of Axial Distance from the Atomizer during Laboratory Spray Drying of 60% (w/w) Aqueous Sucrose Solution, with and without Foaming by Desorption of Dissolved Carbon Dioxide. (500 ppm (w/w) Initial Acetate Concentration; 200 C Air Inlet Temperature; 7.0 MPa Atomizer Pressure; 49.5 C Liquid Feed Temperature) (ref. 26).

Existence of an Oil Phase in the Feed. Zakarian and King (ref. 29) investigated the influence of an emulsified, extractive oil phase on volatiles loss. There are two principal effects. First, extraction of volatile solutes into the oil phase serves to reduce the concentration of the volatile component in the continuous aqueous phase and thereby decreases the percentage loss of the solute during drying. This factor can be offset by extraction of the volatile substance into the oil in the reconstituted product, thereby suppressing the olfactory response for a given solute concentration. The net effect depends upon the relative dilutions of the feed to the dryer and the reconstituted product (ref. 29).

The second effect of an emulsified oil phase is to cause earlier break-up of the sheet, again through a perforation mechanism. This can reduce sheet losses and produces larger drops for a given atomizer and atomizer pressure. Because of similarity considerations, the change in drop size has little effect upon the percentage volatiles loss for a given percentage water removal (ref. 29).

   Feed Composition: Additives Affecting Particle Morphology. To
the extent that changes in particle morphology during drying
engender additional volatiles loss, it should be possible to
increase volatiles retention through use of additives which alter
the changes in morphology. Since there is essentially no
experimental information on the effect of morphological changes on
volatiles loss, this avenue is still a speculative one.

FLOW DYNAMICS AND MIXING IN SPRAY DRYERS
   Retentions of volatile flavor and aroma components should also
be strongly influenced by flow and mixing patterns within the
dryer. These phenomena determine drop trajectories and therefore
residence times. Even more important, they determine the air
temperature and humidity fields within the dryer, and thereby
determine the driving forces for heat and mass transfer associated
with drying. If the goal is very rapid drying near the atomizer so
as to bring selective diffusion into play as soon as possible, then
it is important to achieve flow and mixing patterns which give high
temperature and low humidity in the immediate vicinity of the
atomizer.
   Flow and mixing patterns can be studied experimentally and
through computer-based modeling. The PSI-Cell model of Crowe and
associates (ref. 30) iterates between trajectory-based solutions
for droplets and grid solutions for the gas phase to describe
two-way interactions between the gas and droplet phases for all
pertinent momentum-, heat-, and mass-transfer phenomena. In
itspresent state this model does not allow for mass-transfer
processes within the drops or particles. It therefore describes
only the evaporation of drops of pure water, or the
constant-activity period of drying. Nonetheless, it proves very
useful for predicting and interpreting flow and mixing patterns
within a spray dryer.
   For a pressure atomizer, the air flow field is dominated by the
pumping action of the spray. Drops initially have the high
velocity of the sheet issuing from the atomizer. As they slow to
their terminal velocities, they exchange momentum with the gas and
thereby draw a substantial flow of air into the spray (ref. 31).
This "pumping" of air by the spray has a number of important
effects (ref. 32):
   1. It serves to bring hot and dry air into the spray from

outside. This hot air increases temperatures and decreases
humidities. It thereby provides greater driving forces for heat
and mass transfer, accelerating drying. As has also been noted by
Schwartzberg (ref. 33), the rate at which hot air is entrained into
the upper spray in this way can be an important overall rate limit
to the early drying process, and therefore a deterrent to the onset
of selective diffusion.

2. It determines the overall flow pattern for the gas phase.
For a cocurrent dryer, a sufficiently high atomizer pressure will
lead to a situation where the volumetric flow of air drawn into the
spray exceeds the feed flow of air. The result is that, below a
certain level in the dryer, cooler and moist air is drawn outward
to the walls from the bottom of the spray, upward along the walls
("backflow"), and radially inward toward the spray ("sideflow").
This situation is shown schematically in Figure 7 for evaporation
of a spray of water. Mixing of this cooler air from below with
warmer air from above at the level of sideflow causes substantial
axial temperature gradients.

3. It forces a time-variant behavior on the flow. Dombrowski
and Wolfsohn (refs. 34,35) note that the irregular manner in which
the conical sheet breaks up causes the radial position of the edge

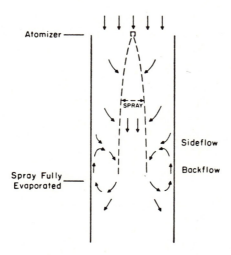

Fig. 7. Schematic of Air Flow Patterns in a Cocurrent Spray Dryer,
based upon Solutions of the PSI-Cell Model (ref. 32).

of the spray to vary over time. This effect causes substantial
temperature oscillations and strong mixing effects. In the region
of sideflow, additional mixing may occur through natural convection
associated with inverse temperature gradients.

Fig. 8 shows experimental radial temperature profiles at
various axial locations below the spray in a laboratory spray
dryer, fed with water. These measurements were made with ultrafine
thermocouple probes (ref. 32). Humidities, as inferred from
comparisons of wet- and dry-bulb thermocouple readings, showed a
behavior similar, but inverse, to that of temperature. The edge
of the spray corresponds to the steep change in temperature
radially.

The temperatures within the spray at levels near the atomizer
are much lower than those outside the spray. Thus the

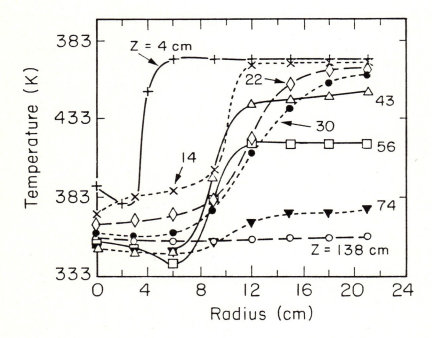

Fig. 8. Measured Air Temperatures vs. Radial Distance from the
Centerline of a Cocurrent Laboratory Spray Dryer Equipped with a
Pressure Atomizer and Fed with Water. Parameter (Z) is Axial
Distance from the Atomizer (cm). (199 C Inlet Air Temperature;
5.34 MPa Atomizer Pressure; 47 C Water Feed Temperature; 21.3 g
Air Fed/g Water Fed) (ref. 32).

heat-transfer driving force for drying is much less inside the
spray than outside. This is a manifestation of the importance of
Point No. 1 above -- the potential rate limit due to the rate of
entrainment of hot air into the spray.

The temperature outside the spray decreases markedly as the
level of sideflow is reached, 56 to 74 cm below the atomizer. Thus
for maximum drying rate near the atomizer it is important that
sideflow not occur at too high a level in the dryer.

Fig. 9 shows another interesting result, found through the
PSI-Cell model for operating conditions similar to those of Fig. 8.
Trajectories of drops of different initial sizes are shown in this
figure, with the end of each curve corresponding to the point at
which the drops fully evaporate. Inertial effects cause larger
drops to be thrown outward more toward the wall, while small drops
are carried inward by the air drawn into the spray.

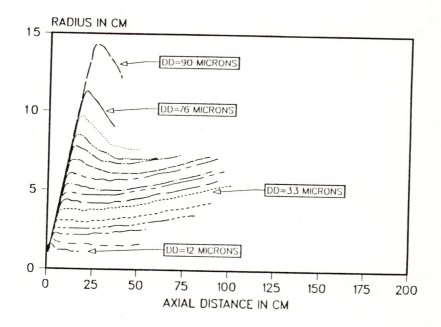

Fig. 9. Droplet Trajectories Predicted by PSI-Cell Model for Drops
of Different Initial Sizes Formed from a Single Water Feed. (202 C
Inlet Air Temperature; 3.69 MPa Atomizer Pressure; 47 C Water Feed
Temperature; 30.7 g Air Fed/g Water Fed) (ref. 32).

The smallest drops, located near the center of the spray, dry most rapidly because of their lesser masses and lower terminal velocities. However, the largest drops reach out into the much higher air temperatures at the edge of the spray (Fig. 8) and experience much larger driving forces. Consequently they evaporate to dryness at a higher level than do the the drops of middle size, which are located further into the spray. Therefore the spray tends to evaporate from the outside inward, because of the much higher temperatures at the edge of the spray. Note also that developing sideflow draws the outer drops in toward the center as they become small enough to follow the air flow.

OPTIMUM ATOMIZER PRESSURE

Higher atomizer pressure decreases initial drop sizes. In addition, changing atomizer pressure has three other effects, all of which influence volatiles retention:

1. As atomizer pressure increases, the liquid sheet emanating from the atomizer becomes shorter, and the sheet velocity becomes greater. Therefore the exposure time of the sheet becomes less, and volatiles loss from the sheet decreases.

2. As atomizer pressure increases, the volumetric flow rate of hot air entrained into the spray becomes greater. This tends to increase temperatures within the spray near the atomizer, thereby increasing drying rates and bringing on selective diffusion at an earlier point in drying.

3. As atomizer pressure increases further and the volumetric flow of air drawn into the spray increases, more backflow along the walls lower in the dryer is needed to supply the entrained air, and the level of sideflow becomes higher. Above some atomizer pressure the level of sideflow should move high enough, and the volume of entrained, cooler air be great enough, to cause the temperatures in the spray near the atomizer to drop again. The lower temperatures would reduce drying rates and delay the onset of selective diffusion.

Factors 1 and 2 lead to improved volatiles retention with increasing atomizer pressure, whereas Factor 3 decreases volatiles retention at very high atomizer pressures. There should therefore be an optimal atomizer pressure for maximum volatiles retention during spray drying.

CONCLUDING STATEMENT

From this discussion it should be apparent that the selective diffusion concept of Hans Thijssen has indeed been seminal, leading to strong physical insight into the factors governing losses of volatile flavor and aroma substances in spray dryers, and leading to a number of different useful avenues for improving the retention of these substances.

Acknowledgement

The research from our own group summarized herein has been supported by a series of grants from the National Science Foundation (Division of Chemical, Biochemical and Thermal Engineering), and by supplemental grants from General Foods Corporation and Merck R&D.

REFERENCES

1 J.L. Bomben, S. Bruin, H.A.C. Thijssen and R.L. Merson, Advances in Food Research, 20, (1973) 2-111.
2 H.A.C. Thijssen, Inaugural Address, Technical Univ., Eindhoven, Netherlands, 1965.
3 H.A.C. Thijssen and W.H. Rulkens, De Ingenieur (The Hague) 80(47) (1968) Ch45-56.
4 H.A.C. Thijssen, J. Appl. Chem. Biotechnol., 21 (1971) 372-376.
5 H. Hikita, S. Asai and Y. Azuma, Canad. J. Chem. Eng., 56 (1978) 371.
6 C.G. Greenwald and C.J. King, AIChE Symp. Ser., 78(218) (1982) 101-110.
7 L.C. Menting, B. Hoogstad and H.A.C. Thijssen, J. Food Technol., 5 (1970) 111-126.
8 S.K. Chandrasekaran and C.J. King, AIChE Jour., 18 (1972) 520-526.
9 P.J.A.M. Kerkhof and H.A.C. Thijssen, AIChE Symp. Ser., 73(163) (1977) 33-46.
10 C.J. King, Freeze Drying of Foods, CRC Press, W. Palm Beach FL, 1971 (Appendix).
11 L.C. Menting and B. Hoogstad, J. Food Sci., 32 (1967) 87-90.
12 P.J.A.M. Kerkhof and W.J.A.H. Schoeber, in Advances in Pre-concentration and Dehydration of Foods, A. Spicer (Ed.), Appl. Sci. Publs., London, 1974, pp. 349-397.
13 D.D. Frey, Ph. D. Dissertation, Univ. of California, Berkeley, 1984.
14 T.G. Kieckbusch and C.J. King, AIChE Jour., 26 (1980) 718-725; 27, (1981) 528.
15 C.J. King, T.G. Kieckbusch and C.G. Greenwald, in Advances in Drying, Vol. 3, A.S. Mujumdar (Ed.), Hemisphere Publ. Co., New York, 1984.
16 T. Furuta, M. Okazaki and R. Toei, Proc. 4th Intl. Drying Symp., Soc. Chem. Engrs., Japan, 1 (1984) 336-342.
17 T.M. El-Sayed, Ph. D. Dissertation, Univ. of California, Berkeley, 1987.
18 S.G. Simpson and S. Lynn, AIChE Jour., 23 (1977) 666-679.

19 D. Hasson, D. Luss and R. Peck, Int. J. Heat Mass Transfer, 7
    (1964) 969.
20 S.K. Chandrasekaran and C.J. King, AIChE Jour., 18 (1972)
    513-520.
21 L.C. Menting, B. Hoogstad and H.A.C. Thijssen, J. Food
    Technol., 5 (1970) 127-139.
22 W.J.A.H. Schoeber and H.A.C. Thijssen, AIChE Symp. Ser.,
    73(163) (1977) 12-24.
23 J.K. Liou and S. Bruin, Int. J. Heat Mass Transfer, 25, (1982)
    1221.
24 H.A.C. Thijssen and W.J. Coumans, Proc. 4th Intl. Drying
    Symp., Soc. Chem. Engrs., Japan, 1 (1984) 22-30.
25 M.R. Etzel and C.J. King, Ind. Eng. Chem. Process Des. &
    Devel., 23 (1983) 705-710.
26 D.D. Frey and C.J. King, Ind. Eng. Chem. Fundam., 25 (1986)
    730-735.
27 H.A.C. Thijssen, Lebensm. Wiss. Tech., 12 (1979) 308-317.
28 D.D. Frey and C. J. King, Ind. Eng. Chem. Fundam., 25 (1986)
    723-730.
29 J.A. Zakarian and C.J. King, Ind. Eng. Chem. Process Des. &
    Devel., 21 (1982) 107-113.
30 C.T. Crowe, in Advances in Drying, Vol. 1, A.S. Mujumdar (Ed.)
    Hemisphere Publ. Co., New York, 1980.
31 F.G.S. Benatt and P. Eisenklam, J. Inst. Fuel, 43 (1969)
    309-315.
32 S.E. Papadakis, Ph. D. dissertation, Univ. of California,
    Berkeley, 1987.
33 H.G. Schwartzberg, Dept. Food Engg., Univ. of Massachusetts,
    Personal Communication, 1987.
34 N. Dombrowski and D.L. Wolfsohn, Trans. Instn. Chem. Engrs.,
    50 (1972) 259-269.
35 N. Dombrowski and D.L. Wolfsohn, J. Inst. Fuel, 46 (1972) 327.

Preconcentration and Drying of Food Materials, edited by S. Bruin
Elsevier Science Publishers B.V., Amsterdam, 1988 — Printed in The Netherlands

EVALUATION AND PREDICTION OF EXPERIMENTAL DRYING CURVES OF SLABS

W.J. COUMANS[1] and K.Ch.A.M. LUYBEN[2]

[1]Faculty of Chemical Engineering, Eindhoven University of Technology,
Postbox 513, 5600 MB Eindhoven
[2]Faculty of Chemical Engineering, Delft University of Technology

SUMMARY
A short-cut-method for the calculation of drying times of bodies with a slab geometry is given. For the experimental determination of drying curves (weight versus time) a drying apparatus has been developed. The relatively simple equations of the short-cut-method are used to evaluate the experimental drying curves in order to obtain the relevant model parameters. Next the same equations are used to predict drying curves at different drying conditions. A comparison is made between predicted and experimental drying curves.

INTRODUCTION

In solids drying the "exact" calculation of drying rates and drying times is complicated by the concentration dependence of the diffusion coefficient and the shrinkage of the drying body due to the moisture loss. Coumans and Thijssen (refs. 1-3) developed easily to handle short-cut-approximations, which are applicable to slabs, massive and hollow cylinders and spheres, irrespective of their degree of shrinkage. These approximations are based on a *power law dependence* of the diffusion coefficient on the moisture concentration. Previous research in this field has been done by Schoeber (refs. 4-5), Luyben, Olieman, Bruin and Liou (refs. 6-9).

This contribution only deals with the short-cut-method for slabs. It will be shown how the method should be used in practice.

DESCRIPTION OF SHORT-CUT-CALCULATION METHOD

Physical model

Mass transfer in shrinking and non-shrinking slabs is regarded as a pseudo binary diffusion process, with an effective diffusion coefficient D (m^2/s) and with components moisture (m) and solids (s). In real systems mass transfer may occur by several mechanisms, therefore the diffusion coefficient, which will depend strongly on moisture concentration and temperature, should be considered as a lump parameter. It is assumed that the slab has a constant and uniform temperature (isothermal drying) and a uniform initial moisture concentration.

The external boundary condition of the slab depends on the equilibrium sorption properties of the material being dried and the conditions of the gas phase carrying off the moisture.

164

The following drying stages can be distinguished:

I   constant surface water activity ($\longrightarrow$ constant surface flux for slabs);

II   decreasing surface water activity and surface water concentration;

III constant surface water concentration (nearly equilibrium at surface).

Each of the three main stages can be split up into two substages, namely:

- *Penetration Period* (PP), during which the centre concentration changes hardly from the initial value (e.g. $m_{centre} \geq 0.9$).

- *Regular Regime* (RR), during which the centre concentration changes significantly from its initial value (e.g. $m_{centre} < 0.9$).

This paper deals with drying processes with a *high initial flux*; in such processes a Penetration Period with a constant surface activity (I-PP) is succeeded by drying stage II, next by a Penetration Period with a constant surface concentration (III-PP) and eventually by a Regular Regime (III-RR). It is assumed that drying stage II takes a neglible time interval with respect to the total drying time.

Definitions of dimensionless parameters (for slabs)

The dimensionless concentration m:

$$m = \frac{u - u_*}{u_0 - u_*} \qquad \text{with } 0 \leq m \leq 1 \tag{1}$$

where u = solids based concentration (kg m/kg s); u_0 refers to the initial value and u_* to the equilibrium value. u is related to the volume based concentrations ρ_m (kg moisture/m^3) and ρ_s (kg solid/m^3) according to $u = \rho_m/\rho_s$

The averaged drying efficiency E:

$$E = \frac{u_0 - \bar{u}}{u_0 - u_*} = 1 - \bar{m} \tag{2}$$

where $\bar{u}$ and $\bar{m}$ are averaged values; thus E is fraction of moisture removed.

The dimensionless diffusion coefficient D_r:

$$D_r = \frac{D\rho_s^2}{D_0 \rho_{s0}^2} \tag{3}$$

in which D is the actual diffusion coefficient (m^2/s); D_0 represents the value of the diffusion coefficient at ρ_{m0}. A power law dependence of the diffusion coefficient with concentration was put forward (see Introduction):

$$D\rho_s^2 = b \left[\frac{\rho_m}{\rho_s} - \frac{\rho_{m*}}{\rho_{s*}} \right]^a = b(u - u_*)^a \tag{4}$$

where a and b are fitting parameters. From eqns. 1, 3 and 4 the *dimensionless power law relation* follows:

$$D_r = m^a \tag{5}$$

The dimensionless time τ:

$$\tau = \frac{D_0\, t}{R_0^2} \tag{6}$$

where t=time (s) and R_0 = initial thickness of a one-sided drying slab (m). The dimensionless flux parameter F:

$$F = \frac{j_{mi}^s \rho_{s0} R_0}{D_0 \rho_{s0}^2 (u_0 - u_*)} \tag{7}$$

where j_{mi}^s = moisture flux through the interface = drying flux (kg/m^{2}s).

Mass Balance and Drying Time

The moisture balance over the drying slab during a time interval dt reads:

$$j_{mi}^s\, A\, dt = -\bar{\rho}_s V\, d(\bar{\rho}_m/\bar{\rho}_s) \tag{8}$$

where A = mass exchanging area (m^2); V = volume of drying slab (m^3). Putting the mass balance in a dimensionless form:

$$Fd\tau = dE \tag{9}$$

and the drying time (isothermal) is calculated with:

$$\tau = \int_0^E \frac{dE}{F} \tag{10}$$

This integration requires the relationship between F and E.

Short-Cut-Equations

If drying starts with a high initial flux then the constant activity period will end during its Penetration Period (drying stage I-PP). The integration of the mass balance is simple, because now $F = F_{ca} \approx$ constant. The upper integration limit $E = E_{ca}$, where E_{ca} is the averaged efficiency at the end of this drying stage, is found from the so-called *critical point curve* (E_{ca} versus F_{ca}). For drying stage I-PP this curve may be approximated with

$$F_{ca} = G_{0,ca} \frac{(E'_{i,cr})^2}{E_{ca}} \qquad \text{with } G_{0,ca} = \frac{\pi}{4}\left[\frac{1.45}{a+1.45}\right]^{1.89} \tag{11}$$

if the critical surface efficiency $E'_{i,cr} > 0.8$

During the *Penetration Period* of drying stage III-PP:

$$F = G_0 \frac{1}{E} \qquad \text{with } G_0 = \frac{2}{\pi}\left[\frac{1.42}{a+1.42}\right]^{1.98} \quad \text{and } E \leq E_T = \frac{1}{a+2} \tag{12}$$

During the *Regular Regime* of drying stage III-RR:

$$F = \frac{1}{2}\frac{Sh_d}{a+1}(1-E)^{a+1} \qquad \text{with } Sh_d = 4.935+2.454\frac{a}{a+2} \quad \text{and } E > E_T = \frac{1}{a+2} \tag{13}$$

Calculation of Drying Time

The drying time t, needed to attain a certain efficiency E, can be calculated with eqns. 10 –13 if the parameters a, D_0, F_{ca}, R_0, $E'_{i,cr}$, and E are known. The duration of the constant activity period (t_{ca}) follows from:

$$t_{ca} = \frac{R_0^2 G_{0,ca}}{D_0 F_{ca}^2} \tag{14}$$

For the Penetration Period of drying stage III-PP ($E \leq E_T$):

$$t = t_{ca} + \frac{R_0^2}{2G_0 D_0}(E^2 - E_{ca}^2) \tag{15}$$

and for the Regular Regime of drying stage III-RR ($E > E_T$):

$$t = t_T + \frac{2R_0^2}{Sh_d D_0}\frac{a+1}{a}\left[\frac{1}{(1-E)^a} - \frac{1}{(1-E_T)^a}\right] \quad \text{if } a \neq 0 \tag{16}$$

and

$$t = t_T + \frac{2R_0^2}{Sh_d D_0}\ln\left[\frac{1-E_T}{1-E}\right] \quad \text{if } a = 0 \tag{17}$$

The above short-cut-equations for drying fluxes and drying times can be used for the evaluation, reconstruction and prediction of drying curves.

Evaluation of a and D_0 from Regular Regime

Values of a and D_0 are evaluated from the Regular Regime (III-RR) because this drying stage contributes dominantly to the total drying time. Moreover, during this stage the effects of undesired initial experimental faults will have been extinghuished. From mass balance and definiton of τ (eqns. 6 and 9):

$$F = \frac{R_0^2}{D_0} \frac{dE}{dt} \tag{18}$$

and combining eqns. 13 and 18 gives:

$$\ln(\frac{dE}{dt}) = \ln\left[\frac{1}{2} \frac{Sh_d}{a+1} \frac{D_0}{R_0^2}\right] + (a+1)\ln(1-E) \tag{19}$$

From experimental drying curves (E versus t) values of a and D_0 can be derived by linear regression of $\ln(dE/dt)$ versus $\ln(1-E)$.

EXPERIMENTAL

In this paper the experimental drying curves of gelled malto-dextrin solutions are studied at different initial moisture contents and different temperatures. In a vacuum drying apparatus a sample with a slab geometry is *isothermally* dried at *a high initial flux*. During the experiment the weight of the sample is registrated.

Description of Drying Apparatus

The drying apparatus (Figure 1) consists of two horizontal cylindrical chambers, one on top of the other. The sample holder in the lower chamber is connected to an electronic precision balance in the upper chamber. To dilute the evaporated moisture a clean and dry air stream (R_3) is blown as evenly as possible over the sample. In order to avoid uneven drying of the slab a sieve plate is placed between the sample and the air stream. The temperature of the sample is kept constant by an electrically heated radiation source and a temperature controller. The absolute pressure in the chambers is kept constant by means of a vacuum pump and a pressure controller, which activates the servo motor of a needle valve (R_2). The initial rate of drying depends on the slab temperature, absolute pressure in the chambers and the distance between sample holder and sieve plate.

For data-acquisition the digital weight balance, the temperature controller, the pressure controller and several thermocouples are connected to a microcomputer. From the momentary, initial and final weight of the sample the drying efficiency E can be calculated quite simply and the basic experimental results are represented as E versus t.

In Table 1 the conditions used in the various drying experiments are summarized.

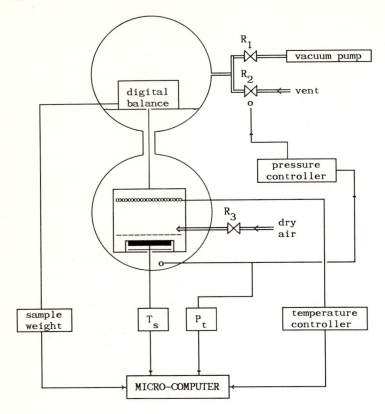

FIGURE 1. Vacuum drying apparatus

████ = sample; --- = sieve plate; ∞∞∞ = radiation source;

T_s= sample temperature; P_t= total pressure

TABLE 1.
Survey of drying experiments of gelled maltodextrin/water layers.
(R_0=2.50 mm, d_s=1610 kg/m^3, u_*=0 kg/kg, P_t=12400 N/m^2)

exp. number	temp. (°C)	u_0 (kg/kg)	ρ_{s0} (kg/m^3)	$E'_{i,cr}$ (-/-)	a (-/-)	D_0 (m^2/s)	F_{ca} (-/-)
5	41.4	2.40	331	0.833	−0.092	3.88E−10	21.563
6	32.8	2.40	331	0.842	+0.076	3.99E−10	5.951
7	26.4	2.40	331	0.850	+0.292	5.03E−10	3.888
8	35.8	4.85	183	0.922	−0.087	9.27E−10	4.254
9	26.7	4.85	183	0.926	+0.075	1.00E−09	2.187

all values of a and D_0 are derived from experiment 9 (see text)

RECONSTRUCTION OF EXPERIMENTAL DRYING CURVE

The reconstruction of a single drying experiment will be shown from experiment 9 as a typical example. In Figure 2 some characteristic relations, derived from this experiment, are represented.

From a first examination of the Regular Regime drying curve it was estimated that a$\approx$0. Therefore Regular Regime behaviour was assumed for E$\geq$0.5. Linear regression of ln(dE/dt) versus ln(1-E), including all data points in this range, gives a better value for a and thus a better estimate for the pertinent concentration range; after two or three iterations: a = 0.075 and D_0 = 1.00E-09 m^2/s.

The imposed initial drying flux dE/dt = 3.50E-04/s is obtained by linear regression of E versus t in the arbitrarily chosen range 0$\leq$E$\leq$0.2. The initial value of the flux parameter F_{ca} = 2.187 follows from eqn. 18.

From the sorption isotherm the critical surface concentration u_{cr} = 0.362 kg/kg and thus $E'_{i,cr}$ = 0.925. Now all required input data (a, D_0, F_{ca}, R_0 and $E'_{i,cr}$) are known and the drying curve can be reconstructed according to eqns. 14-17. Some typical figures are: E_{ca}=0.263, t_{ca}=751 s, E_T=0.482 and t_T=1638 s.

A comparison of measured and calculated drying times shows, that maximum deviations are about 10% , which is typical for all drying experiments.

DIFFUSION BEHAVIOUR OF MALTODEXTRIN/WATER SOLUTIONS

The exponent a of the power law relation can be obtained from the experiments in several ways:

1) from a single drying experiment by linear regression of Regular Regime data
   (eqn. 19); moreover also values of D_0 are obtained.
2) from experiments at different initial moisture concentrations by:
   a) correlating values of D_0 with u_0 (eqn. 4)
   b) correlating values of G_0D_0 with u_0 , where G_0D_0 is obtained by linear
      regression of E^2 versus t with data from the Penetration Period (eqn. 15)
Method 1 does not produce one single value of exponent a for all experiments. Methods 2a and 2b give negative values (see Table 2), which strongly deviate from those of method 1. This inconsistency of results means, that the power law relation (eqn. 4) does not fit the whole concentration range of the system maltodextrin/water. It can be argued that putting $D\rho_s^2$ versus ρ_m/ρ_s may show a maximum, and indeed such a dependence can not be expressed by a power law relation. One may wonder now why the reconstruction of drying curves, based on the power law concept, gives such satisfying results. The answer to this question might be, that drying behaviour is fully controlled by the lower concentrations at the interface, whereas the concentration dependence of the diffusion coefficient at the higher concentrations in the drying material is of minor impor-

tance then. In the range of rate controlling concentrations apparently a power
law dependence of the diffusion coefficient may be assumed.

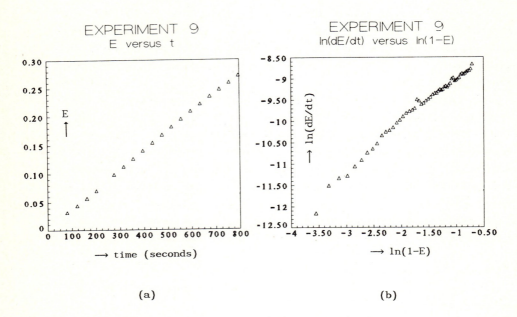

(a)   (b)

FIGURE 2   Characteristic data plots from experiment 9:

  (a) constant activity period or constant flux period

  (b) Regular Regime with constant surface concentration

TABLE 2
a-values calculated from drying experiments at different initial
moisture concentrations.

exp no.	u_0 (kg/kg)	ρ_{s0} (kg/m^3)	$G_0 D_0$ from PP (m^2/s)	a (-/-)	D_0 from RR (m^2/s)	a (-/-)
7	2.40	331	2.37E–10		5.03E–10	
				–0.61		–0.71
9	4.85	183	5.04E–10		1.00E–09	

PREDICTION OF EXPERIMENTAL DRYING CURVES

(i) <u>Drying curves at higher initial moisture contents</u> can be predicted from
drying curves at lower initial moisture contents. This will be illustrated by
predicting the drying curve of experiment 7 (u_0= 2.40 kg/kg) from the Regular
Regime drying curve of experiment 9 (u_0= 4.85 kg/kg).

The values of a and D_0 for the prediction of experiment 7 are derived from
the Regular Regime of experiment 9. Assuming a = 0.075 (so, E_T= 0.482) the concentration range of the Regular Regime of experiment 7 is: $0 \leq u \leq 1.16$. Linear
regression of ln(dE/dt) versus ln(1-E) with all data points from experiment 9
in this range gives a better a-value and thus a better estimate of the relevant
concentration range; linear regression is repeated, etc.. After only two iterations: a = 0.292 and D_0= 5.03E-10 m^2/s. Linear regression of E versus t in the
range $0 \leq E \leq 0.1$ gives dE/dt = 3.13E-04/s and the initial flux in experiment 7 is
F_{ca}= 3.888. Similarly to the method described previously, the drying times of
experiment 7 are calculated. The maximum deviation between measured and calculated drying times appears to be 20%

(ii) <u>The temperature dependence of dE/dt versus $\bar{u}$</u>, can be expressed with an
Arrhenius-type relation (ref. 4):

$$\left[\frac{dE}{dt}\right]_T = \left[\frac{dE}{dt}\right]_{T_1} \exp\left[-\frac{A_F}{R}\left(\frac{1}{T}-\frac{1}{T_1}\right)\right] \tag{20}$$

in which R = 8.314 (J/mol ^{o}K); T = temperature (^{o}K) and A_F = activation energy
of the flux (Joule/mol). The activation energy A_F, which depends on the moisture concentration, can be derived from at least two isothermal drying experiments with the same initial concentration, but with different temperatures. The
concentration dependence of the activation energy A_F can be described very well
by a correlation of the type (ref. 6):

$$A_F = A \exp(-B\,\bar{u}) + C \tag{21}$$

in which for maltodextrin/water the fitting parameters are found from experiments 8 and 9: A = 48 kJ/mol, B = -2.40 kg/kg, C = 18.8 kJ/mol.

(iii) <u>Drying curves at different temperatures</u> and different initial concentrations can be predicted from experiment 9 as follows:
<u>first</u>, the Regular Regime of experiment 9 is translated to the desired tempera-
ture by using eqns. 20-21.
<u>second</u>, the parameters a and D_0 at this temperature and initial concentration
are obtained by linear regression of ln(dE/dt) versus ln(1-E) in the

concentration range of interest. Because exponent a is not known beforehand, some iterations (in most cases two) are required.

third, the drying curve at the desired temperature level and desired initial concentration can be calculated by means of eqns. 14–17.

The above procedure has been applied to predict the drying curves of experiments 5 and 6 (in fact also 7 and 8) from the Regular Regime drying curve of experiment 9 (see Table 1). Deviations between predicted and measured drying times vary from a few percent to 30%

CONCLUSIONS

The whole drying history of a slab can be reconstructed from experimental data of the Regular Regime only. Drying curves at lower initial moisture concentrations can be predicted from the Regular Regime data of drying curves at higher initial moisture concentrations. Power law diffusion does not apply strictly to maltodextrin/water solutions. Though drying curves can be described and predicted fairly well by means of the short-cut-equations, the model parameters a and D_0 should be considered as fitting parameters with a limited physical meaning.

REFERENCES

1. W.J. Coumans, _Power law diffusion in drying processes_, Ph.D. Thesis, Eindhoven University of Technology, the Netherlands (1987)
2. W.J. Coumans and H.A.C. Thijssen, _A simplified calculation method for the isothermal drying of solid and hollow systems with any degree of shrinkage"_ Proc. 5th Int. Drying Symp., Boston, pp. 49–56, Hemisph. Publ. Corp. (1986)
3. H.A.C. Thijssen and W.J. Coumans, _Concise procedure for the calculation of isothermal drying rates of non-shrinking solid and hollow particles_, Proc. World Congr. III of Chem. Eng., Tokyo, (1986)
4. W.J.A.H. Schoeber, _Regular regimes in sorption processes_, Ph.D. Thesis, Eindhoven University of Technology, the Netherlands (1976)
5. W.J.A.H. Schoeber, _A short cut method for the calculation of drying rates in case of a concentration dependent diffusion coefficient_, Proc. 1st Int. Drying Symp., Montreal, pp. 1–9, Hemisphere Publ.Corp. (1978)
6. K.Ch.A.M. Luyben, J.J. Olieman and S. Bruin, _Concentration dependent diffusion coefficients derived from experimental drying curves_, Proc. 2nd Int. Drying Symp., Montreal, Vol. 2, 233–243, Hemisph. Publ.Corp. (1980)
7. K.Ch.A.M. Luyben, J.K. Liou and S. Bruin, _Enzyme degradation during drying_, Proc. Int. Symp. Food Process Engineering, Helsinki, Vol. 2, pp. 192–209, Applied Science Publ. (1979)
8. J.K. Liou, _An approximate method for nonlinear diffusion applied to enzyme inactivitation during drying_, Ph. D. Thesis, Agricultural University, Wageningen, the Netherlands (1982).
9. J.K. Liou and S. Bruin, _An approximate method for the nonlinear diffusion problem with a power relation between diffusion coefficient and concentration. Part I: computation of desorption times_,
             Part II: computation of concentration profiles
    Int. J. Heat and Mass Transfer, 25 (1982); pp. 1209–1229

Preconcentration and Drying of Food Materials, edited by S. Bruin
Elsevier Science Publishers B.V., Amsterdam, 1988 — Printed in The Netherlands

THE MODELLING AND MEASUREMENT OF SEGREGATION OF SOLUTE MATERIAL DURING DRYING OF FOOD SYSTEMS

G. MEERDINK, K. van 't RIET, W.A. BEVERLOO, J. de KONING and J.J. DOMMERSHUIJZEN

Food- and Bioengineering Group, Department of Food Science, Wageningen Agricultural University, De Dreijen 12, 6703 BC Wageningen (The Netherlands)

SUMMARY

In view of the large differences in the values of the diffusivities of various components in food systems, segregation is expected to occur during drying. Drying experiments with a food model system(water, sucrose and sodium caseinate) were performed. In these drying experiments a number of slabs of the model system were dried simultaneously and cut in thin slices after different times. The concentration profiles in the slabs, as a function of time, show that segregation occurs during drying. All experiments show that during drying the ratio of the sodium caseinate and sucrose concentrations near the surface increases. In the centre of the slab the ratio decreases. The theory of multicomponent diffusion is used to develop a simple model to describe this segregation. Simulations with the diffusion model, using literature data for the values of the diffusivities, confirm qualitatively the experimental results.

INTRODUCTION

In drying calculations liquid foods are often considered as binary systems, with water and dry solids as the two components. Foods are however multicomponent systems. This multicomponent character of foods implies that during drying of, for instance, a simple ternary system(water and two non-volatile dissolved components i and j), there is not only a water concentration gradient, but there are also concentration gradients of the components i and j(figure 1a). This is neglected in the binary approach. In general the diffusivities of the components i and j are not equal and segregation will occur. The ratio between i and j will become a function of the distance from the surface(figure 1b). The concentration of the component with the smallest diffusivity will be relatively high at the surface compared with the other component, in the centre the reverse situation will exist. The extent of this segregation will depend on the difference between the diffusivities and the drying conditions. Foods often consist of components with largely different diffusivities. Segregation during drying of liquid foods can be expected accordingly.

In literature on drying very little attention is paid to segregation of non-aqueous components and relevant information is almost non-existing. An important exception is the retention of aroma components during drying of foods(ref. 1,2). A few fundamental studies are reported on dilute non- electrolyte ternary

174

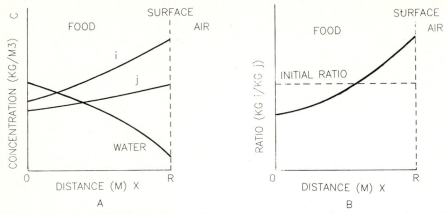

Fig. 1. (a) Concentration profiles of the components i,j and water during drying. (b) Ratio-profile of the components i and j during drying.

mixtures in water(ref. 3-5). In these studies multicomponent diffusivities were measured usually at a single composition of the mixture.

Our research aims are the measurement and modelling of the extent of this segregation and the determination of the consequences for the product quality of dried foods.

In this paper we will discuss the measurement of segregation during drying of a ternary food model system and a simple mathematical model describing the segregation.

MULTICOMPONENT DRYING MODEL

The description of multicomponent diffusion can be based either on the generalized Stefan-Maxwell relations or on flux relations derived from irreversible thermodynamics(ref. 6). It can be shown that these descriptions are equivalent(ref. 6). In this paper the flux equations derived from irreversible thermodynamics are used. The general form of these flux equations is:

$$j_i^V = - \sum_{j=1}^{N-1} D_{ij} \nabla c_j \tag{1}$$

,where j_i^V = flux of component i relative to the volume-average velocity(kg m^{-2} s^{-1}); n = number of components; D_{ij} = diffusivity(m^2 s^{-1}); and c_j = concentration of component j(kg m^{-3}). There are (n-1) independent flux equations.

Application of these flux equations on the modelling of a non-isothermal drying process of a ternary mixture, including shrinkage effects and concentration dependence of the diffusivities, leads to a complex mathematical model. Moreover literature data on or formulas for the prediction of multicomponent diffusivities in foods are lacking. Therefore a simple drying model was developed for an isothermal non-shrinking ternary system(water and two dissolved non-volatile components i and j), with constant diffusivities. The sorption isotherm was linearized.

The diffusion equations describing the transport of water and one of the dissolved components in a slab are:

$$\frac{\partial c_i}{\partial t} = D_{iw} \frac{\partial^2 c_w}{\partial r^2} + D_{ii} \frac{\partial^2 c_i}{\partial r^2} \tag{2}$$

$$\frac{\partial c_w}{\partial t} = D_{ww} \frac{\partial^2 c_w}{\partial r^2} + D_{wi} \frac{\partial^2 c_i}{\partial r^2} \tag{3}$$

, where c_w = water concentration(kg m^{-3}); c_i = concentration of component i(kg m^{-3}) ; r = space coordinate(m).

The initial and boundary conditions are :

$$t = 0 \qquad 0 \leq r \leq R \qquad c_w = c_{wo} \quad ; \quad c_i = c_{io} \tag{4}$$

$$t > 0 \qquad r = 0 \qquad \frac{\partial c_w}{\partial r} = 0 \quad ; \quad \frac{\partial c_i}{\partial r} = 0 \tag{5}$$

$$r = R \quad - D_{ww} \frac{\partial c_w}{\partial r} - D_{wi} \frac{\partial c_i}{\partial r} = n_w = k \, (\rho_{w,i} - \rho_{w,b}) \tag{6}$$

$$- D_{iw} \frac{\partial c_w}{\partial r} - D_{ii} \frac{\partial c_i}{\partial r} = -\beta \, n_w \tag{7}$$

, where c_{w0} = initial waterconcentration(kg m^{-3}); c_{i0} = initial concentration of component i(kg m^{-3}); $\rho_{w,i}$ = interfacial gas phase water concentration(kg m^{-3}); $\rho_{w,i}$ = bulk gas phase water concentration(kg m^{-3}); k = mass tranfer coefficient(m s^{-1}); β = constant.

The parameter β in equation 7 reflects the assumption that the volume averaged velocity is zero(no shrinking effects). As a consequence of this assumption the components i and j have formally to be supplied to the system at the interface, to replace the volume of water lost during the drying process. The components have to be supplied in the initial ratio in order to keep the average ratio of i and j in the system constant during the drying process. In a similar way the shrinking behaviour of a real drying system can be modelled. The two coupled partial differential equations are numerically solved by using a modified Crank-Nicolson's method with variable implicitness(ref. 1). The two partial differential equations can be solved analytically in some cases by defining two linear combinations of the real concentrations as variables(ref. 7,8). For boundary conditions of the first and second kind this procedure leads to two uncoupled partial differential equations. For these equations standard solutions are available(ref. 9). These analytical solutions are used to test the numerical algorithm.

As stated before data on multicomponent diffusivities are scarce. In the simulations diffusivity data are used which have been measured in a dilute mixture of glycine and sucrose in water(ref. 4). The diffusivity in an infinite dilute solution at 25 °C is for sucrose(mol weight = 342 g mol^{-1}) 0.52 10^{-9} m^2 s^{-1} and for glycine(mol weight = 75 g mol^{-1}) 1.06 10^{-9} m^2 s^{-1}(ref. 10).

Experimental Set-up

The drying experiments were performed with a food model system, consisting of water(demineralised), sucrose(Merck) and sodium-caseinate(DMV Campina). To avoid internal bulk flow and to symplify the experimental procedure, the model system is jellified by adding a small amount of agar-agar(Merck, 0.4% on total basis). The ratio between the sodium caseinate and the sucrose concentration was 0.50. The diffusivity of sucrose is at least one order of magnitude larger than that of sodium caseinate.

Fig. 2. Experimental procedure

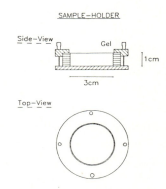

Fig. 3. Sample holder

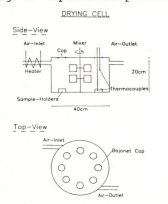

Fig. 4. Drying cell

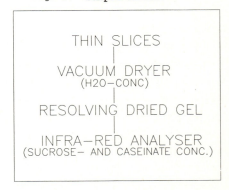

Fig. 5. Analysis procedure

The experimental procedure used in the drying experiments is given in figure 2. Slabs of the jellified food model system (thickness 10 mm.)were dried simultaneously in 8 sample holders(fig 3), placed in a drying cell(fig 4). At different times during the drying experiment a sample holder was removed from the cell. A sample holder consisted of a stack of 7 flat rings and after removal from the cell, the sample holder was disassembled ring by ring. Each slice protruding after one ring removal was cut off. Analysis of the slices gave the concentration profiles of water, sucrose and sodium caseinate in the slab . The shrinkage was quite uniform throughout the slab. The temperature in the drying cell was controlled and the external mass tranfer could be influenced by changing the stirrer speed. A constant flow of dry air was used as drying medium.

The analysis consisted of two steps, see figure 5. The moisture content was determined by means of a vacuum dryer, in which the slices were dried at 70 °C for two days. The sucrose and sodium caseinate concentrations in the slices were determined, after dissolution and dilution, by an automatic infrared analyser, type Milkoscan 104 A/B(Foss Electric, Danmark, ref. 11). The accuracy of the analysis depended on the initial dry solids content of the model system. At an initial dry solids content of 15.9% on total basis, the difference between dry solids content in the slices as determined in the vacuum dryer ,or calculated on basis of the concentrations determined by the infrared analyser, was less than 3%. The error in the ratio between sodium caseinate and sucrose was less than 5% for that initial dry solids content. In general the accuracy decreased at lower dry solids contents.

The results of the experiments were only qualitatively reproducible, because it was impossible to cut slices with exactly the same thickness and to maintain completly identical drying conditons.

In the drying experiments performed, the dry solids content of the model system varied between 5% and 25%. The temperature of the drying air was 50 °C.

RESULTS and DISCUSSION

Drying experiments

The results of a drying experiment with an initial dry solids content of 15.9 % (on total basis) are given in the figures 6, 7, 8 and 9. In figure 6 the waterconcentration profiles are given at 3 drying times. The dimensionless distance X is defined as:

$$X = \frac{\int_0^r c_c \, dr}{\int_0^R c_c \, dr} \tag{8}$$

, where R = slab thickness(m); r = space coordinate(m); c_c = sodium caseinate concentration(kg m^{-3}). The water concentration profiles and the profiles in the other figures are given in the form of bar graphs, because only the average

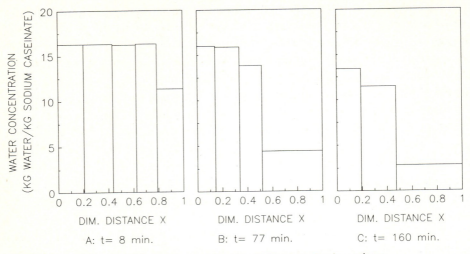

Fig. 6. Water concentration profiles at different drying times.

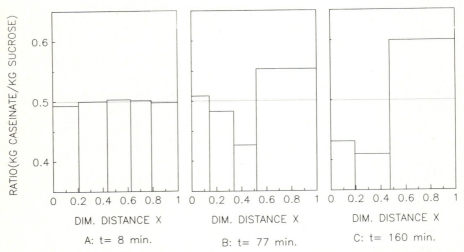

Fig. 7. Ratio-profiles(cas. conc./sucr. conc) at different drying times.

concentration in a thin slice was measured. The ratio between the sodium
caseinate and sucrose concentration is given in figure 7. The initial ratio was
0.50(kg sodium caseinate/kg sucrose). In the figures 8 and 9 the deviations of
the measured from the segregation free concentrations are given. The calculation
of the latter is based on the assumption that during drying no segregation
occurs .

In the earliest part of the drying process the orginally flat water concentration profile has changed only near the surface(fig. 6a) and no segrega-

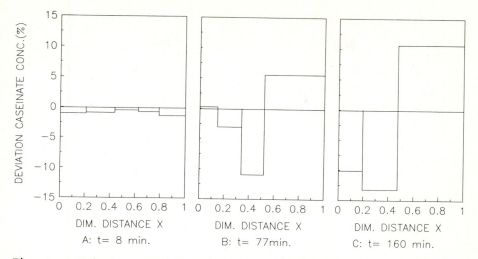

Fig. 8. Deviations from the segregation-free sodium caseinate concentrations at different drying times.

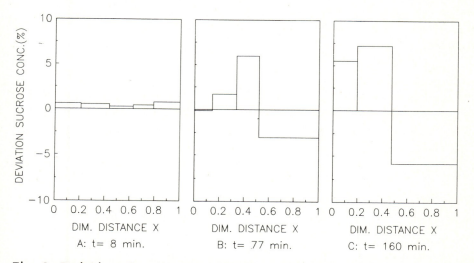

Fig. 9. Deviations from the segregation-free sucrose concentrations at different drying times.

tion is measured(fig. 7a). There is no significant deviation from the initial ratio of the two solutes. In the second part(still in the penetration period) the waterconcentration profile is very steep, however the bottom concentration still has not changed(fig. 6b); a considerable degree of segregation occurs(fig 7b). Near the surface the ratio between the sodium caseinate and sucrose concentrations increases from the initial ratio and attains a value of 0.55. In the centre of the slab the situation is reversed, whereas at the bottom no segregation is found. In the last part(regular regime) the water concentration profile flattens and the bottom concentration decreases(fig. 6c). The ratio between the dry solids components at the bottom decreases now from the initial ratio and the ratio-profile moves inward(fig. 7c). The ratio near the surface is 0.60. The profiles in the figures 8 and 9 give a similar image as figure 7. The maximum deviation in the concentration near the surface is for sodium caseinate +11% and for sucrose -6%. The experimental set-up makes it impossible to measure exactly the segration at the surface of the slab. It is expected however, when one looks at the shape of the ratio-profile, that the ratio at the surface is higher than 0.60 and that the deviations from the segregation free concentrations are more pronounced.

The experimental results agree with our theoretical considerations: that a water concentration gradient causes a considerable segregation when there is a large difference in diffusivities. The concentration at the surface of the component with the smallest diffusivity(sodium caseinate) is relatively high as compared with the other component(sucrose).

Drying experiments with other initial dry solids concentrations indicate that the extent of segregation decreases when the dry solids content increases, as expected.

Drying model simulations

The isothermal drying of a non-shrinking slab is simulated. The data used in the simulation are given in table 1. In figure 10 the water concentration profiles are given at different drying times. The ratio-profiles of the sucrose and glycine concentrations are given in figure 11. The initial ratio(kg sucrose/kg glycine) is 1. In the first part of the drying process the degree of segregation

Table 1. Simulation data.

concentrations   diffusivities

initial water(w) conc.	:	845 kg m^{-3}
initial sucrose(s) conc.	:	125 kg m^{-3}
initial glycine(g) conc.	:	125 kg m^{-3}
equilibrium water conc.	:	0 kg m^{-3}
bulk water conc. gas phase	:	0 kg m^{-3}

$D_{ww} = 0.39 \ 10^{-9} \ m^2 \ s^{-1}$
$D_{wg} = -0.18 \ 10^{-9} \ m^2 \ s^{-1}$
$D_{gg} = 0.57 \ 10^{-9} \ m^2 \ s^{-1}$
$D_{gw} = -0.95 \ 10^{-10} \ m^2 \ s^{-1}$

external mass transfer coefficient : 0.04 m s^{-1}
ß   : 0.806

linearized sorption isotherm : $c_w > 250$ kg m^{-3} , $\rho_w = 0.025$ kg m^{-3}
                                 $c_w < 250$ kg m^{-3} , $\rho_w = c_w/10000$ kg m^{-3}
where, c_w = equilibrium water concentration in the solid phase(kg m^{-3}) and ρ_w = equilibrium water concentration in the gas phase(kg m^{-3})

drying temperature   : 25 °C
half thickness   : 10 mm.

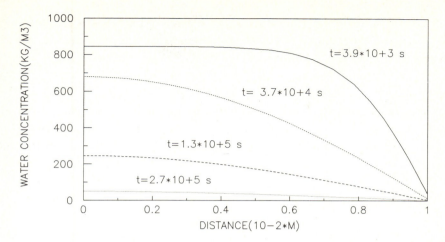

Fig. 10. Computed water concentration profiles at different drying times.

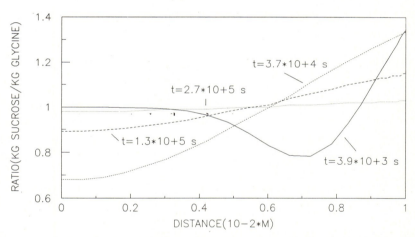

Fig. 11. Computed ratio-profiles(sucrose conc./glycine conc.) at different drying times.

increases, whereas in the second part the segregation decreases and finally will disappear(as expected). The concentration at the surface of the component with the smallest diffusivity (sucrose) is relatively higher than the concentration of the other component(glycine).

The simulation results during the first phase of the drying process agree qualitatively with the experimental results. The disappearance of the segrega-tion in the second fase, is not found experimentally. This is due to the strong water concentration dependence of the diffusivities, not allowed for in the model. The degree of segregation will in reality be "fixed" at some stage because the diffusivities become very low at low water contents.

The qualitative agreement of the experimental and modelling results indicates that the multicomponent diffusion theory can adequately describe and explain the measured segregation.

CONCLUSIONS

The developed experimental method is suitable to measure segregation. In the food model system used a considerable degree of segregation occurs during drying. Simulations with a simple drying model, based on the theory of multicomponent diffusion, resulted in a qualitative agreement with the drying experiments.

REFERENCES

1. P.J.A.M. Kerkhof, A quantitative study on the effect of process variables on the retention of volatile trace components in drying, Ph.D. thesis, Technical University Eindhoven, The Netherlands, 1975.
2. S.K. Chandrasekaran, Volatiles Retention during Drying of Food Liquids, Ph.D. Thesis, University of California, Berkeley, 1970.
3. P.J. Dunlop, Interacting Flows in diffusion of the system Raffinose-Urea-Water, The Journal of Physical Chemistry, 61(12) (1957) 1619-1622.
4. P.J. Dunlop and L.J. Gosting, Diffusion Coefficients for One Composition of the System Water-Sucrose-Glycine, The Journal of Physical Chemistry, 68(12) (1964) 3874-3876.
5. H.D. Ellerton and P.J. Dunlop, Diffusion and Frictional Coefficients for Four Compositions of the System Water-Sucrose-Mannitol at 25 °C. Tests of the Onsager Reciprocal Relation, The Journal of Physical Chemistry, 71(5) (1967) 1291-1297.
6. E.L. Cussler, Multicomponent Diffusion, Chemical Engineering Monographs, Vol. 3, Elsevier, Amsterdam, 1976.
7. H.L. Toor, Solution of the Linearized Equations of Multicomponent Mass Transfer: I, A.I.Ch.E. Journal, 10(4) (1964) 448-455.
8. H.L. Toor, Solution of the Linearized Equations of Multicomponent Mass Transfer: II. Matrix Methods, A.I.Ch.E. Journal, 10(4) (1964) 460-465.
9. A. Luikov, Analytical Heat Diffusion Theory, Academic Press, London, 1968.
10. R.C. Weast, Handbook of Chemistry and Physics, 57th edition, CRC Press, Cleveland, Ohio, 1976, F-62.
11. J.D.S. Goulden, Analysis of milk by infra-red absorption, J. Dairy Res., 31(1964) 273-284.

HEAT AND MASS TRANSFER MODELING DURING PASTA DRYING. APPLICATION TO CRACK FORMA-
TION RISK PREDICTION.

J. ANDRIEU[1], M. BOIVIN[2], A. STAMATOPOULOS[3]
[1]Laboratoire de Génie Chimique, Université de LYON I - 69622 VILLEURBANNE CEDEX
[2]Laboratoire de Mécanique des Solides - INSA LYON - 69621 VILLEURBANNE CEDEX
[3]Laboratoire de Génie Chimique et Alimentaire - Université de Montpellier II
34060 MONTPELLIER CEDEX

SUMMARY
    Data presented in this paper concern the theoretical and experimental study
of coupled heat, mass and rheological phenomena during durum wheat pasta convective drying by hot air. Temperature and humidity profiles evolution has been
interpreted by a simplified LUIKOV'S model neglecting thermomigration with evaporation near the solid external surface. This model was extended to cylindric
geometry (spaghetti) in order to calculate internal humidity profile evolution.
Then these data were used to calculate the triaxial stress field induced by the
pasta shrinkage during the drying. The simulation shows two critical phases :

    - on the pasta surface at the beginning of the drying
    - inside the pasta core at the end of the drying.

INTRODUCTION

    It is well known by pasta dryer designers that drying step is the most dif-
ficult operation during pasta manufacture process because air operating conditions (temperature, humidity, velocity) have a strong influence on organoleptic
and nutritional properties (color, taste, cooking behaviour , ...) and on mechanical properties (Young modulus, breaking strenght, surface state, etc ...) of
dry product.

    Due to apparition in the industry of new drying processes named "high tempe-
rature" or "very high temperature" - which could divide by 2 or 3 the drying
time without altering organoleptic properties - there exist a new interest for
a scientific analysis of the drying phenomena and for a quantitative description
of the interaction between drying climatic conditions and dry product quality.

    The first results concerning drying kinetics of durum wheat pasta were obtai-
ned by A. STAMATOPOULOS [1, 2, 4], then were confirmed by A. ZAFIROPOULOS as
concern a new product of the same kind i.e. corn base pasta [5, 7].

    These data show that for this hygroscopic, isotropic and homogeneous product
of very low porosity, the drying rate is independent of hydrodynamic air conditions and is mainly a function of :

    - the air temperature and hygrometry
    - the shape and thickness of the sample.

These observations have been done for products of the same texture like gels, soaps, gelatins, etc ... for which the vapor phase transport is negligible [5]. Besides, in a previous work, A. STAMATOPOULOS [3, 4] showed that temperature and humidity profiles evolution inside pasta (slab geometry) could be interpreted by a simplified LUIKOV'S model neglecting thermomigration with evaporation near the solid external area [9, 10, 11]. Thus, by comparing theoretical and experimental profiles we concluded that drying process is quite isothermal and entirely controlled by mass transfer resistance inside pasta.

In the industry during pasta drying process, it is necessary to slow down the drying in order to obtain the homogeneization of the internal humidity profile responsible of the apparition of mechanical stresses. This "sweating" period corresponds generally to an increase of air humidity and/or a decrease of dry air temperature.

In the present work, we extended the previous data concerning temperature and humidity profiles evolution in the case of slab geometry to cylindric geometry (spaghetti). So, the humidity profile obtained by this simulation, associated with pasta mechanical properties (shrinkage coefficient, elasticity and plasticity modulus, etc ...) let us to calculate triaxial stress field [3, 4, 8]. So it is possible to approach quantitatively the very difficult problem of the prediction of cracks formation risks – which is an important quality factor – by presenting some qualitative rules for dryer operators.

PASTA RHEOLOGICAL PROPERTIES :
Shrinkage :
During the drying, pasta shrinks linearly with a linear coefficient $\alpha = 0.44$. Volumic shrinkage, characterized by a coefficient $\beta = 3\alpha = 1.32$, is quite equal to water volume eliminated during the drying.

Rheological properties :
These properties are necessary to quantify mechanical stresses induced by the drying and responsible of the mechanical deformations.

These data have been measured by traction runs with an INSTROM apparatus. For example, as concern breaking strenght these data are shown on figure 1 [4, 12] where one can see their evolution from a plastic state to an elastic state.

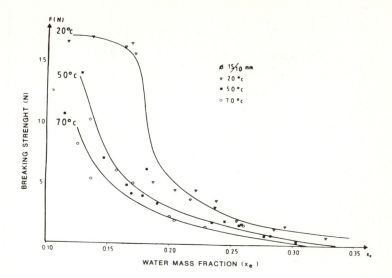

Fig. 1. Pasta breaking strenght as a function of humidity and temperature

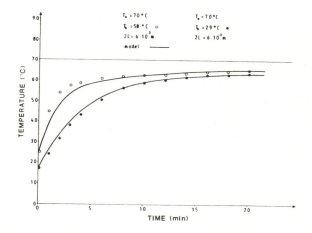

Fig. 2. Core pasta temperature evolution with drying time. Influence of wet bulb temperature.

THEORY

Heat and mass transfer inside pasta [10, 11] :

Among various models describing heat and mass transfer inside porous media, we chose a LUIKOV'S type model. With this model, the heterogeneous solid at microscopic scale, is represented by a continuous media. Due to pasta intrinsic properties, we admit the following hypothesis :

- transfer is unidirectional (radial in spaghetti case)
- desorption enthalpy is negligible
- total pressure is constant
- thermomigration is negligible ($\delta' = 0$)
- evaporation takes place near the external surface so that $\varepsilon' = 0$ if $r < R$ and $\varepsilon' = 1$ if $r = R$.

Mass and heat conservation principles lead to the following equations :

$$\frac{\partial X}{\partial t} = \frac{1}{R} \frac{\partial}{\partial r} \{r.D \ (\frac{\partial X}{\partial r} + \delta' \ . \ \frac{\partial T}{\partial r})\} \tag{1}$$

$$\frac{\partial T}{\partial t} = \frac{1}{\rho_p.c_p.r} \frac{\partial}{\partial r} \{r.\lambda. \ \frac{\partial T}{\partial r}\} + \frac{\varepsilon'\Delta H_v}{\rho_p.c_p} \ . \ \rho_s \ \frac{\partial X}{\partial t} \tag{2}$$

Initial and boundary conditions can be written :

I.C.

$$t = 0 \qquad T = T_o \qquad X = \overline{X}_o \qquad \text{for } \forall \ r \ (\text{flat profile}) \tag{3}$$

B.C.

Center :

$$t = 0 \qquad \frac{\partial X}{\partial r} = \frac{\partial T}{\partial r} = 0 \qquad (\text{symmetry}) \tag{4}$$

Surface :

$$r = R \qquad X = X_e \ \text{with} \ X_e = f(a_w, T_{r=R}) \tag{5}$$

$$r = R \qquad -\lambda \ (\frac{\partial T}{\partial r}) + h \ (T_a - T_{r=R}) - \Delta H_v \ . \ J_m = 0 \tag{6}$$

Equation (5) states that the spaghetti external surface humidity is always in equilibrium with bulk gas humidity (no mass transfer resistance inside the boundary layer).

Equation (6) is based on the thermal flux continuity at the solid surface, with a term source, $\Delta H_v.J_m$, expressed as a function of the experimental value of the mass flux density obtained from drying curves.

A similar system has been defined and integrated in the case of plane geometry [3, 4]. Due to parameter dependance with temperature and humidity, the system defined by equations (1) to (6) was integrated numerically using finite difference method [3, 4, 10].

Stress profile inside pasta :

Internal stress profile evolution inside the pasta during the process was calculated by a mechanical approach. The humidity gradient inside the pasta, which is the main driving force for mass transfer, induces different shrinkage between core and surface zones leading to plastic strains ; so at the end of the drying period, a triaxial residual stress field remains. We used the well known method of "successive elastic solutions" precisely described by MENDELSON [13] and recently used by ourselves [14] for solving a similar problem by numerical calculation of residual stress in quenched bars.

An incremental method was programmed with a micro-computer ; this calculation, at any time, was coupled with the humidity profile determination previously presented. For this purpose, we used pasta mechanical properties obtained as a function of temperature and humidity by traction tests on spaghetti [4]. So, we calculated stress evolution during spaghetti drying for different climatic operating conditions (T_a, H.R.).

RESULTS AND DISCUSSIONS

Temperature and humidity profiles :

Any experiment being impossible with spaghetti, the model validation was done by comparison of the theoretical and experimental temperature and humidity profiles obtained with slab geometry [3, 4].

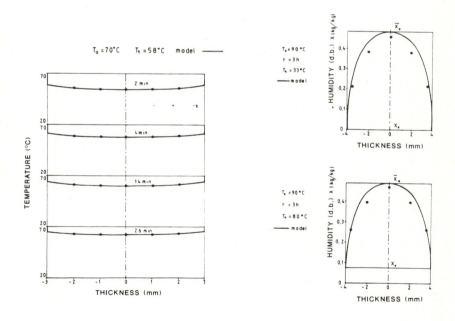

Fig. 3. Temperature profile inside pasta.

Fig. 4. Comparison of experimental and theoretical humidity profiles.

For example, on figure 2 we can see that the model predicts reasonably well the sample core temperature evolution ; this temperature reaches rapidly (t = 10 min) a value very close to the air dry bulb temperature. This figure shows also that heat penetration increases with air humidity that is to say with wet bulb temperature, all the other parameters being equal.

This observation can be easily explained by the importance of the term source in equation (6), the numerical value of this term decreasing when air humidity increases. Besides, figure 3 shows that there is at any time no significant temperature gradient inside the pasta (flat profile) which is predicted by the model and by the mean value of BIOT number, $Bi_c = 4$. This result shows that heat transfer is much more rapid than mass transfer and that drying can be considered as isothermal.

A similar comparison has been done as concern humidity profiles inside pasta as shown on figure 4 ; one can see that local humidity decreases continuously from the core to the external surface (parabolic variation [4]) and, in the other hand, that there doesn't exist any dried zone with a receding front inside the material. Due to pasta very low porosity and to the exponential variation of water diffusivity with the temperature [1, 2] (ARRHENIUS type law) in the other hand, it seems that liquid transport inside pasta takes place mainly in liquid or adsorbed phase [2, 6].

A numerical integration of the equation system (1) to (6) - cylindric geometry - gives the humidity profile inside the spaghetti. This simulation shows that air humidity has a strong influence on surface humidity gradient i.e. on mechanical stresses induce by the drying [3, 4]. (cf. figure 5).

Stress profile :

Stress profil evolution - axial, radial, tangential and equivalent stress - was calculated for constant air operating conditions (differential drying). The VON MISES equivalent stress, frequently used to characterize loading intensity was defined by the relation :

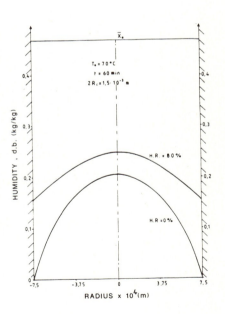

Fig. 5. Radial humidity profile (spaghetti), X(r).

$$\sigma_{eq} = \frac{1}{\sqrt{2}} \cdot \sqrt{(\sigma_r - \sigma_\theta)^2 + (\sigma_\theta - \sigma_z)^2 + (\sigma_z - \sigma_r)^2} \qquad (7)$$

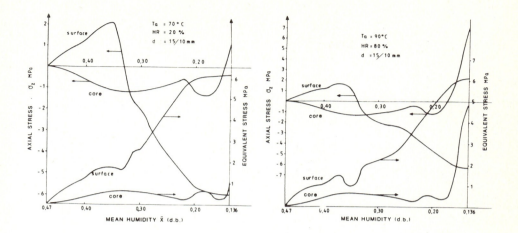

Fig. 6. Variation of axial and equi-   Fig. 7. Variation of axial and equiva-
valent stress with humidity (T_a = 70°C) lent stress with humidity (T_a = 90°C)

So, on figure 6 and 7 we presented few results corresponding to two sets of
extreme values :

   — T_a = 70°C ; H.R. = 20 %
   — T_a = 80°C ; H.R. = 80 %
   We observe :

   a) An inversion in the stress direction during the process : at the beginning of the drying the pasta surface is in tension, whereas at the drying end
this zone is in compression. Inversaly, the spaghetti core zone is first in
compression and then in traction. Besides, tension stress being the most dan-
gerous, there are two critical periods as concern the risks of cracks formation :
   – at the drying beginning, on the external spaghetti surface.
   – at the drying end, on the spaghetti core.

   b) The experimental conditions (T_a = 90°C ; H.R. = 80 %) leads to an equivalent stress value higher than the conditions (T_a = 70°C , H.R. = 20 %) so that
it may exist optimal operating conditions.

   On figure 8 and 9, we plotted at the drying end, the axial, radial, tangential
stress profile for the set of operating conditions presented before. One can
observe, that an increase of dry air temperature even with very humid air, gives
an important axial stress in the spaghetti core.

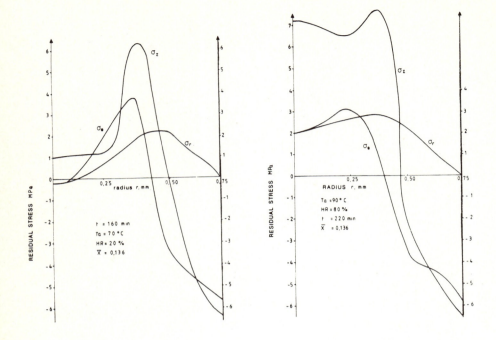

Fig. 8. Residual stress distribution after drying (T_a = 70°C ;
H.R. = 20 %).

Fig. 9. Residual stress distribution
after drying (T_a = 90°C ; H.R. = 80 %)

Finally, the programm written allows to simulate an industrial drying diagram
with periods at different air temperatures and humidities.

CONCLUSIONS

A simplified LUIKOV'S model - in the case of non porous durum wheat pasta
material - can be used to predict experimental temperature and humidity profiles
inside the solid.

These theoretical and experimental data confirm that heat transfer during
drying is much more rapid than mass transfer. For practical applications, drying
can be considered isothermal and entirely controlled by internal mass transfer
resistance.

Stress field simulation during the drying allows to set a quantitative approach to the very difficult problem of the prediction of cracks formation risks
induced by the process.

REFERENCES

1 J. ANDRIEU and A. STAMATOPOULOS, Diffusion model applied to pasta drying kinetics, Proceedings of I.D.S. '84, Kyoto, Japan, Volume 1, p. 290-294 (1984)
2 J. ANDRIEU and A. STAMATOPOULOS, Durum wheat pasta drying kinetics, Lebensm. Wiss. Technol. , 19, (1986) p. 448-456
3 J. ANDRIEU and A. STAMATOPOULOS, Heat and mass transfer modelling during durum wheat pasta drying, Proceedings of I.D.S.'86, Boston, Volume 2, p. 492-498, (1986)
4 A. STAMATOPOULOS, Contribution à l'étude expérimentale et théorique du séchage des pâtes alimentaires, Thèse d'Etat, Université de Montpellier II (1986)
5 J. ANDRIEU, A. STAMATOPOULOS and M. ZAFIROPOULOS, Cinétique de séchage des pâtes à base de maïs, J.I.Th., Lyon, Volume 1, p. 328-335 (1987)
6 KAMEI and Coll. in KRISHER O. et KROLL K., Traduction française par CETIAT, 1963, vol. IV, p. 390-391
7 M. ZAFIROPOULOS, Contribution à l'étude du séchage des pâtes à base de maïs, Thèse de Docteur-Ingénieur, U.S.T.L. Montpellier II, (1987)
8 P. GORLING, Getreide and Mehl., 4, p. 39-43 (1960)
9 A.V. LUIKOV, Heat and mass transfer in capillary porous bodies. Ed. Pergamon Press (1966)
10 A.V. LUIKOV, Analytical heat and diffusion theory, Ed. Academic Press (1968)
11 R.B. KEEY, Drying principles and practice, Ed. Pergamon Press (1972)
12 J. ANDRIEU and A. STAMATOPOULOS , Rapport de fin de convention "séchage T.H.T. des pâtes alimentaires" (1987)
13 A. MENDELSON, Plasticity : theory and application, The MacMillan Compagny, New York (1968)
14 R. HABACHOU and M. BOIVIN, Modélisation de la trempe et du détensionnement par traction de barres cylindriques d'alliage d'aluminium. Journal de Mécanique Théorique et Appliquée, vol. 4, n° 5, p. 701-723 (1985)

NOMENCLATURE

a_w	Water activity	
Bi_c	BIOT number	
c_p	specific heat	J/Kg.K
d	sample diameter	m
D	mass apparent diffusivity	$m^2.s^{-1}$
E	YOUNG modulus	Pa
J_m	drying rate by surface unity	$Kg/m^2.s^{-1}$
h	heat transfer coefficient	$Watt.m^{-2}.K^{-1}$
ΔH_v	vaporization latent heat (water)	J/Kg
H.R.	relative humidity	
r,R	radial abscissa or spaghetti radius	m
t	time	s
T	temperature	K or °C
T_h	wet bulb temperature	°C
x_e	water mass fraction	
X	solid water content (d.b.)	Kg/Kg
$\overline{X}$	mean solid humidity (d.b.)	Kg/Kg
Y	air absolute humidity	Kg/Kg

Greek letters

α, β	linear and volumic shrinkage coefficients	
δ'	thermomigration coefficient	
ε'	phase transition ratio	
λ	pasta thermal conductivity	Watt m^{-1}K^{-1}
ρ_p	pasta density	Kg/m^3
ρ_s	dry matter density	Kg/m^3
σ_r	radial stress	Pa
σ_z	axial stress	Pa
σ_θ	tangential stress	Pa
σ_{eq}	equivalent stress	Pa

Subscripts

a	ambient air
e	equilibrium

P.S.

The authors are grateful to A.C.B. - ALSTHOM, D.I.A., C.F.S.I., I.T.C.F., O.N.I.C., S.I.F.P.A.F. and I.N.R.A. for the material aid that they received.

Preconcentration and Drying of Food Materials, edited by S. Bruin
Elsevier Science Publishers B.V., Amsterdam, 1988 — Printed in The Netherlands

SPRAY DRYING OF CONCENTRATED MILK: RELATION BETWEEN INITIAL DROPLET SIZE AND FINAL PARTICLE SIZE

P.J.J.M. van Mil, G. Hols and H.J. Klok
NIZO, P.O. Box 20, 6710 BA Ede, the Netherlands.

ABSTRACT
Droplet sizes were measured with a Malvern instrument (light diffraction) in sprays of concentrated skim milk atomized by a centrifugal pressure nozzle. Size distributions ranged from log-normal at a pressure of 10 MPa to bi-modal at 20 MPa. The median of the distribution was proportional to $P^{-1/3}$. The size distribution was not influenced by age-thickening of the milk (increase of viscosity at low shear rate) nor by addition of sweet-cream buttermilk which contains surface-active phospholipids. Drying of the droplets led to powder particles which were somewhat agglomerated.
Calculation of the droplet diameter thus gave values which were 80 % higher than the measured values.

INTRODUCTION

The principal step in the process of spray drying is the formation of a spray of droplets by atomization. A large surface area is created to accomplish maximum water and heat flux and to mix the fine spray with drying air.

The initial droplet size (or the specific surface·area) has an influence on the drying process and therefore determines many of the final powder properties (particle size, particle density, moisture content etc.).

With a technique which makes use of the detection of light that is scattered by droplets in a forward direction and computes a size distribution from the light intensity pattern [1], the droplet sizes are measured in a spray of concentrated milk atomized by a centrifugal pressure nozzle. The spray is often inhomogeneous i.e. the concentration of droplets is higher inside the spray cone (solid cone) or lower inside the spray cone (hollow cone) and larger droplet sizes occur at the boundary of the cone due to differences in velocity between large and small droplets. However, for centrifugal pressure nozzles droplet size distributions should follow a Rosin Rammler or upper limit log-normal distribution [2], or a square-root-normal distribution [3].

After drying the milkpowder particles have sizes that are used to calculate the droplet size distribution assuming that only uniform shrinkage or vacuole formation has taken place [4]. An equation that is used for this purpose is:

$$d_d/d_p = [\rho_p/\rho_d \times X_p/X_d]^{1/3} \qquad\qquad (1)$$

The droplet diameter is denoted by d_d, the particle diameter by d_p, for droplet density and particle density ρ_d and ρ_p are used, X_d and X_p are the weight fractions of solids per unit weight for droplet and particle, respectively.

Because drying time should be limited, to avoid heat damage to the milk solids, the spray of milk droplets is intensively mixed with drying air. Collision of droplets and dried particles will lead to agglomerates and the relation between droplet size and particle size will not be as proposed by the equation mentioned above.

EXPERIMENTAL

Skim milk or a mixture of skim milk and sweet cream buttermilk (50/50, pre-heattreatment 1 minute 85 °C) was concentrated with a 4-effect falling film evaporator to a fluid with approximately 45 % total milksolids. The viscosity was measured at 3917 s^{-1} with a Haake RV2, NV-system, MK500. At a temperature of 55 °C the concentrated milk was atomized by a centrifugal pressure nozzle (Spraying Systems type SX 77/220). Various pressures were applied (7.5 - 20 MPa), flow rates were measured between 35 and 45 l/h.

The spray of droplets concentrated milk was dried to milk powder by inserting the nozzle in a drying chamber of the pilot plant of NIZO. The water evaporating capacity was 25 kg per hour, the temperature of the inlet air was varied from 160 to 200 °C at an amount of 1100 kg/h.

Droplet size measurement

A particle size analyzer (PSA, Malvern 2600 D) was used to assess the droplet size distribution. The sizer was operated in the Model Independent mode and equipped with a lens of 300 mm focal length. Each measurement was repeated five times and the average result reported. After drying of a spray the droplet size was measured again. The experimental set-up was checked by blowing glass ballottini, with a certified size distribution, through the laser beam and measuring its size distribution.

Particle size measurement

The particle size distribution of the milk powder was measured with the PSA. The powder was dispersed in isopropanol and subjected to ultrasound for three minutes to disintegrate any accidental agglomerates [5].

Properties of the milk powder, viz. particle density, insolubility index, moisture content, were assessed by analysis according to international methods.

RESULTS AND DISCUSSION

The size distribution of the spray of droplets of concentrated milk was measured at various distances from the nozzle (longitudinal) in a horizontal plane. Figure 1 shows the volume/surface diameter (Sauter mean) of the size distribution when concentrated milk of 45 % total solids is atomized with a pressure of 10 MPa. The Sauter mean in the middle of the spray is lower than at the outer regions. There are three possible explanations for this phenomenon.

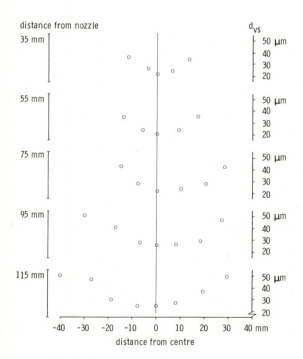

Fig. 1. Sauter mean (d_{vs}) of the droplet size distribution of a vertically positioned nozzle measured at five distinct horizontal levels and various distances from the centre of the cone (pressure 10 MPa, total solids 45 %).

1. Because differences in concentration of droplets occur when the laser light travels through the center or at the outside of the spraycone the obscuration of light is different. The high concentration causes multiple scattering which leads to an underestimation of the size at high obscurations [6]. Corrections can be made by determination of the relation between concentration and Sauter mean with a suitable particulate system. For obscurations in the range of 0.1 to 0.5 the Sauter mean decreased 0.8 μm when the obscuration was increased with 0.1. Therefore, this will not give an explanation of the difference in size in the outer and inner region of the spray.

2. Since the spray is a hollow cone the size distribution of the frontside of the spray is superimposed by the sizes of the droplets at the backside [7]. Laboratory experiments with two portions of particles placed in the laser beam to simulate a hollow cone revealed that this procedure did not have influence on the original size distribution when measured with one portion.

3. There is an actual difference in size inside the spray (which appears not be to hollow): small droplets in the inner regions of the cone, large droplets are to be seen at the outer regions. Characterization of the spray can thus be be given best by the Sauter mean of the size distribution in the centre of the spray where, because of the symmetry of the cone, two identical size distributions are measured.

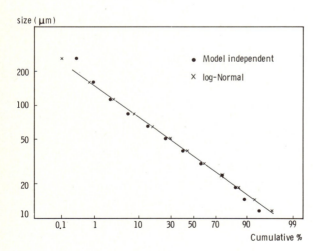

Fig. 2. Droplet size distribution plotted on log-probability paper. Spheres are values obtained in the Model Independent mode, crosses are values calculated from the log-normal mode.

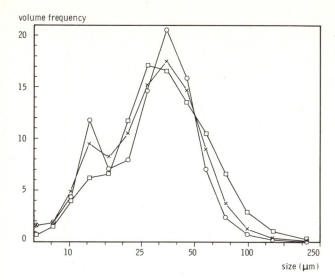

volume frequency

size (μm)

Fig. 3. Volume frequency graph of skim milk spray (45 % total solids). Nozzle pressure: □ 10 MPa, × 15 MPa, o 20 MPa.

The distribution of sizes of the droplets in a spray is often given by a Rosin-Rammler type of distribution, or by a (upper limit) log-normal distribution [2]. In figure 2 the sizes of the droplets from measurements at 115 mm from the nozzle are shown on a log-probability graph. It is very likely that in this case they follow the log-normal or even better an upper   limit log-normal distribution. Fitting of the data to Rosin Rammler or square-root-normal distributions gave poor results. If the conditions of atomization are altered, however, the distribution can become multimodal [7]. If the pressure for atomization is increased, the spray will contain finer droplets, but, as can be seen in Figure 3, the size distribution becomes bi-modal. From the size distribution the Sauter mean was calculated. In Figure 4a the relation between Sauter mean and pressure for this batch of concentrated milk (45 % total solids, viscosity at 3917 s^{-1} 19 mPa.s.) was

d_{vs} = 93 - 14.3 ln P.

Plotting the logarithm of the median versus the logarithm of the pressure yields a coefficient for log P of -0.34 which was also suggested by Masters [4] and Matsumoto et al. (see reference no. 16 in [7]). The flow of

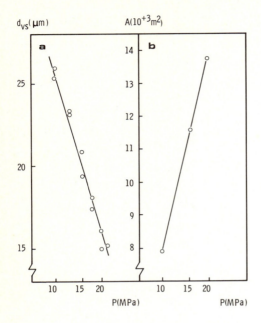

Fig 4. (a) Sauter mean (d_{vs}) of droplet size distribution versus the nozzle pressure. (b) Total surface area calculated from Sauter mean and flow at three nozzle pressures.

concentrated milk was measured at nozzle pressures of 10, 15 and 20 MPa and the total surface area per unit of time available for heat and water flux was calculated:

$$A = 6 * Flow / d_{vs} \qquad (2)$$

In Figure 4b the lineair relationship between applied pressure and surface area is shown. These graphs could be useful if drying efficiency has to be calculated.

The droplet size is also determined by the viscosity of the liquid. When kept at temperatures of above 50 °C, concentrated milk with a high solids content (>40%) can become more viscous [8]. Applying high shear rates to the concentrated milk, e.g. at atomization, will disrupt the structural viscosity. Figure 5 shows the volume frequency size distribution of a spray from concentrated milk before and after age-thickening at two positions in the spray (pressure 10 MPa, total solids 44,7 %, pre-heat treatment 15 s at 85 °C).

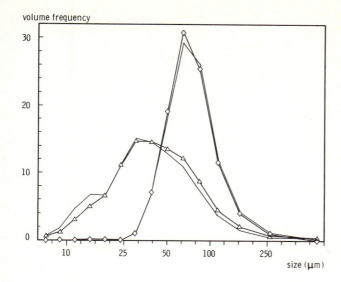

Fig. 5. Droplet size distributions of skim milk (no symbols used) and skim milk after age-thickening at two positions in the spray ($\triangle$ and $\diamond$). The viscosity before and after age-thickening was 28 and 87 mPa.s, respectively, at a shear rate of 173 s^{-1}.

The viscosity of the concentrated milk was 28 mPa.s at a shear rate of 173 s^{-1} and 21 mPa.s at 3917 s^{-1}. After age-thickening the viscosity was 87 mPa.s and 22 mPa.s, respectively. It is clear that age-thickening has no influence on the droplet size distribution.

If the surface tension of a liquid is low, droplet size in the spray will be fine. Sweet cream buttermilk, which contains phospholipids that can lower the surface tension, is said to have an effect on particle size. However, Figure 6a shows that addition of 50 % of sweet cream buttermilk to skim milk has no effect on the droplet size distribution (pressure 15 MPa, total solids 44.5 % and 43 %, viscosity at 3917 s^{-1} 13.4 and 14.1 mPa.s for skim milk and the sweet cream buttermilk/skim milk concentrate, respectively). In these cases the time for diffusion of surface-active agents to the surface to lower the surface tension is too short compared to the time it takes to disrupt the fluid. The figure (6b) also shows that in this case the particle size distribution in the skim milk powder is not different from the size distribution in the milk powder with sweet cream buttermilk solids. When other atomization pressures were applied (i.e. 10 and 20 MPa) similar graphs could be drawn.

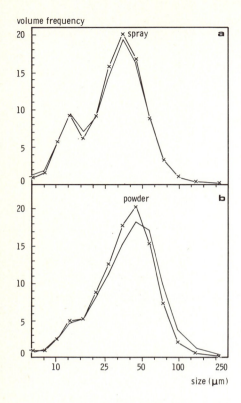

Fig 6. (a) Droplet size distribution of skim milk (no symbols used) and of a mix (50/50) of skim milk and sweet cream buttermilk (x). (b) Particle size distribution after drying of the sprays mentioned in figure 6a.

The droplet size distribution of a spray is often calculated from the size distribution of the particles in the powder [4,9]. Calculations of the droplet size can only be made if the primary particle size is known. Agglomerates will lead to erroneous droplet sizes. Table 1 shows the Sauter mean of the droplet and particle size distribution of concentrated and dried skim milk, both measured. Calculation of the droplet diameter showed that the Sauter mean for droplets at nozzle pressures of 10, 15 and 20 MPa should have been 43, 37 and 34 µm, which is 80 % above the measured values. The particle diameters are larger than droplet diameters which can only be caused by agglomeration of the particles. The milk powder particles, when seen through a microscope, were indeed agglomerated and not spherical. Small droplets are caught by large droplets (cf. figure 6) and since the size distributions that were measured

Table 1. Effect of nozzle pressure and inlet air temperature on spray and powder properties (concentrated skim milk: 45.1 % total solids, viscosity 19 mPa. s).

pressure (MPa)	temperature (°C)	Sauter mean		particle density (kg/m³)	moisture content (%)
		droplets (μm)	particles (μm)		
10	160	24.4	30.2	1261	3.3
	180		29.8	1120	2.1
	200		37.3	1032	1.8
15	160	19.6	28	1272	3.4
	180		26.3	1180	2.3
	200		27.8	1064	2.0
20	160	18.4	22.7	1300	3.7
	180		26.7	1162	2.6
	200		26.8	1159	2.1

are volume distributions, a small increase of the diameter of large particles will lead to a relatively large increase in Sauter mean of the particle distribution. This shows that calculation of the droplet diameter from the particle diameter is extremely hazardous, especially when agglomeration occurs which is unavoidable in industrial spray driers.

CONCLUSION

Assessment of the droplet size distribution in a spray of concentrated milk should be measured through the centre of the spray. Viscosity increase by age-thickening of skim milk or addition of sweet cream buttermilk did not change the size distribution of the droplets. Droplet sizes that were calculated from powder particles were higher than measured droplet sizes due to agglomeration of the particles. It is advised to use measured droplet sizes for calculation of drying efficiency.

REFERENCES

1. E.D. Hirleman, Particle Sizing by Optical, Nonimaging Techniques, in: 'Liquid Particle Size Measurement Techniques', ASTM STP 848, J.M. Tishkoff, R.D. Ingebo and J.B. Kennedy (Eds.), American Society for Testing Materials, Philadelphia, 1984.
2. C.E. Goering, L.E. Bode and D.B. Smith, Characterization of Spray Droplet Size Distributions, in: Proceedings of the First International Conference on Liquid Atomization and Spray Systems (ICLAS 78), The Fuel Society of Japan, Tokyo, 1978.
3. P.A. Nelson and W.F. Stevens, Size distribution of droplets from centrifugal spray nozzles, A. I. Ch. E. Journal 7 (1961) 80-86.
4. K. Masters, Spray Drying Handbook, 4th edition, George Godwin, London, 1985.
5. P.J.J.M. van Mil, H.J. Klok and A.J. Damman, Het meten van de deeltjesgrootteverdeling in zuivelprodukten (Measurement of the particle size distribution in dairy products), Zuivelzicht 78(1986)336-338, 436-438; Voedingsmiddelentechnologie 19(1986)(9)35-37, (12)23-25.
6. P.G. Felton, A.A. Hamadi and A.K. Aigal, Measurement of drop size distributions in dense sprays by laser diffraction, in: ICLASS-85 Proceedings, 1985.
7. E. Sada, K. Takahashi, K. Morikawa and S. Ito, Drop size distribution for spray by full cone nozzle, Can. J. Chem. Eng. 56 (1978) 455-459.
8. T.H.M. Snoeren, A.J. Damman and H.J. Klok, The viscosity of skimmilk concentrates, Neth. Milk Dairy J. 36(1982)305-316.
9. E.J. Crosby and W.R. Marshall, Effects of drying conditions on the properties of spray-dried particles, Chem. Eng. Prog. 54(1958)56-63.

Preconcentration and Drying of Food Materials, edited by S. Bruin
Elsevier Science Publishers B.V., Amsterdam, 1988 — Printed in The Netherlands

MODELING GRAPE DRYING KINETICS

P. MASI[1] and M. RIVA[2]

[1] *Dipartimento di Ingegneria Chimica, Università degli Studi di Napoli, 80125 Napoli, Italy*
[2] *D. I. S. T. A. M., Università degli Studi di Milano, 20133 Milano, Italy*

ABSTRACT

This paper presents an approach for modeling grape drying kinetics. The behaviour of six seedless grape varieties in forced convection drying experiments was analyzed and the influence of ethyloleate pretreatment on the drying rate was investigated. The drying process occurred at a variable rate which decreased with decreasing grape moisture content. The observed behaviour indicated that dipping the grapes in an ethyloleate solution modifies the water permeability of the grape skin but does not affect the internal water diffusion mechanism. The drying process was modeled by taking into account the geometrical changes related to the shrinkage of the berries and by assuming that a) water diffusion is the limiting stage of the overall process and b) water transport within the berry follows a Fickian diffusion mechanism governed by a variable diffusion coefficient. The variation of the effective diffusion coefficient during the process was estimated from the experimental data and was found to correlate with temperature and to the actual glucose content of the berry in a way similar to that reported in the literature regarding the diffusion coefficient of water in glucose-water solutions. Volumetric change of the berries was found to be independent of the grape variety and to correlate linearly with grape moisture content. The performance of the model in predicting drying kinetics is analyzed and discussed.

INTRODUCTION

Exposing grape to direct sunlight has been for centuries the way to prepare raisins in several Mediterranean countries. However in recent years this procedure has been widely replaced, for economic and quality considerations, by drying in forced air convection oven.

Grape drying is a composite process which involves simultaneous heat and mass transfer phenomena. The process partially develops under unsteady conditions. During the early stages of the process the temperature of the berries rises, approaching thermal equilibrium conditions. While the transient stage lasts 3-4 hours, the entire drying operation requires much longer time, usually between 24 and 48 hours, depending on the variety of the grape and process conditions. Because of this, for practical purposes one can assume isothermal conditions and that the only governing mechanism is the water permeation process.

In the course of the drying operation the berries remain at a temperature an a_w levels which favor considerable darkening of the grape due to the enzyme activities (1,2). Moreover, in drying operations energy consumption is together with the cost of the raw material, the main factor which determining the overall operating cost. Therefore, a proper design of a drying operation cannot but be based on an appropriate optimization procedure in order to select process conditions which result in minimum energy consumption and thermal damage to the product.

In order to optimize the process in terms of product quality and operating costs suitable models which allows the prediction of the drying time and performance of the product are needed.

Because of the complexity of the physical phenomena involved in the process, the common way to proceed has been a semi-empirical approach i.e., experimental drying data are correlated with simple mathematical equations without taking into account the physical laws which govern the phenomena involved in the process. Although this simple procedure has been often useful for practical applications, it is inadequate for a complete analysis of process kinetics and inadequate to clarify the nature of the phenomena which occur in the course of the drying process.

A previous work reported the influence of some process parameters and pretreatment on water permeation kinetics through grape skin (3). Though water permeation through the skin is one of the most important steps in grape drying mechanism modeling care should be paid also to chemical and physical modifications of the berries during the drying process, as these changes may affect water mobility.

In this work the main phenomena which take place during drying have been analyzed and described in mathematical terms and incorporated in a model to predict water loss kinetics in the course of grape drying.

MATERIALS AND METHODS

Six seedless grape varieties were used after harvesting at full maturity followed by a few days of storage in a cold room at 5 °C. The grapes were different in composition and geometry. Their composition and geometrical characteristics are summarized in table 1.

Sample were prepared for drying tests by hand-removing the stems and subsequent sulphuring in a confined atmosphere under SO_2 vapour for 6 h. Some of the samples were also dipped in a solution containing 3% ethyloleate and 2.5% K_2CO_3 for three minutes at 40 °C, followed by free draining.

Air drying was carried out under forced-convection tangential flow conditions in a cabinet equipped with trays in parallel at a constant temperature: 50 °C, relative humidity: 20% and air velocity: 2.2 m/s. During the tests the temperature near the centers of the berries were monitored by means of Cu-Const. thermocouples. Water loss was periodically measured by removing the trays and weighting them. Also their positions in the cabinet were changed in order to obtain completely comparable experimental conditions. The experiments were stopped when the weight loss during the last hour was less than 0.1%

The average volume shrinkage of the berries was estimated by measuring the average volume reduction at different stages of the process by a displacement method (picnometer) by using toluene at room temperature.

Rehydration of the grape at different stages of drying was evaluated by immersing a set of ten berries removed from the cabinet at different times in a water solution containing a small amount of SO_2. The weight gain of the sample was periodically measured and the experiment stopped when the weight variation was less than 0.1%.

Sample area was estimated by assuming the berry to be a rotational ellipsoid and measuring the two main diameters by means of a cursor caliper.

TABLE I

	Cent.	Emer.	K.Rub	Nede.	Ruby	Sul.B.
Moisture g/100 g	81.40	79.86	81.94	79.77	80.91	77.55
Red. sugar g/100 g	8.16	13.96	15.94	13.85	17.09	15.23
Tot. acid. g/100 g	1.03	0.50	0.59	0.49	0.45	0.37
Tot. SO2 mg/100 g	84.90	69.90	84.30	45.80	84.10	76.20
Free SO2 mg/100 g	38.97	24.13	44.80	13.40	27.07	16.84
Weight g	2.26	3.73	2.70	4.29	2.64	2.60
Skin Thick. mm	0.220	0.223	0.296	0.271	0.210	0.222
Volume ml	1.34	3.16	2.10	3.60	2.10	2.06
Surface sq.cm	6.09	10.45	7.93	10.77	7.97	7.98

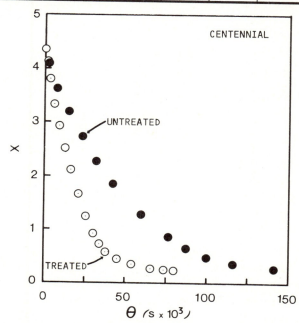

Figure 1: Drying curves of Centennial grape at 50 °C

Moisture, total acidity, reducing sugar content, total and free SO_2 were determined according to the Italian Official Methods of Analysis for must and wine (4).

RESULTS AND DISCUSSION

Figure 1 shows the characteristic drying curve of untreated grapes and grapes which were treated with ethyloleate solution. Dipping the grape into an ethyloleate solution reduced markedly the resistance of the skin to water permeation (5); the time required to complete the drying operation was also reduced considerably. For the Centennial variety, shown in the figure, steady state conditions was reached in less than 22 hours while for the untreated sample a drying time twice as long was needed. In addition to the evident advantage of reduced energy consumption, shorter drying times result in products with improved organoleptic characteristics. Rapidly increasing sugar concentration inhibits the reactions responsible for grape darkening (6) making it possible to obtain better quality products, lighter in color with a brilliant surface appearance (7).

A lower residual moisture content was obtained in the case of the pretreated samples. This can be explained by recognizing that rapid drying reduces internal resistance phenomena giving rise to more porous structures which, in turn, favour water mobility in the final stage of the process. This is also in agreement with the higher weight gain observed during the rehydration of pretreated samples (table II).

Table II: Percentage increment of rehydratability.
Weight gain of treated samples/weight gain of untreated samples.

Variety	%
CENTENNIAL	29
EMERALD	21
KING'S RUBY	45
NEDELTCHEFF	100
SULTANA BLACK	51
RUBY	30

Figure 2 shows the experimental grape drying rate vs the moisture content of the grape. Three distinct drying periods can be detected: an initial transition period, a first period during which drying proceeds at decreasing velocity and a second falling rate period characterized by a more rapid decrement of the drying velocity. No region at constant velocity was observed for any of the analyzed grape varieties, which confirm that under the process conditions usually used in grape drying operations the overall process is governed only by internal diffusion phenomena. The unsteady state period is probably related to the temperature rise of the grape during the initial stage of the process (figure 3). For untreated grapes the transition period was very short compared with the treated sample, suggesting that the external wax layer which was removed by the alkali treatment while acted as a resistance for mass transfer improves heat propagation.

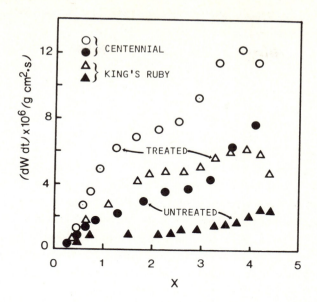

Figure 2: Grape drying rate vs absolute moisture content of the grape, X (kg water/kg dry solids)

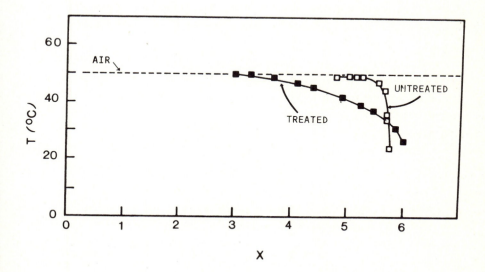

Figure 3: Temperature at the center of the berry during drying at 50 °C.

In the literature, drying kinetics of fruits and vegetables are often described by means of a simplified form of Fick's law of the type :

$$(X_t - X_e)/(X_o - X_e) = \exp(-k\Theta) \tag{1}$$

where X_e is the mean moisture content of the sample at the drying time Θ.

The main advantage of this approach is related to the mathematical form of equation 1. In a semi-logarithmic diagram, plotting the data according to eq. 1 results in a straight line, permitting the estimation of long term product performance from short time experiment. In addition, by treating the equilibrium moisture content, X_e, as a parameter linear regression analysis of experimental data allows one to estimate the equilibrium moisture content of the grape, avoiding the experimental difficulties usually associated with the direct determination of this quantity.

Figure 4 shows for two grape varieties linear plots which were obtained by plotting the experimental data according to eq. 1. Unfortunately this simple approach appears to be inadequate to describe the drying kinetics of grapes. In some cases, in fact, large departures from linearity are observed, pointing out the risk of a generalized use of this method.

In the course of drying operation water removal from grapes occurs by means of processes which take place in series. Water diffuses from the internal region to the grape skin, permeate through it and emerges at the external surface from which it is removed by the circulating air. At the explored air flow rates the external resistance to mass transfer were negligible compared to the internal resistance (Biot number >>1). Therefore when modeling grape drying kinetics one can assume that the limiting phenomena which govern the overall process are those related to internal mass transfer, i. e. : water diffusion inside the grape and permeation through the skin.

In defining the features of the model the geometrical variations which occur during drying cannot be ignored. Shrinkage of the berry during drying, in fact, will modify considerably the external exchange area affecting the flux of vapour removed by the air. At the same time the progressive concentration and precipitation of solutes as well as the formation of colloidal structures will affect the internal mobility of the water molecules.

Assuming that the ellipsoidal shape of the berries can be approximated with equivalent spheres and isothermal conditions, drying kinetics of grape can be described by applying Fick's unsteady state equations for spheres;

$$\frac{\partial X}{\partial t} = \frac{1}{4\pi r^2} \frac{\partial}{\partial r} \left[4\pi r^2 \; D \; \frac{\partial X}{\partial r} \right] \tag{2}$$

under the following boundary and initial conditions accounting for a) uniform initial moisture content and b) symmetrical radial diffusion:

$$\begin{array}{cccc} t=0 & \forall r & X = X_o \\ \forall t & r = 0 & dX/dr = 0 \end{array} \tag{3}$$

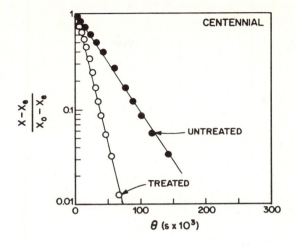

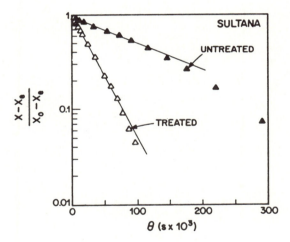

Figure 4: Linear plot of grape drying kinetics according to eq. 1

Moreover, in order to properly take into account the structural changes which occur during drying and their influence on mass transfer mechanisms discussed earlier, the following additional conditions should be imposed:

1) the diffusivity coefficient in eq. 2 is not a constant but varies with varying moisture content in the berry.
2) the berry surface area varies with varying moisture content of the berry.
3) surface water concentration is constant during the process and is equal to zero.

In order to integrate the above set of equations it is necessary to express the above conditions in a suitable mathematical form. Once the mathematical form of the above conditions is provided, equation 2 can be solved by means of a finite difference method (8) or equivalent numerical methods to provide drying kinetics of grape.

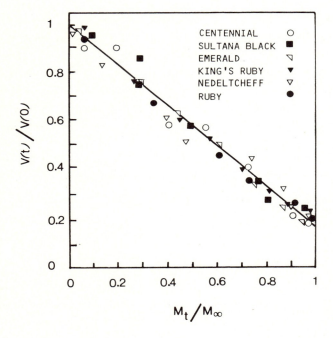

Figure 5: Average volume shrinkage of grape as a function of free water content. M_t = moisture desorbed at time t, M_∞ = moisture desorbed at steady state.

Figure 5 shows the percentage volume reduction of the berries as a function of the relative content of free water, M_t/M_∞ the ratio between the volume reduction of the berries at the drying time t and the initial volume of the sample decreases linearly as free water content decreases. The average volume of the grape at the end of the process will be almost 1/6 of the initial volume. The volumetric change during the process can be predicted by the equation:

$$V(t)/V(0) = 1 - (5/6)\ M_t/M_\infty \qquad (4)$$

A similar result has been reported for Sultana grape variety (9). Moreover it is noteworthy that the same straight line correlates the experimental data of all of the grape varieties analyzed, suggesting that equation 4 has a general validity and is independent of the grape variety.

The experimental measurement of the external area of the berry at different stages in the drying process is quite difficult since berry shrinkage during drying is accompanied by considerable wrinkling of the skin. A common way to proceed has been to assume that the ellipsoid shape of the berries can be approximated with spheres of equivalent volume calculating an equivalent diameter by using the formula: $d_e = (6V/\pi)^{1/3}$.

This, however implies that during shrinkage the shape of the berry does not changes. This may happen only if the skin is completely elastic. On the other hand, if the skin is completely inelastic, water losses will cause only the depleting of the berry and the skin surface will remain constant. The real situation is a compromise between these two extreme cases.

In order to evaluate the skin surface during drying ten berries at a time were removed from the oven at different stages of the process and kept in water until the weight gain reached equilibrium. The swelling of the grape subsequent to rehydration eliminates the skin wrinkles allowing the accurate determination of the sample geometrical dimensions. Figure 6 shows the variation of the skin surface with respect to the initial area as a function of the relative amount of free water contained in the berries. Again the ratio between the area of the skin at a drying time t and the initial surface area of the berries decreases linearly with decreasing relative moisture content and can be predicted by the equation:

$$A(t)/A(0) = 1 - 0.5\ M_t/M_\infty \qquad (5)$$

The effective diffusivity at a certain moisture content can be estimated by the method of slopes of the experimental and theoretical curves (10). For this purpose equation 2 was numerically solved assuming the diffusivity to be constant within a certain moisture range, with volume and surface of the berry varying according to eq. 4 and ed. 5 respectively.

The effective diffusivity of moisture at a certain moisture content was estimated from the following equation (8):

$$D_{eff} = (Slope_{exp}/Slope_{th})\ (d_e/2)^2 \qquad (6)$$

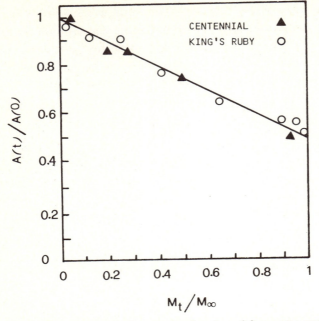

Figure 6: Average surface area of grape as a function of free water content. M_t= moisture desorbed at time t, M_∞= moisture desorbed at steady state.

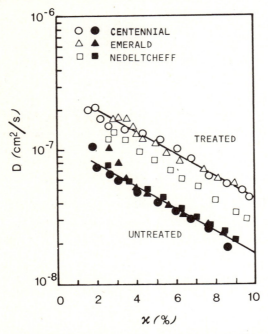

Figure 7: Effective diffusivity coefficient vs molar glucose content in the grape χ

where d_e is the equivalent diameter of the grape berry at the given moisture content.

Figure 7 shows for three different grape varieties the effective diffusion coefficient as a function of the molar glucose concentration within the berry at a given moisture content.

For the grape varieties analyzed plotting the diffusivity coefficient on a logarithmic scale against the molar concentration gives a linear relationship which may be described in mathematical form by the equation:

$$\log D = - K_1 - K_2 \chi \qquad (7)$$

which is of the same type as that proposed in the literature to describe the binary diffusion coefficient in glucose-water solutions (11).

It is interesting to note that all the data relative to untreated grapes fall on the same straight line suggesting that the mechanism with which water diffuses through the berry is the same for all of the grape variety considered in this work. Treated grapes exhibited a higher water mobility compared to the untreated ones. the curves which correlate the experimental data are parallel to each other. This is in agreement with the hypothesis that ethyloleate acts on the wax layer reducing its resistance to water transport but does not affect the mechanism of internal diffusion. Differences in diffusivity among treated grape varieties may be explained in terms of different effectiveness of the treatment due to differences in quantity and composition of the external layer of wax which exists among the different grape varieties.

Figure 8 compares the experimental drying curve with the model prediction. The agreement between the experimental data and the model prediction is quite good, confirming the validity of the proposed approach. Departure from the model prediction which are noticed at the very early stages of the process are probably related to the thermal transition which take place at the beginning of the drying stage and which has been ignored in the present analysis.

Although further refinement of the model is still required to eliminate same discrepancies, the proposed approach appears to be a promising tool in predicting grape drying kinetics and can be successfully extended to other waxy fruits and to product which undergo severe geometrical changes in the course of drying.

ACKNOWLEDGEMENT

Research work supported by CNR - Italy. Special grant IPRA - Subproject 3. Paper n. 1602

214

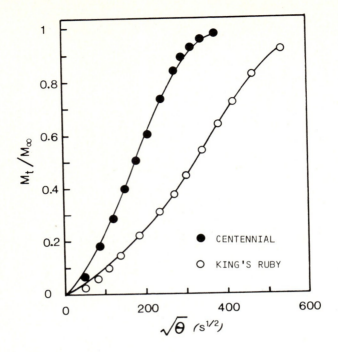

Figure 8: Comparison between experimental data (dots) and model prediction (solid line).

REFERENCES

1 **D. Barnett,** Dried grapes: the involvement of lipids and their production, CSIRO Food Research Quarterly, 40 (1980) 16–22.
2 **M.Grncarevic and J. J. Hawker,** Browning of Sultana grapes berries during drying, J. Sci. Food Agr., 22 (1971) 270–272.
3 **M. Riva and P. Masi,** Permeability to water of grape skin, in A. Mujumdar (Ed) Drying 86, Hemisphere Pub. Corp., Washington, 1986, vol. 1 pp.454–460.
4 **Ministero Agricoltura e Foreste,** Metodi Ufficiali di Analisi per vini, mosti e aceti, MAF , Roma, 1964.
5 **J. D. Pointing and D. M. McBean,** Temperature and dipping treatment effects on drying rates and drying times of grapes, prunes and other waxy fruits, Food Technol., 24 (1970) 1403–1406.
6 **F. Radler,** The prevention of browning during drying by cold dipping treatment of Sultana grapes, J. Sci. Food Agr., 12 (1964) 864–869.
7 **M. Riva, C. Per and R. Lovino,** Effects of pretreatments on kinetics of grapes drying, in: Le Maguer and P. Jelen (Ed.s) Food Engineering and Process applications, Elsevier Appl. Si. Pub. Ltd, Barking, England 1986, pp. 461–472.
8 **J. Crank,** The mathematics of diffusion, Claredon Press, Oxford 1975, cp. 8, pp. 137–160.
9 **G. D. Saravacos and G. S. Raouzeos,** in: A. Mujumdar (Ed) Drying 86, op. cit. vol. 2, pp. 487–491.
10 **R. H. Perry and D. Green,** Perry's Chemical Engineering Handbook, 6th Ed., Mc Graw Hill, New York 1984, pp. 20.13–20.14.
11 **J. van der Lijn,** Simulation of heat and mass transfer in spray drying. Ph.D. Thesis, Centre for agricultural Pub. and Documentation, Wageningen 1976, Appendix B: physical properties of model components, pp. 72–85

DRYING OF FOOD MATERIALS:
PROCESSES AND OPTIMISATION

Preconcentration and Drying of Food Materials, edited by S. Bruin
Elsevier Science Publishers B.V., Amsterdam, 1988 — Printed in The Netherlands

OPTIMIZING THE HEAT SENSITIVE MATERIALS IN CONCENTRATION AND DRYING
by Marcus Karel

Department of Applied Biological Sciences Massachusetts Institute of
Technology, Cambridge, MA   02139 USA

Paper to be presented at:
 The Thijssen Memorial Symposium Eindhoven, The Netherlands November 6, 1987

ABSTRACT

The present paper outlines the approaches to the optimization of food
quality and drug/(enzyme) potency in drying and concentration. The specific
topics include:

   1. Development of kinetic models of dependence of reaction rates on
       temperature and on water content.
   2. Effect of constraints.
   3. The role of indicators.
   4. Examples of optimization:
   5. Difficult problems requiring new approaches and techniques

I.   INTRODUCTION

Quantitative analysis of quality losses in any product during preparation, processing and storage requires certain initial assumptions, as well as
a set of real or assumed data. The first assumption is that there exists an
index of quality Q which can be measured and which corresponds and correlates
with quality of the products. In order to be able to simulate and predict
quality losses, this index has to be sensitive enough to express the effect
of the environmental factors on the quality composition.

When a single measurement (e.g., concentration of a given component) is
not in itself adequate to describe the "quality" of the product, it is still
possible to define an index of deterioration, or an index of quality based on
a weighted set of measurements. Each defect in the product may be assigned
an arbitrary value. A scoring system of this type is widely used for bread
quality (ref. 1).

The quantitative analysis of quality changes requires further that we
describe the changes in Q as a result of processing, storage, and

preparation conditions in a manner which allows prediction or simulation of these changes. An approach which has been evolved by several researchers over the last 30 years is to obtain differential equations relating rate of change of quality to significant processing or storage conditions, as shown in the generalized equation

$$\frac{dQ}{dt} = f(E_i) \tag{1}$$

where: E_i = environmental or compositional factor.

In order to analyze the quality change, we also require the knowledge of how each of the pertinent variables changes with time:

$$E_i = f(t) \tag{2}$$

II. DEVELOPMENT OF APPROPRIATE KINETIC MODELS

In concentration and in drying the most important factors are concentration, temperature and water content.

A. Concentration of Heat-Sensitive Components

In many cases it is possible to correlate quality losses with the loss of a particular component, such as a vitamin, a pigment, or enzyme. In such cases these concentrations are chosen as the index of quality. The dependence of quality loss may then be represented as:

$$\frac{-dQ}{dt} = -dC_s/dt = k\ C_1^{n_1}\ C_2^{n_2} \ldots \tag{3}$$

where: C_s — concentration of the heat sensitive component.

Various orders of reaction may be involved. Non-enzymatic browning very often follows zero order kinetics. First order reactions have been observed in many changes occurring during de-watering of foods and biological systems. (refs. 5-6). Second order kinetics in protein denaturation were observed by Barzana et al. (ref. 7), who studied inactivation of alcohol oxidase during air drying, and by Manji and Kakuda (ref. 8).

B. Temperature Effects

To relate the rate of quality losses to temperature, the most common and generally valid assumption is that temperature-dependence will follow the Arrhenius equation:

$$k = k_o \exp(-Ea/RT) \tag{4}$$

where: k_o = constant, independent of temperature (also known as
pre-exponential frequency factor or collision factor)

E_a = activation energy

R = ideal gas constant

T = absolute temperature

The use of equation (4) constitutes the soundest approach to modeling temperature-dependence, but there are limitations to its precision. (refs. 9-10)

C. Water Content and Water Activity

Water influences reactions causing heat-sensitivity of foods. The equilibrium relationship between water activity a_w and moisture content is expressed by a sorption isotherm and may be used to specify local moisture contents, or to calculate average m.

$$a_w = f(m) \tag{5}$$

where: m = moisture content

$$a_w = (p/p°)_T$$

where: p = partial pressure of water in food
p° = vapor pressure of water at temperature T.

$$m = f(x,y,z,t) \tag{6}$$

$$a_w = f(x,y,z,t) \tag{7}$$

where: x,y,z are the coordinates specifying position.

In many foods and biological systems the above relationships are inadequate because physical, and/or chemical changes occur concurrently with, and often caused by, sorption of water. The kinetic model requires the knowledge of dependence of reaction rate constants on either m or a_w. These relations can be extremely complex, and simplified relations must be obtained, such as:

$$\ln(k) = C_1 + C_2 M \tag{8}$$

or

$$\ln(k) = C_3 + C_4 a_w \tag{9}$$

where: k is the appropriate reaction rate constant (zero or first order)

c_1, c_2, c_3, c_4 are constants

In many oxidative reactions at very low values of m a useful model is:

$$k = b/m^n \qquad (10)$$

where: b is a constant

n is an exponent with a value usually close to 1.0

III. PROCESS STATE EQUATION

Kinetic models of deteriorative reactions occurring in de-watering processes have the form:

$$\frac{-dQ}{dt} = k \qquad (11)$$

$$k = f(m, T, c) \quad \text{or} \quad f(a_w, T, c) \qquad (12)$$

In order to apply a given kinetic model to a process we must obtain equations describing the distribution of m, T and c with time and location. This is achieved by analyzing heat and mass transfer during the process. What is required as a minimum is the sorption isotherm and the appropriate transfer equations: (ref. 11)

$$g = -\lambda \nabla T \qquad (13)$$

where: g = heat transfer rate
         = heat transfer coefficient

$$n_w = -D_w \nabla W \qquad (14)$$

where: n_w = mass transfer rate for water

W = volumetric concentration of water

D_w = diffusion coefficient

The problem may be complicated when λ and D_w depend on temperature and concentration. Justifiable assumptions and the use of computer-assisted numerical analysis have made the prediction of temperature and moisture distribution quite manageable, even for complex cellular materials (refs. 12-14).

IV. DYNAMIC TESTS FOR MODEL DEVELOPMENT

Traditionally, static tests were and still are by far the most common way of obtaining kinetic data. Static tests are designed to follow quality deterioration under many, but constant, environmental conditions. These experiments require a balanced matrix of tests in which the degradation rate is measured at each combination of stress conditions. The effect of each environmental factor is fitted to some mathematical/kinetic model. The concept of evaluating chemical stability by using dynamic thermal conditions has grown out of the pharmaceutical industry, and has been demonstrated in relatively simple systems. Rogers (ref. 15) showed how the parameters k_o and E_a of the Arrhenius equation can be derived from storage tests conducted under non-isothermal temperature changes, and was able to obtain agreement with static tests for the first-order decomposition of riboflavin and of sucrose. In a non-isothermal accelerated kinetic study, the degradation (e.g., quality loss, drug decomposition, nutrient loss, etc.) is monitored while the temperature of the system is increased in a predetermined specific path. This makes it possible to determine the kinetic parameters from a single experiment (ref. 16).

Different time-temperature programs have been used in the non-isothermal kinetic studies within the pharmaceutical industry. Some more advanced parameter estimation methods have been suggested, since the dominance of the digital computer (ref. 17). Non-isothermal tests applied to food were also investigated (refs. 18-20).

More recently dynamic methods have been applied to conditions relevant to dehydration. This approach was used in the dynamic method first proposed by Saguy et. al. (ref. 21). The dynamic method for determining nutrient degradation kinetics, under conditions representative of drying, requires the acquisition of moisture, temperature, and nutrient concentration data during actual drying experiments. We investigated the use of the method in the development of models for degradation of vitamin C in potatoes.

The form of the kinetic model was assumed a priori:

$$\frac{-dC}{dt} = kC \tag{15}$$

where: C - concentration of ascorbic acid. It was also assumed that the Arrhenius equation applies to the temperature dependence: (equation 4), with k_o and E_a assumed to be functions of moisture content(m). A series of drying experiments was carried out in which m, T and C varied, and were determined as a function of time. The time course of changes in m, T and C in one of such experiments is shown in Figure 1.

222

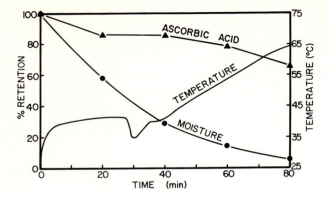

Fig. 1. Time profiles for moisture, temperature, and ascorbic acid concentration for one of the experiments used to collect data for dynamic model
building.

The results were used to determine the parameters P_1 to P_7 in the
functions:

$$\ln k_o = P_1 + P_2 m + P_3 m^2 \tag{16}$$

$$E_a = P_4 + P_5 m + P_6 m^2 + P_7 m^3 \tag{17}$$

in this particular study the model parameters were derived using the
average moisture content of potato disks of a specific geometry, thus
ignoring local moisture effects. Such a model, although very effective for
a particular case, might be less representative for other shapes and sizes.

V. DEVELOPMENT OF INTEGRATING INDICATORS AND THEIR ROLE IN
   DYNAMIC TESTS FOR QUALITY CHANGES

One of the drawbacks of dynamic tests is that because of additional
degrees of freedom (due to variation of stress factors with time) the
associated uncertainty in results is increased and to compensate additional
samples must be prepared and tested. Dynamic modeling would be facilitated
if samples obtained under actual process (or storage) conditions, which are
tested routinely for quality control purposes, could be incorporated in
modeling. This requires knowledge of the stress-time history of the sample,
which is difficult to obtain in many process conditions. However, if
integrating indicators of such stress-time history could be found, and used,
dynamic testing would be enhanced. A number of such indicators have been
developed. One of these, the Lifeline system, appears to offer advantages
for the purposes discussed here. This system utilizes a polymer strip which
is incorporated into a "bar code" strip. The bar codes contain machine
readable marketing for automatic identification of the product. The polymer

strips are diacetylenes which gradually and irreversibly change color in response to cumulative temperature exposure. That is, at higher temperatures the color change progresses more rapidly than it does at lower temperatures. Because of the small area required for scanning, appropriate polymer strips weighing less than 10^{-3} grams could be placed <u>within</u> products undergoing heating or drying. The strips may be "read" after retrieval using a hand-held computer with optical wand for reading the bar code, measuring the color of the polymer and calculating the remaining life of the product. The unit can store up to 3,000 indicator label readings in its memory before being downloaded to a host computer. The kinetics of the color change of the polymer exhibit first order kinetics with Arrhenius-type dependence over a wide temperature range. Several types of indicators are available with somewhat different sensitivities. Data obtained at several temperatures show that for a given indicator type a single activation energy describes the temperature dependence over the range of 30° – 90°C (ref. 22). In Figure 2, an Arrhenius-type plot of time to reach 50% reflectance versus temperature is shown for the range of activation energies available.

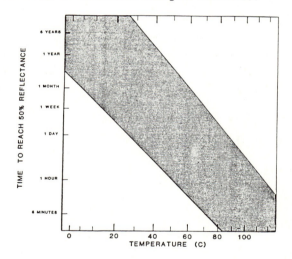

Figure 2. Temperature versus time to reach 50% reflectance for "Lifelines" indicators (with permission of Lifeines Technology, Inc.)

The distributor of this indicator system recommends the prediction of quality changes in foods by using T^* (defined in Figure 3). Strictly speaking this approach allows the establishment of relative severity of a process only for products which have the same activation energy as the indicator (the polymer has E_a's in the 20 to 30 Kcal/mole range). Development of indicators with different E_a's is likely to improve the precision of this approach.

Definition of virtual temperature T^*

Let T = temperature

k_R = "effective rate constant"

t_I = time at transient $T = T_I$

E = activation energy

t = total time

R = gas constant

Define: $f_I = \exp(-E/RT_I)$

Then : $k = k_R \left[\Sigma(t_I f_I) / (f_R t) \right]$

$T^* = (-E/R) / \left[\ln \Sigma (t_I f_I)/t \right]$

Figure 3. Definition of virtual temperature

Another important development is the development of self-contained microcircuit probes which acquire time-temperature records during processing (Cross and Lesley, 1985). They can be placed within or outside the container. Unfortunately, the are still bulky (approximately 2" x 1.5").

VI. APPROACHES TO OPTIMIZATION

A. Analysis of Thermal Damage in Concentration Processes

Professor Thijssen, to whose memory this symposium is dedicated, was distinguished by his extraordinary flair for simplifying the analysis of complex physicochemical processes in a way yielding useful engineering approximation. Thijssen's contributions are exemplified by the paper by Thijssen and Van Oyen presented here in Eindhoven almost exactly 10 years ago on September 23, 1977. He compared the costs (both monetary and those due to lost quality), and value added of different concentration processes for liquid foods. The approach to optimization was outlined as follows: (ref. 24)

"The ratio of: (1) the product of the 'net added value' resulting from concentration and the total tons of feed processed per year; and (2) the capital to be invested in the concentration equipment (installed costs of equipment and cost of the building to be used for the process) has to be maximized. The net added value per ton of feed, S_{net}, is the difference between the gross added value per ton of feed, S_{gross}, and the costs, C_f, of the concentration process per ton of feed.

$$S_{net} = S_{gross} - C_f \qquad (18)$$

The gross added value is the difference in sales value,
expressed per ton of feed ex factory, between the
concentrated product and the not concentrated liquid
(feed). The concentration costs include capital costs,
utility costs, labour costs."

In considering the gross value, the following process-induced changes
were considered:

1) selective physical losses (e.g., aroma loss)

2) physical changes (e.g., rheological changes)

3) chemical changes (e.g., browning)

4) concentration factor

By characterizing key physical and chemical reactions by their typical
rate constants at 100°C, and their activation energies (Table 1), they
constructed plots of constant "thermal damage" which will remain constant
if the following condition is satisfied

$$\ln t = b_i + \frac{E_i}{RT}$$

(19)

in which t is the residence time at process temperature T and b_i, is a
constant for a given product. Consequently when the product residence time
in the process equipment is plotted against the reciprocal of the absolute
process temperature, straight lines with slope E indicate the conditions
yielding equal thermal degradations for those values of E. The resulting
graphical comparison of processes is shown in Figure 4.

Table I

Rate constants and activation energies
(after Thijssen and Van Oyen, 1977)

	k, at 100°C (s^{-1})	E (KJ/mole)
Physical processes	variable	8-40
Enzymatic reaction	–	17-60
Chemical reactions	10^{-6} to 10^{-4}	30-200

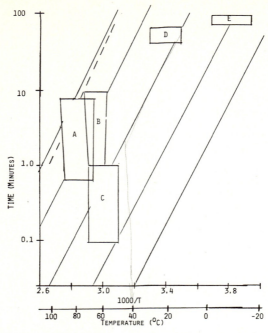

Figure 4. Relationship between residence time and temperatures in various concentration processes. Each solid line represents conditions of equal thermal degradation for E=83⋅6 KJ/mole and various values of k. Broken line represents damage to orange juice.

A. Plate evaporators; B. Falling film evaporators; C. Centrifugal evaporators; D. Membrane processes; E. Free concentration.

(After Thijssen and Van Oyen, 1977)

They proposed an equivalence relation for sensory quality and chemical reactivity:

$$\text{Sensory Quality} = \text{Constant} \times (K_i t)^n \tag{20}$$

They also analyzed the cost components of the various concentration processes (Figure 5), and they also provided data on one of the key constraints in optimization of concentration processes, namely the maximum viscosities which can be handled in concentrators (Table 2). The time was not quite ripe in 1977 for formal optimization of the processes, but the necessary components for such optimization were developed, and the plots given in Figures 4 and 5 were excellent engineering tools for concentration process design and selection.

Table 2

Maximum concentrate viscosity
(After Thijssen and Van Oyen, 1977)

Concentration process	Viscosity (cP)
scraped film evaporator	40,000
centrifugal film evaporator	20,000
plate evaporator	400
falling film-long tube evaporator	200
freeze concentration	200
reverse osmosis	50

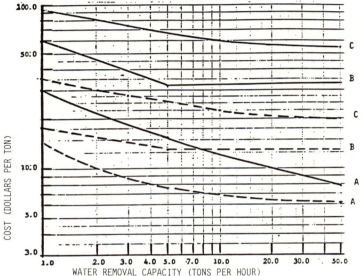

Figure 5. Dewatering costs in dollars per ton for water removal with aroma
recovery (After Thijssen and Van Oyen, 1977) A. Falling film evaporator;
B. Freeze concentration; C. Reverse osmosis (3.51 m^{-2} h^{-1})

Solid lines represent an operation of 2,000 hrs/yr
Broken lines represent an operation of 7,000 hrs/yr

B.   Optimization of Dehydration With Respect To Quality

In one of our studies we combined drying theory, and reaction rate
kinetics to models of the course of a given deteriorative reaction during
drying, and we used such models to optimize the process (refs. 25-27). We
specifically considered:

a) Minimizing vitamin C loss in white potatoes

b) Minimizing browning in white potatoes;

c) Above two objectives when one of them is used as a constraint;

d) Minimizing vitamin loss while assuring a specific level of enzyme
inactivation in a model system.

The model of mass transfer was based on Fick's Law with temperature-dependent diffusion coefficient. The temperature of the potato disks was modeled using an algebraic approximation of the heat balance, and was verified experimentally. Area and thickness of the disks were considered to change according to a model of shrinkage.

The kinetic model representative of ascorbic acid degradation during air-drying of white potato disks was obtained using a dynamic test (ref. 28). An empirical first-order kinetic model was used. (Equ. 17) The first-order rate constant has Arrhenius temperature dependence, (Equ. 4) with the constants k_o and E_a having moisture functionality.

The model for browning was pseudo-zero order:

$$\frac{dB}{dt} = k_b \tag{21}$$

$$k_b = k_{b_0} \exp E_a/RT) \tag{22}$$

$$E_a = b_1 m + b_2 \tag{23}$$

$$\ln k_{b_0} = b_3 \ln m + b_2 \tag{24}$$

where m is the moisture content.

The kinetic model for inactivation of catalase in the model was assumed to be identical to that of Luyben (ref. 6).

$$k_c = k_1 \exp[E_a/RT] \tag{25}$$

$$\ln k_1 = a_1 - a_2 \exp(m) \tag{26}$$

$$E_a = a_3 - a_4 \exp(m) \tag{27}$$

Drying was treated as a batch process with dry bulb temperature (T_{db}) control. Figure 6 illustrates the effect of simultaneous consideration of several objectives. Optimal profile A is for minimizing browning in an 180 minute process without regard to vitamin loss. The resulting final quality was 0.021 Browning Units (arbitrary units) and 24.4% retention of vitamin C. Profile B is for maximizing vitamin C retention, while restricting browning to 0.025 units. Under these conditions vitamin C

retention is 29.9%. Profile C is for maximizing vitamin retention with no

restriction on browning. The resulting vitamin retention is 84.5% and the

browning is 0.032 units.

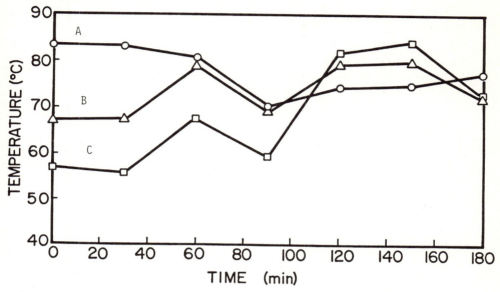

Figure 6. Optimal temperature control profile for a given process.
(Karel, 1984). With permission of ZFL

A. Minimizng browning; B. Minimizing vitamin C loss, constraint on
browning; C. Minimizing vitamin C loss, no constrataint on browning

Figure 7 shows optimization of vitamin C retention in a model. As a
consequence of the different temperature sensitivity of the enzyme and the
vitamin C the optimal process without a constraint on the amount of enzyme
to be inactivated is quite different from the optimal program in the presence of a constraint. We performed optimizations for three stage drying
processes with air temperature control for different drying times.
Figure 7 shows the optimal process specifying a final moisture content of
0.05 g/g solids and 360 minutes of drying. The optimal program for process
in which the drying was similarly constrained with respect to drying time,
and the final moisture content, but in which the additional constraint was
imposed requiring 99% inactivation of the enzyme is shown in Figure 8.

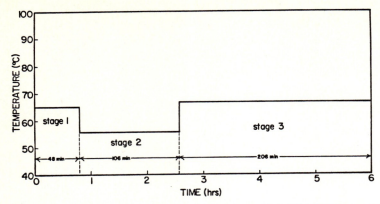

Figure 7. Optimal 3-stage drying process for minimizing ascorbic acid destruction for 6 hour process.

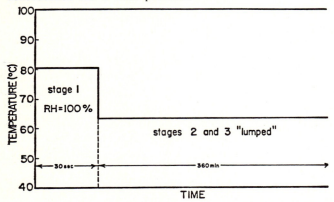

Figure 8. Optimal 3-stage drying process for minimizing ascorbic acid destructuion with constrained final catalase activity for 6 hour process.

VII. PROBLEMS ARISING FROM COMPLEX KINETIC OR PHYSICAL PHENOMENA

Optimization of retention of heat sensitive materials becomes very difficult when the reaction kinetics cannot be described simply, or when the properties of the materials being heated and/or dried change dramatically during the process.

A. Free radical reactions

Many of the reactions causing deterioration of food quality involve free radicals, and the kinetics are those of chain reactions. These kinetics

may be simplified by focusing on only one of the several potential indicators of oxidation and by making simplifying assumptions. Under these circumstances, it is possible to write the somewhat simplified equations shown
in Table 3.

Table 3

Simplified Oxidation Kinetics

R_O = RATE OF OXYGEN ABSORPTION
R_I = RATE ON INITIATION
NO ANTIOXIDANT, HIGH O_2 PRESSURE
$$R_O = K_1 (RH) (R_I)^{1/2}$$
NO ANTIOXIDANT, LOW O_2 PRESSURE
$$R_O = K_2 (O_2) (R_I)^{1/2}$$
ANTIOXIDANT, LOW O_2 PRESSURE
$$R_O = K_3 (O_2) (AH)^{-1} (R_I)$$
RATE OF LOSS OF ANTIOXIDANT = R_A
$$R_A = R_I$$

A typical and more difficult problem involving degradation of B-
carotene in drying conditions was studied by us (refs. 29, 30). The kinetics depended initial concentration of carotene C_o in a complex way. For a
given C_o the integrated rate equation has the form:

$$\ln [1 + (1-C/C_o)^{0.5}/(1-C/C_o)^{0.5}] = rt \qquad (28)$$

where r is an effective rate constant. It was found that r is a function
of water temperature and oxygen. As an example at a constant temperature
of 35°C, r in a model system was given by:

$$r = (k_o + k_1 [O_2] \exp (k_2 a_w) \qquad (29)$$

where $[O_2]$ = oxygen concentration

a_w = water activity

k_o, k_1, k_2 = constants

Simulation and optimization of free radical reactions of this degree of
complexity is practically impossible given the compounding of errors in
determination of so many parameters. New approaches, perhaps combining new
sensors and new computer techniques will be required.

B. Effect of glass transitions and structural changes.

Changes in structure and in particular glass transitions have a
profound effect on rates or chemical reactions of heat-sensitive materials,
and water content affects these transitions very substantially. In a
pioneering study reported some 25 years ago, Duckworth and Smith (ref. 31)
measured diffusion of radio labelled glucose (C^{14}) and sulphate (S^{35}) in

pieces of dry vegetables. Diffusion of sugars is important to non-enzymic browning. Enormous amount of work has been conducted in this area and summarized recently by Eichner et. al. (ref. 32). Considerable work has been done in connection with diffusion of water and of flavors during drying. This work is well reviewed by Bruin & Luyben (ref. 33). The diffusion coefficient for organic compounds drops even more rapidly than that for water. This phenomenon is the basis of the "selective diffusion" theory which was formulated by Thijssen which, with some modifications, is generally accepted as the basis for encapsulation and flavor retention in drying.

The transitions in freeze-dried materials have been studied in particular by the groups of King et. al. (ref. 34), Thijssen (ref. 35) Karel and Flink (ref. 36), and Toei (ref. 37), and are usually described as "structure collapse." Most recently, this subject has been reviewed by Levine and Slade (ref. 38). The collapse phenomena have also profound effects on various chemicals reactions. Plasticizing a system based on sugar glasses facilitates diffusion of oxygen to droplets of linoleic acid entrapped in such glasses and allows rapid oxidation of this lipid (ref. 39).

VIII. FUTURE DIRECTIONS

The complexity of the phenomena involved in destruction of heat-sensitive material during concentration and drying is obvious. Optimization of such process is therefore difficult. The approach used in traditional food technology to this problem was based on employing well-experienced craftsmen, who could make decisions on a case-by-case basis using a combination of objective and subjective criteria "integrated" into a decision in their brains. Quite often it is difficult to train new experts of this type, even within a given organization, and even when the "instructors" are themselves capable of making such decisions on the basis of their experience. It is impossible to transmit such instruction through handbooks, manuals and academic training. Yet modern food technology makes it imperative that solutions be found which will allow optimization of complex processes with respect to complex quality factors.

The path to such solutions may lie in combination of on-line-sensors with Expert Systems. Artificial intelligence is reaching a stage where

applications to industrial problems are mushrooming, and on-line-sensors
can now be found which will feed the necessary data for the decision
making. The computer has revolutionized food inventory control, ingredient
metering and distribution control. It has made possible drastic changes in
process control, but the revolution is yet to come.

REFERENCES

1. Matz, S. A., 1960. Bakery Technology and Engineering, Avi, Westport,
   Conn.

2. Karel, M. and Nickerson, J.T.R., 1964. Food Technol., 18, 104.

3. Mauron, J., 1981. Prog. Food Nutr. Sci., 5, 5.

4. Labuza, T.P. and Saltmarch, M., 1982. J. Food Sci., 47, 92.

5. Labuza, T.P., 1972. CRC Crit. Rev. Food Technol 3 (2), 217.

6. Luyben, K.Ch.A.M., Liou, J.K. and Bruin, S., 1980. in Food Process
   Engineering: Enzyme Engineering in Food Processing. Linko, P.,
   et. al., Eds., 1980, Vol. 2, 192.

7. Barzana-Garcia E., Klibanov, A. and Karel, M., 1986.
   IN: Mujumdar A (ed) Drying '86. Hemisphere Pub. Corp.,
   Washington, DC, Vol I, pp 428-431.

8. Manji, B. and Y. Kakuda, 1986. Can. Inst. Food Sci. Tech. J. 19, (4),
   163.

9. Davis, O.L., and Hudson, H.E., Stability of drugs: Accelerated
   storage tests, in Statistics in the Pharmaceutical Industry.
   Buncher, C.R. and Tsay, J.-Y. Eds., Marcel Dekker, New York, 1981.

10. Malhotra, A. and A. Sadana, 1987. Biotech, Bioeng. 30, 108.

11. Rotstein, E., 1986. IN: Mujumdar, A., ed. Drying '86. Vol. I, p. 1.

12. Chirife, J. 1983. Adv in Drying, 2, 73.

13 Toei, R., 1983. Adv. in Drying. 2, 269.

14. Rogers, A.R., J. Pharm. Pharmacol. 15, 101.

15. Zoglio, M.A., Windheuser, J.J., Vatti, R., Maulding, H.V.,
    Kornblum, S.S., Jacobs, A. and Hamot, H., 1968. J. Pharm.
    Sci., 57(12), 2080.

16. Yang, W-H., 1983. Drug Dev. and Ind. Pharm. 9(5), 821.

17. Kamman, J.F., Labuza, T.P. and Warthesen, J.J., 1983.
    J. Food Sci., 46, 1457.

18. Chen, J.Y., Bohnsack, K. and Labuza, T.P., 1983.
    J. Food Sci., 48, 460.

19. Mizrahi, S., and Karel, M., 1978. J. Food Sci 42, 958.

234

20. Saguy, I., Mizrahi, S., Villota, R. and Karel, M., 1978.
J. Food Sci 43, 1861.

21. Fields, S.C. and Prusik, T., "Shelf Life Estimation of Beverage and
Food Products Using Bar Coded Time-Temperature Indicator Labels,"
Proceedings of the IV International Flavors Conference, Rhodes,
Greece, July 1985, Elsevier Science Publishers B.V., Amsterdam,
The Netherlands (publication pending).

22. Cross, W. R. and D. R. Lesley, 1985. Food Technol. 39, (12), 36.

23. Thijssen, H.A.C. and Van Oyen, N.S.M., 1977. Proc 7th European Symp.
IUFoST Eindhoven, Step. 1977, p.231.

24. Mishkin, M., Saguy, I. and Karel, M., 1984 a. J. Food Sci 49, 1267.

25. Mishkin, M., Saguy, I. and Karel, M., 1983 a. J. Food Sci 48, 1617.

26. Karel, M., Saguy, I. and Mishkin, M., 1985
IN: Toei, R. and Mujumdar, A. (eds) Drying '85. Hemisphere
Pub. Corp., Washington, DC, pp 303-307.

27. Mishkin, M., Saguy, I. and Karel, M., 1984 b. J. Food Sci 49, 1262.

28. Stefanovich, A.F. and Karel, M., 1982. J Food Process Preserv 6, 227.

29. Saguy, I., Goldman, M. and Karel, M, 1985. J Food Sci 50, 526.

30. Duckworth, R.B. and Smith, G.M., 1963. Proc Nutr Soc 22, 182.

31. Eichner, K., Laible, R. and Wolf, W., 1985. In "Properties of Water
in Foods" Simatos, D. and Multon, J.L., eds, Nijhoff Publ,
Dordrecht p. 191.

32. Bruin, S. and K. Ch.A.M. Luyben, 1980. Adv. in Drying 1, 55.

33. King, C.J., Carn, R.M. and Jones, R.L., 1976. J. Food Sci 41, 614.

34. Rulkens, W.H. and Thijssen, H.A.C., 1972, J Food Tech 7, 79.

35. Karel, M. and Flink, J.C., 1983. Adv Drying, Vol 2, p. 103.

36. Toei, R., 1986. IN: Mujumdar, A., ed., Drying '86, vol. 2 p. 880.

37. Levine, H. and Slade, L., 1986. Carbohyd Polymers 6, 213

38. Geil-Hansen, F. and J. M. Flink, 1977. J. Food Sci., 42, 1049.

Preconcentration and Drying of Food Materials, edited by S. Bruin
Elsevier Science Publishers B.V., Amsterdam, 1988 — Printed in The Netherlands

235

A DYNAMIC MECHANISTIC MODEL OF A SPRAY-DRYING TOWER

CONSTRUCTED FOR CONTROL AND OPTIMISATION PURPOSES

M.E. Paoli[1], P.L.J. Swinkels[2], T.J.A. Wagenaar[2], W.L. de Koning[3]

[1]Development & Application Centre (D.A.C.), P.O. Box 10
 3600 AA Maarsen, the Netherlands

[2]Unilever Research Laboratorium Vlaardingen, P.O. Box 114
 3130 AC Vlaardingen, the Netherlands

[3]Department of Applied Mathematics, Delft University of Technology
 Julianalaan 132, 2628 BL Delft, the Netherlands

SUMMARY

As a first step in developing a computer controller for controlling the powder moisture content of spray-dried detergent powder, a dynamic mechanistic (based on physical and chemical phenomena) model of the spray-drying process has been constructed. In the model construction, the emphasis is on the macroscopic behaviour of the process. The drying process is subdivided into four processes; the most important, i.e. the spray-drying tower itself, will be discussed in this paper.

The dynamic equations of the spray-tower's sub-model describe the relevant physical mechanisms, like convective heat and mass transport, heat losses to the environment via the tower wall and the insulation, and the water transport from the drying detergent particles to the drying air. This tower model accurately simulates the experimentally-observed dynamic behaviour of the measurable output variables when step changes are made to the slurry flow rate, the inlet drying air flow rate and the inlet drying air temperature. The model developed is expected to be sufficiently accurate for the construction of the controller.

INTRODUCTION

Spray-drying is a very important step in the production of most detergent powders. This powder generally contains liquids (i.e. surfactants, water etc.) and solids (i.e. builder salts). Other components of the finished powder are heat-sensitive ingredients like enzymes and bleach systems. These are post-dosed to the spray-dried base powder in granular form.

In order to improve product quality and the energy efficiency of the spray-drying process, the powder has to be produced at a very constant moisture content. For this purpose, a computer controller is being developed for a pilot plant spray-tower.

As a first step, a dynamic mechanistic model was constructed, on which the controller will be developed. The model equations describe the most important macroscopic physical phenomena taking place in the various subsystems of the overall spray-drying process. The submodel of the key part of the process, the spray tower itself, will be discussed in this paper.

PROCESS DESCRIPTION AND MODELLING APPROACH

Process description

A schematic diagram of the spray-drying process for the production of a detergent base powder is given in Fig. 1.

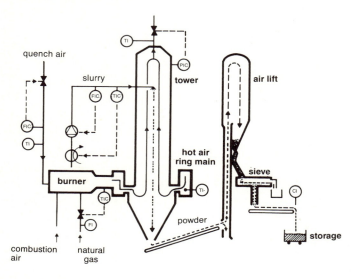

Fig. 1 Spray-drying process for production of detergent base powder

In the slurry making process, the various base powder components like surfactants and salts are dispersed and dissolved in water at elevated temperature. This slurry is then atomised in the tower by pressure atomisers. The atomised slurry droplets are dried in counter-current with hot air injected near the tower bottom. The hot air is generated by a burner in which natural gas is combusted together with an excess flow of air. The resulting hot gas mixture is quenched with atmospheric air. This well-mixed gas mixture is evenly distributed and injected over the circumference of the tower by a hot air ring main. The exhaust drying air is vented to the atmosphere after the fine powder particles have been separated in cyclones and in a scrubber. The dried powder is transported from the tower bottom to an air-lift by conveyor belts. In the air-lift, any powder lumps are broken up and the powder is cooled. Oversized particles are sieved off and the remaining powder is stored or fed to the post-dosing line.

A large number of process input and output variables relevant to the construction of the model are monitored on-line: the slurry temperature and mass flow rate, the quench air mass flow rate and temperature (before the burner, after the burner, in the hot air ring main), the natural gas mass flow rate, the exhaust air temperature, the moisture content of the powder ex sieve, and the pressure in the tower. The local controllers, which are standard in the plant, will be used in the control strategy discussed below for controlling slurry mass flow rate, slurry temperature, quench air mass flow rate, air temperature from burner (by adjusting natural gas input), and the pressure in the tower. All data acquisitions and local control actions are performed by a central process computer.

Modelling approach

In order to develop the supervisory computer controller, which will control the spray-drying process by adjusting the setpoint values of the various local controllers, a dynamic mathematical model has been constructed for the entire spray-drying operation. This model correlates the time-dependent changes of the process output variables to the time-dependent changes in the input variables by differential equations, describing the main chemical and physical phenomena taking place. Starting from this model and selecting cost criteria for optimising the process, a controller can subsequently be developed to calculate the optimal values for all the local controller setpoints.

The advantage of this approach over a black-box approach is, that all the relevant dynamic phenomena are included and that all the model coefficients have a physical meaning. The model is suitable for chemical and control engineers. Physical changes during spray-drying as well as off-line changes (e.g. other slurry formulation or scale-up) are taken into account in the model parameter values.

The main emphasis is on macroscopic behaviour (overall dynamic heat and mass balances).

The overall model can be subdivided into 4 submodels corresponding with the four subsystems of the process: spray-tower, burner, hot air ring main, and powder transport including air-lift and sieve (see Fig. 1). With respect to dynamics, this subdivision is allowed because the subsystems are only related by mass flows.

In modelling the spray-tower, the following microscopic phenomena, which could be significant for changes in moisture content on a macroscopic scale, were considered:
- specific surface area creation by atomisation of primary particles and sub-
  sequent agglomeration

- drying behaviour of one single droplet (heat and mass transport within the particle, heat and mass transport through boundary layer between particles and continuous gas phase)
- flow patterns of both disperse and continuous gas phase (mixing, residence time distribution).

TOWER MODEL

Dynamic heat and mass balances

Fig. 2 shows a diagram of the spray-tower indicating all its inlet and outlet flows. The tower has a thermally-insulated steel wall. The inlet flows are: slurry, inlet air and leak air. The leak air flow is a relatively small atmospheric air flow, sucked into the tower via the tower bottom outlet by the underpressure in the tower. The outlet flows are: powder, exhaust air and heat losses.

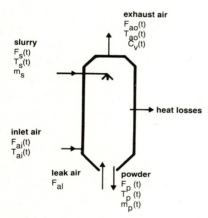

Fig. 2 Inlet and outlet flows of spray-tower

In order to come to a simple macroscopic description of the spray-tower, the following assumptions were made in constructing the model equations:
1. the continuous gas phase in the tower is ideally mixed, both with respect to temperature and composition (water vapour and dry air);
2. the disperse phase in the tower (the powder particles) is ideally mixed in relation to temperature, powder moisture concentration (water) and powder solids concentration;
3. there is no accumulation of dry air in the tower;
4. the mean residence time of the powder in the tower is constant and the flow rates of slurry and powder based on dry solids are equal;

5. the temperatures of the disperse and the gas phases are equal;
6. the overall evaporation rate of water in the tower is dependent on the disperse-phase temperature;
7. the heat transfer from the inside of the tower to the wall occurs by forced convection. Neglecting the heat resistance of the metal wall and the heat capacity of the insulation, the overall heat transfer coefficient from the wall to the environment is, therefore, the summation of the reciprocals of the heat resistance of the insulation and that of the insulation to the environment (caused by free convection).

A few effects have been omitted: the change in dry air concentration as a consequence of changing vapour concentration, the place dependence of the wall temperature and the vapour concentration of the inlet air. The specific heat capacities, the leak air mass flow, the slurry moisture content and the environmental temperature are kept constant during one experiment.

These assumptions can be made plausible as follows. The temperature of the gas phase in the tower is rather independent of place. Significant changes in the moisture content of the powder have periods much longer than the mean residence times of the powder and the air in the tower. So the quick variations due to the residence time distributions, are not relevant. During the drying process, the temperature of the powder particles varies between the wet bulb temperature and the dry bulb temperature of the air in the tower. Because the last period of drying is significant for calculating the evaporation rate and the temperature of the particles will approximate the air temperature in the tower during this period, the temperatures of the disperse and continuous phases are assumed to be equal to a first approximation. This assumption becomes more acceptable when realising that the stationary influence of the powder enthalpy is not large, in contrast to the dynamic influence. Therefore, changes in the powder temperature are more significant than the absolute value.

The following four dynamic equations can be constructed using the assumptions mentioned.

The dynamic mass balance over the water (dispersed as moisture in the disperse phase) in the tower;

$$\frac{V dC_w(t)}{dt} = F_s(t) m_s - F_p(t) m_p(t) - F_{evap}(t) \qquad |1|$$

The dynamic mass balance over the water vapour in the tower;

$$\frac{VdC_v(t)}{dt} = F_{evap}(t) - F_{ao}(t)\frac{C_v(t)}{\rho_a(t)}$$
|2|

The dynamic heat balance over the metal tower wall;

$$\frac{M_m c_m dT_m(t)}{dt} = A_i\alpha_i(t)[T_{ao}(t) - T_m(t)] - A_e U_e[T_m(t) - T_{ae}]$$
|3|

The dynamic heat balance over the two phases in the tower:

$$\frac{Vd}{dt}[C_w(t)c_w T_{ao}(t) + C_v(t)[c_v T_{ao}(t) + R_0] + \rho_a(t)c_a T_{ao}(t) +$$

$$+ C_p(t)c_p T_{ao}(t)] =$$

$$F_s(t)T_s(t)[m_s c_w + c_p] + F_{ai}(t)T_{ai}(t)c_a +$$

$$+ F_{al}T_{ae}c_a - F_p(t)T_{ao}(t)[m_p(t)c_w + c_p] - F_{ao}(t)[T_{ao}(t)c_a +$$

$$+ \frac{C_v(t)}{\rho_a(t)}[T_{ao}(t)c_v + R_0]] - A_i\alpha_i(t)[T_{ao}(t) - T_m(t)]$$
|4|

The remaining assumptions can be inserted in these equations. Note that the α_i-coefficient is both temperature and air mass flow dependent, according to changes in the Reynolds and the Nusselt number. This dependency is related to a reference α_i-value ($\alpha_{i,ref}$) for a constant air mass flow rate (1 kg/s) and for a constant temperature (100°C).
This results in a set of four dynamic equations with four independent variables determining the state of the process (C_w, C_v, T_m and T_{ao}: the state variables). The time-dependent input variables are F_s, T_s, F_{ai} and T_{ai} , which can be used for control purposes. The measurable output variables are T_{ao} and m_p (C_w/C_p).

Calculation of the overall evaporation rate $F_{evap}(t)$

The $F_{evap}(t)$ term in the dynamic equations in the previous paragraph represents the overall drying rate of the particles in the tower. An explicit expression for $F_{evap}(t)$ will be derived, based on experimental data on the drying behaviour of a detergent slurry.

As generally known, drying particles pass through several stages falling within the constant and falling rate periods; the latter period can be subdivided into the penetration period and the regular regime. The drying behaviour (expressed as the dimensionless drying rate versus the average material moisture content) for the drying of spherical slurry particles can be derived from slab drying experiments according to the following approach.

The description of the mass transport in a drying disperse phase during the falling rate period as a Fickian diffusion process, has been used successfully by a number of workers (Refs. 1-6,8). This diffusion problem can be described by a diffusion equation scaled on dry solids centred coordinates and using dimensionless variables and a geometry factor (Refs. 3, 4, 7). By this approach, the dimensionless drying rate is defined as:

$$F = \frac{J_{\omega,i} d_p R_p}{D_0 \rho_{p,0}^2}$$

|5|

where

$$D_0 \rho_{p,0}^2 = 1$$

|6|

A graph of the dimensionless drying rate F versus the average material moisture content $\bar{\omega}$ is called a drying curve. Liou (Ref. 4) developed an approximate method to calculate isothermal (with respect to material temperature) drying curves for the diffusion problem by restricting the dependence of the diffusion coefficient on the material moisture content to a power law dependence. By also assuming an Arrhenius dependence of the dimensionless drying rate related to the material temperature, as proposed by Schoeber (Ref. 3) and Luyben (Ref. 7), the drying rate is expressed as:

$$F(\bar{\omega}, T_2) = F(\bar{\omega}, T_1) \exp \left[\frac{-E_a(\bar{\omega})}{R} \left(\frac{1}{T_2} - \frac{1}{T_1} \right) \right]$$

|7|

Simple non-isothermal slurry slab drying experiments (using drying air of a constant temperature and humidity, and monitoring simultaneously the material temperature and the amount of moisture evaporated as a function of time) can be used to calculate isothermal drying curves for spherical slurry droplets. For a detergent slurry, the falling rate drying curve for spherical particles is shown in Fig. 3.

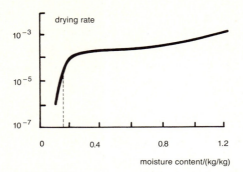

Fig. 3. Isothermal drying curve for spherical detergent particles; material temperature 100°C.

The dependence of the activation energy E_a in equation |7| on the average material moisture content $\bar{\omega}$ can be determined by carrying out slab drying experiments at different drying air temperatures. The dependence of E_a as a function of $\bar{\omega}$ for a certain slurry is shown in Fig. 4.

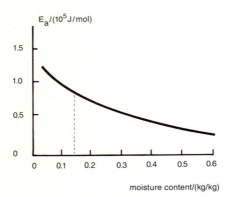

Fig. 4. Activation energy (E_a) as a function of moisture content.

In order to derive an explicit expression for the overall evaporation rate F_{evap}, we first define an average isothermal drying rate per unit change in moisture content ($\bar{F}$):

$$\bar{F}(m_p(t),\ T_{ao}(t)) = \frac{1}{m_s - m_p(t)} \int_{m_p(t)}^{m_s} F(\bar{\omega}, T_{ao})\ d\bar{\omega} \qquad |8|$$

In this equation, the integral boundaries are the slurry moisture content (m_s) and the moisture content of the powder from the tower (m_p). Furthermore, it was already assumed that the disperse phase temperature in the tower equals the exhaust air temperature (T_{ao}), implying an isothermal drying process. Combining equations |7| and |8| and using T=100°C as a reference temperature, we find:

$$\bar{F}\,(m_p(t),T_{ao}(t)) = \frac{1}{m_s - m_p(t)} \int_{m_p(t)}^{m_s} F(\bar{\omega},\ 373)\ \exp\ [\frac{-E_a(\bar{\omega})}{R}(\frac{1}{373} +$$

$$- \frac{1}{273 + T_{ao}})]\ d\bar{\omega} \qquad\qquad |9|$$

Using the data from Figs. 3 and 4, the integral in equation |9| can be approximated. From Fig. 4 it is evident that for the detergent slurry investigated, the activation energy E_a is rather constant for $\bar{\omega}$-values bigger than $\bar{\omega} = 0.15$. Below this value, the activation energy increases significantly, indicating a high resistance to mass transfer at low moisture contents. As a consequence, the drying rate decreases dramatically for $\bar{\omega}$-values below 0.15 as well. This means that the contribution of the part of the integral for $\bar{\omega}$ smaller than 0.15 can be neglected with regard to the part of the integral for the $\bar{\omega}$-interval from 0.15 to m_s. Because in practical spray-drying operations, the moisture content of the detergent powder from the tower is always lower than 0.15, equation |9| can be rewritten as:

$$\bar{F}\,(m_p(t),T_{ao}(t)) = \frac{1}{m_s - m_p}\ \exp\ [\frac{-E_a}{R}(\frac{1}{373} - \frac{1}{273 + T_{ao}(t)})]\ \cdot$$

$$\cdot \int_{0.15}^{m_s} F(\bar{\omega},373)\ d\bar{\omega} \qquad\qquad |10|$$

From equations |5| and |10| and the assumption that all powder particles in the tower are perfect spheres with the same radius, the overall evaporation rate can be calculated:

$$F_{evap}(t) = J_{\omega,i}\ A_p = [m_s - m_p(t)]\ \bar{F}\ \frac{D_0\rho_{p,0}^2}{d_p R_p}\ \cdot\ \frac{3F_s(t)\tau_p}{Vd_p R_p} =$$

$$= C_1\ F_s(t)\ \exp\ [-C_2\ (\frac{1}{373} - \frac{1}{273 + T_{ao}(t)})] \qquad\qquad |11|$$

where:

$$C_1 = \frac{3^r p}{d_p^2 R_p^2 V} \cdot \int_{0.15}^{m_s} F(\bar{\omega}, 373) \, d\bar{\omega}$$ |12|

$$C_2 = - E_a/R$$ |13|

The C_1 coefficient depends on the composition of the slurry (the drying behaviour of the slurry and the dry solids specific density) and on the atomisation conditions (particle radius). The C_2 coefficient is dependent on the activation energy.

TOWER MODEL VALIDATION

Validation of the tower model described was carried out by analysing the results of the spray-drying experiments with detergent slurry, performed on a pilot-plant scale under practical conditions. Input variables, which may be changed during actual operations (slurry mass flow rate, drying air inlet temperature and mass flow rate), were changed stepwise. During these experiments, the local controllers described before were used. The measurable input and output variables were monitored every 15 seconds and subsequently used to carry out computer simulations of the experiments. For this purpose, the dynamic model equations were implemented in a VAX-computer using the dynamic simulation package ISIS (Ref. 9). The time-dependent process input variables monitored during the experiments, served as input data for the simulation model. Model parameters such as physical constants and constants determined by equipment dimensions served as input values for the model as well. For the two heat transfer coefficients ($\alpha_{i,ref}$ and U_e), approximate values were determined by using the well-known chemical engineering relationships for turbulent pipe flow and free convection. Furthermore, rough estimates were made for the coefficients C_1 and C_2 in the evaporation rate equation, by using a number of experimentally observed steady-state values of the process variables.

In this way, the dynamic behaviour of the state variables and output variables of the process caused by time-dependent changes in the process input variables during the experiments, can be calculated. The approximated values of the heat transfer coefficients on the one hand and the evaporation coefficients on the other, were optimised independently, as described below.

For optimising the heat transfer coefficients, the measured powder moisture content was used together with the measured input variables as input in the dynamic equations. This input was changed at every integration interval, which was equal to the sampling period of 15 seconds. In this way, the remaining output variable (the exhaust air temperature) could be calculated and compared with the measured exhaust temperature. This comparison was done by integrating (simultaneously with the dynamic equations) the quadratic deviation between the measured and simulated values of the exhaust temperature. The heat transfer coefficients were then optimised until this quadratic deviation reached a minimum value.

Optimisation of the evaporation coefficients was done in a similar way. The measured exhaust air temperature was input together with the input variables in the model, and the quadratic deviation between measured and simulated powder moisture contents was minimised by optimising the C_1 and C_2 values.

Experimental

Two spray-drying experiments are analysed here. In experiment 1, step changes were made in the slurry mass flow and the inlet air mass flow. Almost at the end of the experiment, also a step change in the burner temperature setpoint (T_{sp}) was made. Due to the dynamics of the burner and the hot air ring main, a step change in the burner temperature setpoint does not result in a step change in the temperature of the air entering the tower, but in a more gradual change. The settings of these three input variables during this experiment are listed in Table 1.

TABLE 1 Values of input variables during experiment 1.

time [s]	T_{sp} [°C]	F_s [kg/s]	F_{ai} [kg/s]
0	195	.0868	2.36
500	195	.0723	2.36
2800	195	.0723	1.94
5500	275	.0723	1.94

In experiment 2, only a step change in the burner temperature setpoint was made. The slurry mass flow and inlet air mass flow rates were almost constant. Table 2 lists the burner temperature setpoints during this

246

experiment. When the step changes during both experiments were made, the input and output variables were practically in a steady state.

TABLE 2 Values of the inlet air temperature setpoint before and after the step change at t=0. The inlet air mass flow rate was constant at 2.36 kg/s, the slurry mass flow rate decreased slightly from 0.0785 kg/s to 0.0764 kg/s.

time [s]	T_{sp} [°C]
0	194
0^+	182

Results

Using the measured values of the output variables (exhaust air temperature and powder moisture content) the independent optimisation of the heat transfer coefficients ($\alpha_{i,ref}$ and U_e) on the one hand and of the evaporation coefficients (C_1 and C_2) on the other, was done by the method described before.

After having optimised the two heat transfer coefficients, the plots of the measured and simulated exhaust air temperatures are shown in Fig. 5 for experiment 1 and in Fig. 7 for experiment 2.

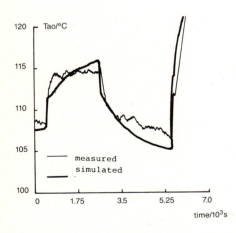

Fig. 5 Exhaust air temperature (T_{ao}) as a function of time - Expt. 1

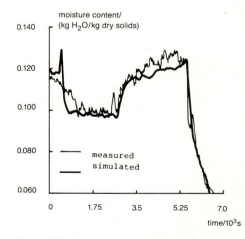

Fig. 6 Moisture content as a function of time - Expt. 1

The average quadratic deviation between the measured and simulated exhaust air temperatures is for the first experiment 4.4 K^2 and for the second 0.22 K^2. The values of the optimised heat transfer coefficients for both experiments and the approximated ones are listed in Table 3.

TABLE 3 Calculated and optimised values of the heat transfer and evaporation coefficients for both experiments.

	calculated	experiment 1	experiment 2
$\alpha_{i,ref}[J/m^2sK]$	5.2	25 ($\pm$ 5)	10 ($\pm$ 2)
U_e [J/m^2sK]	.37	1.7 ($\pm$ .1)	3.0 ($\pm$ .1)
c_1 [kg H_2O/kg ds]	.400	.404 ($\pm$.001)	.377 ($\pm$.002)
c_2 [K]	600	600 ($\pm$25)	480 ($\pm$ 10)

After having optimised the two evaporation constants, the plots of the measured and simulated powder moisture contents are shown in Figs. 6 (experiment 1) and 8 (experiment 2).

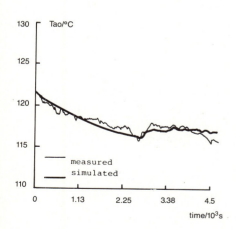

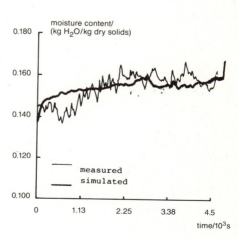

Fig. 7 Exhaust air temperature (T_{ao}) as a function of time - Expt. 2

Fig. 8 Moisture content as a function of time - Expt. 2

The average quadratic deviation between the measured and simulated powder moisture contents is for the first experiment 0.24 (% kg H_2O/kg ds)^2 and for the second 0.29 (% kg H_2O/kg ds)^2 (Table 3).

Discussion

   To interpret the results, three elements should be taken into account. All the physical phenomena occurring during a period of time shorter than the average residence time of the particles or that of the air in the tower were omitted. There were, of course, also disturbances in the process and in the measurements. For the simulation, the start condition was set to the steady-state solution of the differential equations, related to the measured input variables, which was only an approximation of reality.

   In experiment 1, the measured exhaust air temperature clearly shows two effects occurring after a change in the slurry mass flow and in the inlet air mass flow, viz. a new quasi-steady state in the tower itself, which is reached very rapidly, followed by a slow dynamic effect caused by the temperature change of the wall temperature, which has a high time constant. Both phenomena can be simulated quite well. The transient behaviour of the powder moisture is also described quite accurately. The peak-like increase in the powder moisture content at t = 500 s, is caused by the water concentration in the tower increasing temporarily, because there is a time-lag (residence time of powder) before a change in the slurry mass flow has any effect on the output variables. The initial effects for the exhaust air temperature and the powder moisture content after a step change in the burner temperature setpoint can be simulated accurately. For the final stage of the experiment, no reliable con-clusions could be derived because the tower operated far beyond its standard settings.

   In experiment 2, the behaviour of the exhaust air temperature, as a result of a step change in the burner temperature setpoint, is simulated very accurately. Minor changes in the inlet air temperature and the slurry mass flow rate can be followed as well. The main course of the simulated powder moisture content is good. The noise of the measured signal is, however, large in comparison with the changes in this signal.

   The calculated and optimised values of the heat transfer coefficients are of the same order of magnitude. The influence of minor changes in these coefficients on the total quadratic deviation is small.

   For both experiments, the optimised evaporation coefficients are nearly the same, especially in relation to the total quadratic deviation. These values also match very well the values roughly estimated from the four steady-state conditions. A comparison of these values with the calculated values

based on physical data like atomisation conditions and slurry drying behaviour
during constant rate and falling rate periods, was not made because this is
too elaborate an exercise.

CONCLUSIONS

A dynamic mechanistic model of a spray-tower has been developed, based on
the main physical and chemical phenomena taking place. This model accurately
describes the dynamic macroscopic behaviour of the output variables of the
process.

All the coefficients have a physical meaning; almost all of them have fixed
values, because they are related to the physical properties of the process.
Only the heat transfer coefficients and the evaporation coefficients are
roughly approximated and subsequently optimised by experimental data. The
optimised values are of the same order of magnitude as the physically-
approximated ones.

The changes in the input variables (slurry mass flow rate, inlet air
temperature, and inlet air mass flow rate) related to standard operational
conditions, can be simulated quite well. Considering the purpose of this model
to use it as a basis to develop a computer controller for the powder moisture
content, the results are encouraging.

List of symbols

A_i	surface area inside tower wall	$[m^2]$
A_e	surface area outside tower wall	$[m^2]$
A_p	total interfacial surface disperse phase	$[m^2]$
C_1	evaporation constant	$[kg\ H_2O/kg\ ds]$
C_2	evaporation constant	$[K]$
$C_p(t)$	dry solids concentration inside tower	$[kg/m^3]$
$C_v(t)$	water vapour concentration in tower	$[kg/m^3]$
$C_w(t)$	moisture (water) concentration in tower	$[kg/m^3]$
c_a	specific heat dry air	$[J/kgK]$
c_m	specific heat metal	$[J/kgK]$
c_p	specific heat powder dry solids	$[J/kgK]$
c_v	specific heat water vapour	$[J/kgK]$
c_w	specific heat moisture	$[J/kgK]$
$D_0\rho_{p,0}^2$	dimensional constant	$[(kg\ ds)^2/m^4s]$

List of symbols (Contd.)

d_p	dry solids density	$[kg/m^3]$
E_a	activation energy	$[J/mol]$
F	dimensionless drying flux or drying rate	$[-]$
$\bar{F}$	average drying rate per unit change in moisture content	$[-]$
$F_{ai}(t)$	mass flow rate inlet drying air	$[kg/s]$
F_{al}	mass flow rate leak air	$[kg/s]$
$F_{ao}(t)$	mass flow rate exhaust drying air	$[kg/s]$
$F_{evap}(t)$	water evaporation rate	$[kg/s]$
$F_p(t)$	mass flow rate powder dry solids	$[kg/s]$
$F_s(t)$	mass flow rate slurry dry solids	$[kg/s]$
$J_{\omega,i}$	water flux through interface	$[kg/m^2 s]$
M_m	mass tower wall	$[kg]$
$m_p(t)$	powder moisture content, based on dry solids	$[kg\ H_2O/(kg\ ds)]$
m_s	slurry moisture content, based on dry solids	$[kg\ H_2O/(kg\ ds)]$
R	gas constant	$[J/molK]$
R_0	evaporation enthalpy water	$[J/kg]$
R_p	dry solids radius	$[m]$
T_{ae}	temperature environment	$[°C]$
$T_{ai}(t)$	temperature inlet drying air	$[°C]$
$T_{ao}(t)$	temperature exhaust air	$[°C]$
$T_m(t)$	temperature metal tower wall	$[°C]$
$T_s(t)$	temperature slurry	$[°C]$
T_{sp}	temperature set point local burner controller	$[°C]$
U_e	overall heat transfer coefficient from tower wall to environment	$[J/m^2 sK]$
V	internal tower volume	$[m^3]$
$\alpha_i(t)$	heat transfer coëfficient from hot air in tower to metal tower wall	$[J/m^2 sK]$
$\alpha_{i,ref}$	heat transfer coefficient from hot air in tower to metal tower wall related to a mass flow rate of 1 kg/s and an air temperature of 100°C	$[J/m^2 sK]$
ρ_a	dry air density	$[kg/m^3]$

List of symbols (Contd.)

τ_p	mean residence time of powder in the tower	[s]
ω	local moisture content in particle	[kg H$_2$O/(kg ds)]
$\bar{\omega}$	average moisture content in particle	[kg H$_2$O/(kg ds)]

REFERENCES

1. J. van der Lijn, Ph.D. thesis, Wageningen Agricultural University,
   Wageningen, the Netherlands, 1976.
2. P.J.A.M. Kerkhof, Ph.D. thesis, Eindhoven University of Technology,
   Eindhoven, the Netherlands, 1975.
3. W.J.A.H. Schoeber, Ph.D. thesis, Eindhoven University of Technology,
   Eindhoven, the Netherlands, 1976.
4. J.K. Liou, Ph.D. thesis, Wageningen Agricultural University,
   Wageningen, the Netherlands, 1981.
5. S.K. Chandrasekaram, C.J. King, J. Aiche, Vol. 18, No. 3, 1972,
   p. 513-526.
6. H.A.C. Thijssen and W.H. Rulkens, Ingenieur, Vol. 80, 1968, p. 45-56.
7. K.Ch.A.M. Luyben, J.J. Olieman and S. Bruin, Drying '80, Vol. 2,
   Montreal, ed. Mujumbar, 1980.
8. S. Bruin, K.Ch.A.M. Luyben, Drying of food materials: A review of
   recent developments, Advances in drying, ed. Mujumbar, 1980.
9. ISIS manual, Simulation Systems Yatton, 1980.

Preconcentration and Drying of Food Materials, edited by S. Bruin
Elsevier Science Publishers B.V., Amsterdam, 1988 — Printed in The Netherlands

STEAM DRYING OF FOODSTUFFS AND AGRICULTURAL PRODUCTS

by

Claes Münter
President
Svensk Exergiteknik AB
Stampgatan 38, S-411 01 Göteborg, Sweden

SUMMARY

A new drying technique for drying of foodstuffs and agricultural
products and byproducts has recently been commercialized. The technique
improves both the economy of drying and the quality of the final product.
For some materials this also creates possibilitis into new products and
markets.

INTRODUCTION

Svensk Exergiteknik AB was founded in 1981 by Prof. B. Hedström and C.
Münter to continue and commercialize their development of the Steam
Drying Technology at Chalmers University of Technology in Göteborg,
Sweden.

The Company has prospered and today, besides the founders and employees
of the Company, its shareholders include private and institutional in-
vestors, including the Swedish Sugar Company, a part of Volvo Food Division.

The main areas of activity of the Company are process design and
project implementation. A team of highly qualified engineers and technicians is assigned to each project guaranteeing continuity and expe-
dience of the project execution from process design to detailed engineering, from equipment fabrication and supply to its installation and
erection including the plant start-up.

Several of the main components of the drying systems are fabricated in
the Company's workshop, Ekström & Son, which employs approximately 85
people including a staff of 15 engineers and technicians.

The workshop is widely recognized for its high standards of fabrication
of pressure vessels, reactors and heat exchangers in stainless steel and
other alloys.

Most of the process technology and important equipment are patented. In
some cases the patents are related to drying of a certain product so as
to protect both the Company and its Clients.

* In proven applications the Company can offer:
  Feasability studies and price proposals
  Equipment supply or turn-key supply of drying
  process including start-up and education of the
  Client's operators
* For new applications the Company can provide:
  Drying test to adapt the technology to a new product
  Budget proposals and feasability studies
  Quantities of product for further testing, market studies,
  introduction etc.
  Price proposals for the supply of equipment or complete
  installation as agreed with the Client

Besides Steam Drying other processes or products are being developed or
licensed mainly for the Scandinavian market. Such examples includes evaporators for high concentrations and heat pumps using steam.

THE BASIC SYSTEM

The Exergy Dryer is a closed, pressurized system (Fig. 1) where the
material to be dried is suspended and exposed to indirectly heated superheated steam. In the dryer, which consists of transport pipes, heat exchangers, cyclone and fans, superheated steam circulates at a pressure of
1 to 6 bar. The steam serves as a transport media for material in the
dryer. The heat for drying is transferred from the heat exchanger tube
surfaces to the suspension. Primary heating steam is condensed, usually
at pressure between 8 and 15 bar, on the shell side of the heat exchangers.

Dried material and steam are separated in a cyclon and the steam is
recirculated. The excess steam generated during drying is continuously
bled off from the system. This steam is available as process steam at a
pressure of 1 to 6 bar directly or after a reboiler generating clean
steam. Alternatively, generated steam can be used as heating steam for
the dryer after passing a vapour compressor.

Average drying rates in superheated steam are 2 to 3 times greater than
by conventional air drying due to higher heat transfer coefficients for
steam. Typical residence time for the material is 5-60 seconds in the
steam dryer.

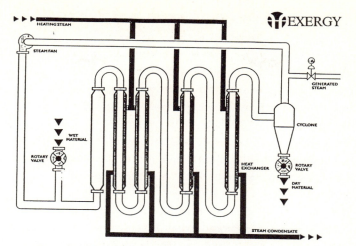

Fig. 1. Exergy Dryer Principle

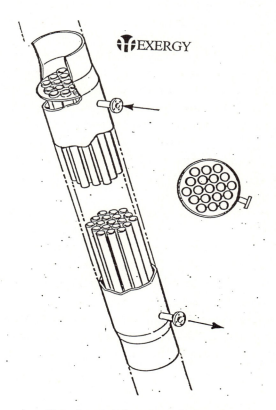

Fig. 2. Tubular Heat Exchanger

EQUIPMENT

Some comments on main equipment in a Steam Drying process:

Feeding and discharge equipment. Several rotary valves can be found in the market. In special cases high density pump or plug screw can be used.

Particle/steam disperser is used for disintegration of lumps. If material is to be mixed with steam a high speed venturi for the material introduction is used.

Heat exchanger design (Fig. 2) is of course very critical. The solid to steam ratio are kept very low, typically 0.1 - 0.8. The suspension is passed inside tubes with diameter 75 - 150 mm. Length of tubes are typically 10 - 20 m.

For abrasive materials inlet tube-sheet is protected by a wear plate.

Empty ducts and elbows are designed after full scale tests to prevent material to settle but to give enough residence time between heat exchangers.

Cyclone for separating carrier steam and dried material is designed for high efficiency performance. Another inertia separator is provided where generated steam is bled-off.

Recycle fans are pressurized centrifugal fans with mechanical seals or labyrinth seals. Typical efficiency is in the range of 70 - 85%.

Pre-superheater for recycle carrier steam is used when paste, concentrated liquor or sticky material is dried. Enough superheat is needed for evaporation of surface moisture in some cases.

MAIN FEATURES OF THE STEAM DRYER
Energy Recovery

60 - 80% of energy for drying is recovered by using generated steam in process or by using vapour recompression.

Safety

Steam atmosphere eliminates the risk of fires or explosions.

No emission

Using closed pressurized steam system there are no flue gases or hot air containing particulates or chemicals vented to the atmosphere.

Ease of operation

Rapid start up, shutdown and response are some benefits of using indirectly heated steam system. From an operator's point of view, the dryer works as a heat exchanger and only steam pressure control valves are necessary for controlling the operation.

Compact Design

The Design of Exergy Dryer is easily adjusted to fit local require-ments. The vertical design is space saving and there are only a few moving parts in a Steam Drying installation.

Highest Product Quality

The unique drying conditions in the Steam Dryer are favourable for drying of many products where quality is critical.
* There are no air or flue gases that can oxidize and contaminate the product.
* Drying in suspension and vapourizing into steam gives a fluffy, porous product where the non-reversible changes due to dehydration, often taking place using air or flue gas drying, are minimized.
* Controlled temperatures and short residence time, 5 - 60 seconds, are two conditions making the dryer particularly suited for drying of heat sensitive products.
* Due to mass and heat transfer in steam atmosphere, a very uniform dryness of the dried product is achieved. In addition, the final moisture can be controlled within a narrow range of, for example, ±0.5% at 90% dryness.

OPERATING INSTALLATIONS
Drying of Paper Pulp

In its first application, the Steam Dryer was developed and used for drying of cellulose fibres, specially CIMP.

The Steam Dryer for CIMP in Rockhammar installed 1979 has recently been modified to increase the capacity from 160 tons of pulp/24 h to about 200.

All design objectives have been met and the benefits of the Exergy Dryer can be summarized as follows:
* Short residence time (15 seconds) and gentle drying conditions (130 - 140°C)

258

* No risk of fires or explosions in steam atmosphere
* Very low energy consumption approx. 150 kWh/ton evaporated water
* High water absorption and brightness of the product
* Accurate final moisture control (±0.5% in 85-95% dryness range)
* No emissions of fibres

Steam Drying to Improve the Use of Biomass

The Steam Drying Technology has been further developed for applications in drying of many different biomass materials such as woodwastes, bark, peat, bagasse, straw.

In one such application at Husum, Sweden, the Steam Dryer was employed to dry bark from the pulp mill for combustion on the grate of a conventional boiler.

The installation of the Steam Dryer 1982 resulted in several immediate benefits to the operation, such as:
* Boiler capacity on bark alone increased from 60 to 100 tons of steam per hour
* Boiler efficiency improved due to less excess air requirement and less fly ash
* Response of the boiler to varying steam demand improved

The development of the technology for this application included bark cleaning and separation, disintegration and classification. (Fig. 3)

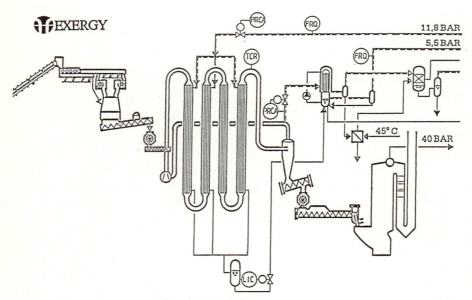

Fig. 3.   Bark Dryer

Sugar Beet Pulp for Use as Dietary Fibre - "Fibrex"

Collaborating with the Swedish Sugar Company, the Steam Drying Techno-
logy was futher developed for use in drying of sugar beet pulp and the
production of a new dietary fibre suitable for human consumption, Fibrex.
Utilization of the Steam Drying Technology in this application has
resulted in excellent product quality characteristics such as:
* Taste and colour
* Microbacterial activity
* Sand content
* Constant dryness for wide range of particle sizes from 0.3 to 3 mm
* Water absorption and water binding capacity

Typical operating and consumption data of the Steam Dryer in this
application are:
* Residence time approximately 60 sec
* Temperature 140° - 160°C
* Net heat consumption, 180 kWh/ton evaporated water
* Net power consumption, 40 kWh/ton evaporated water

Mineral Fibres to Replace Asbestos

To further diversify the use of mineral fibre (Rockwool) a new process
has been developed where fibres are processed in a water system by
cleaning and screening. Besides some applications where fibres can be
used non-dried, a great number of applications require a completely dry
product.

The application of the Steam Drying Technology was instrumental in
achieving some of the important product quality criteria such as:
* High final dryness, more than 99.5%
* Dry product consisting of fluffy individual fibres
* Ease of dispersion in both water and organic solvents without formation
  of nodules

Corn Gluten Fibre as Cattle Feed

In a joint development program with a corn processing company the
Steam Drying Technology has been developed to dry sticky and heat sensitive materials.

The development resulted in a full scale commercial installation
started up in 1986.

260

The main features of this application are:

* Very short residence time in the dryer (8 - 10 seconds)
* Recycle of dry materials enables the addition of concentrated protein rich solutions
* Use of reboiler generating low pressure steam reduces heat consumption to about 30% of conventional dryers
* The product is light in colour, uncontaminated and fluffy.

Drying of Wet Milled Peat using Vapour Recompression

One of the largest peat processing plants is under construction in Sweden, and will be started during 1988. Wet milled peat with 40% dry solids will be processed and dried using the Steam Drying Technology. Two parallell dryers, each with the capacity of about 30 tons evaporated water/h will dry the peat to 90% dryness before baling and transport to a large heat and power plant.

Since there is no external consumer of steam in the peat harvesting area the dryers will be equipped with two turbo compressors increasing the pressure from 3 to 14 bar. (Fig. 4).

The total power consumption including fans etc is about 190 kWh/ton evaporated water. This includes, however supply of district heat of about 3.6 MW to a nearby village.

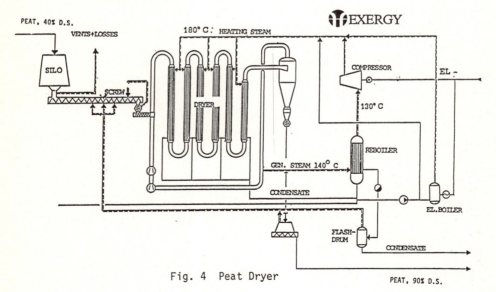

Fig. 4 Peat Dryer

RECENT DEVELOPMENTS

The application of the Exergy Dryer for different substances many times includes the consideration of an increased product quality. Sometimes this even leads to that a new product can be identified.

Acquired knowledge from working with various substances, industries and the Exergy know-how has been applied to areas of food and agricultural industry where drying is not the object.

There are mainly two processes where the same basic technology can be used:

Exergy Extinct for sanitizing or disinfection of granular food ingredients such as spices and herbs, sliced vegetables, grain and dietary fibres etc.

This continuous autoclavation process can replace the use of ethylene-oxide or radiation.

Exergy Digest to modify (increase) digestibility of various cattle feed. The benefit of using steam to hydrolyze cellulose (carbohydrates) was soon found to be very important but also on cattle feed rich in protein important changes of quality has been found. This will be further investigated and used as an argument to promote the use of Steam Drying.

TEST FACILITIES AND EVALUATION

At Chalmers University of Technology, Gothenburg, unique test facilities are available, sponsored by the Swedish Board of Technical Development.

The pilot dryer can evaporate 0.1 - 0.5 tons of water per hour depending upon the product. In connection with testing for dryer design tests of equipment for mixing, dispersion, feeding and discharge are included. Usually 2 - 4 hours test at stationary conditions is enough. If the clients wish to have more product for testing it is possible to run 24 hours a day.

Included in the test evaluation:
- product handling properties
- type of feeder and discharge equipment
- mixing and dispersion equipment
- heat transfer and drying rates for computerized dryer simulation and design

Depending upon dryer configuration heat transfer from tubes to steam and from superheated steam to particles can be calculated.

- Heat Exchanger   - Without Exchanger

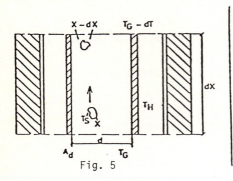

Fig. 5

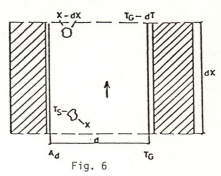

Fig. 6

We define:

$$dQ_{tubes} = \alpha \cdot \pi \cdot dx \cdot T_{ln} \qquad \text{(Fig. 5) (1)}$$

$$dQ_{carrier} = \pm A_d \cdot dx \cdot \varsigma \cdot c_p \cdot dT \text{ (positive or negative) (Fig. 6) (2)}$$

$$dQ_{evaporation} = m_s \cdot (\alpha \cdot a)_s \cdot (T_G - T_S) \cdot t \qquad (3)$$

$$-dX_{moisture\ change} = dQ_{evaporation}/r \qquad (4)$$

From testing in the continuous pilot plant we can determine $(\alpha \cdot a)_s$ as a function of X (moisture content).

Heat transfer $(\alpha \cdot a)_s$ is defined as $\dfrac{kW}{m^2 K} \qquad \dfrac{m^2}{kg\ dry\ substance}$

Preconcentration and Drying of Food Materials, edited by S. Bruin
Elsevier Science Publishers B.V., Amsterdam, 1988 — Printed in The Netherlands

CAKING DEGREE OF SPRAY DRIED COCONUT MILK

by

J.M.C. Da Costa and J. Cal-Vidal
Dept. of Dood Science, ESAL. 37.200 Lavras, MG Brazil

Powdered foods are appearing on the market at an increasing rate. In the present report the production of spray dried coconut milk was investigated and the degree of caking of the final product was considered.

Besides the effect of processing conditions and the addition of anticaking agents the influence of corn starch and of a surface active agent was evaluated.

All treated powders were exposed at two different relative humidity environments and conditioned under different temperatures (5, 15, 25, 35 and 45). The results show relative influences of the processing conditions, having the pretreatments at times some antagonic effects.

The information will be useful in selecting substances to improve the flowability of spray dried food powders.

INTRODUCTION

Food powders are part of a large group of substances that differ in chemical composition and physical characteristics. Among the main factors affecting the free flow property of a powder one may distinguish its surface characteristics, size, size distribution and geometry of the physical system (Peleg, 1977): Karnauskenko, 1984; Pazola & Jankun, 1982). Besides these factors there are others, such as the presence of liquid between particles with the formation of filmes or liquid bridges (Scoville and Peleg, 1981) that are responsible for the formation of caking. Other aspects of interest are the particle radius, water film properties, geometrical changes and a high relative humidity (Santos and Cal-Vidal, 1986).

According to Pruthi et al. (1959) the hygroscopicity is an important characteristic in powdered foods being influenced by the product water content. These authors studied garlic powder and found a product very hygroscopic with a high susceptibility to color changes and caking formation even in conditions of a low relative humidity and temperature. Lazar and Morgan (1966) observed that the tendency of powdered fruits to form caking can be due to the presence of sugars in the amorphous form. Makower and Dye (1956) showed a caking mechanism when the sugar crystallized in the amorphous form released moisture which formed a viscous surface between particles, increasing the rate of crystallization when the moisture content and temperature increased.

De Gois (1981) reported physical changes such as loss of flow and caking formation in freeze dried papaya powder when exposed to relative humidities above 35%. In the case of onion powder, Peleg and Mannheim (1977) concluded that at relative humidities above 40% the time for the samples to reach the equilibrium moisture content was inversaly related to the relative humidity.

A high temperature is also an important factor in powder caking. It promotes an increase in solubility and changes in the moisture distribution through the powder (Mannheim, 1974); Peleg and Mannheim, 1969; Lazar and Morgan, 1966). Peleg and Mannheim (1969) reported that the caking degree of powdered onion increased with the temperature rise and that this product can be stored for a period of six months at 15°C without loss of its physical properties but when stored at 35°C the powder agglomerates in 72 hours.

Other factors of interest in the caking degree of powders are the presence of particles smaller than 10 micra, van der Weals forces and interaction forces (Neuman, 1958). Shoton and Harb (1966) discussed that the cohesion of a powder is affected by the shape of particle, size and size distribution.

The compressibility is an important characteristic for the cohesive properties of food powders. In cohesive powders where the structure is open due to interparticle forces, the compacting pressure is of major significance favoring the structural collapse(Peleg et al., 1973; Moreyra and Peleg, 1980).

In this study it was considered the effect of anticaking agent and surface active agents on the caking degree of spray dried coconut milk.

MATERIALS AND METHODS

Sample preparation

The coconut milk was initially stored at $3^{O}C$ in a cool chamber and then heated up $70^{O}C$, to be homogenized in a Manton-Gaulin Homogenizer Model 125 DJ4 (Massachusetts, USA) of two stages. The objetive being to break and disperse the fat globules present in the material.

After the homogenization anticaking agents, 63FP and 244FP (Grace-Davison Chemical, Baltimore, USA), and surface active agents were added in the proportions of 0.5; 1.0; 1.5; 2.0 % on the basis of total solids on the feeding material and corn starch (Morex) added at the levels of 15 and 20% weight/volume.

Spray-Drying

Two different drying conditions were established in this study as indicated in Table 1.

The disc atomizer was kept constant at 1600 RPM.

Powder conditioning

Aproximately 2 g of the powder sample, in duplicate, with and without the added agent were placed in Petri dishes ($\emptyset$ = 4 cm) and then transfered to

Table 1 - Spray-Drying Conditions

Condition	Inlet Temperature	Outlet Temperature
1	$200 \pm 10^{O}C$	$85 \pm 10^{O}C$
2	$230 \pm 10^{O}C$	$95 \pm 10^{O}C$

desiccators having several levels of relative humidity. These desiccators were
then placed in cabinets set at different temperatures (5, 15, 25, 35 and
45°C). The samples were kept in each condition untill equilibration and then
taken off from the desiccators to determine the amount of water absorbed and
the caking degree.

Water sorption determinations

The several levels of relative humidities inside the desiccators were
obtained with saturated salt solutions as recomended by Rockland (1960) and
O'Brien (1948). The accuracy of the obtained values was confirmed with an
Airguide Hygrometer Model 101 (Airguide Instrument Co. Chicago, Il. USA). The
powder samples were placed in the desiccators which were kept at several
temperature environments, as previously indicated. At preestablished time
intervals gravimetric determinations were made to estimate the degree of water
absorption.

Caking degree

The caking degree was determined using a technique described by Niro
Atomizer (1978). Duplicate samples of about 3g of the powdered coconut milk
were placed in Petric dishes and conditioned at five different temperatures
(5 to 45°C) and two relative humidities (75 and 96%). Immediately after moisture
equilibration the material was exposed in a drying cabinet at 105°C for 30
minutes. Following this procedure and after the evaluation of the initial weight
the samples were transferred for a set of screens Produtest (Telastem Peneiras
para Analises Ltda. São Paulo, Brasil). The degree of caking was estimated using
the screen with an opening of 2 mm. The set of screens was adapted to a vibrator
system also Produtest which was regulated to operate during 5 minutes at its
maximum vibration rate. After such a time the material retained on each screen
was estimated and the caking degree was given by the following expression.

$$\text{Degree of Caking (\%)} = \frac{\text{Weight of Retained Material}}{\text{Original Weight}} \times 100 \qquad (1)$$

RESULTS AND DISCUSSION

Water Content Effects

Fig. 1 to 3 show the influence of water content on the caking degree
of spray dried coconut milk having different amounts of anticaking agents added.
It is observed that increasing the water content there is a corresponding
increase on the values for the caking degree. In addition, it is verified that
temperature plays also an important role with a significant effect on the degree
of caking. This effect is accentuated in the temperature of 45°C (Fig. 3) where
the caking degree rises drastically in a short range of water content.

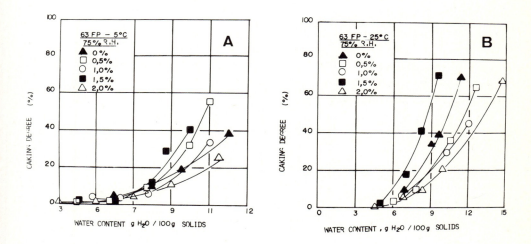

Fig.1. Water content effect on the caking degree of Spray-dried coconut milk powd
containing anticaking agent 63FP at several concentrations conditioned at
5°C (A) and 25°C (B).

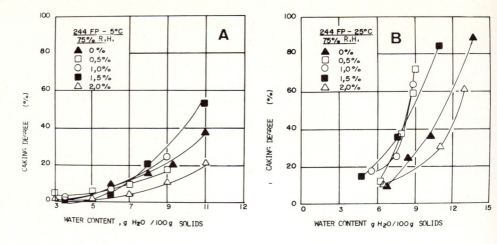

Fig.2. Water content effect on the caking degree of Spray-dried coconut milk powder containing anticaking agent 244FP at several concentrations conditioned at 5°C (A) and 25°C (B).

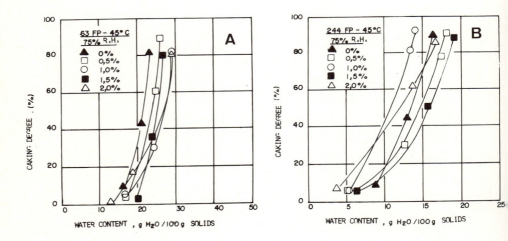

Fig. 3. Water content effect on the caking degree of Spray-dried coconut milk powder containing anticaking agent 63FP (A) and 244FP (B) conditioned at 45°C.

Contidioning Time Effects

      The influence of the conditioning time on the caking degree of coconut
milk powder having corn starch (Morex) added is presented in Fig 4 and 5. Fig 6
shows the behavior of the pure coconut milk powder with the influence of temperature on the reduction of time for caking, mainly at 45°C. These results are in
agreement with those reported by De Gois (1981) and Peleg and Mannheim (1969)
that studied the effect of water activity and temperature on the caking formation
of powdered papaya and powdered onion, respectively. Comparing the degree of
caking at the three temperatures, it can be clearly observed that to reach a
caking degree of 95% at 45°C it is necessary a time of about seven and half hours,
while at 15 and 25°C were spent nine and twenty days, respectively.

      The mathematical expressions of Fig 6 were obtained through polynomial
regression. Fig 4 shows the effect of adding corn starch (Morex) separetely and
in combination with anticaking 244FP. It can be observed (Fig 4-A) that the
combination is effective in reducing the degree of caking of the product. The
same type of behavior can be observed for samples conditioned at 35°C (Fig 5-A).

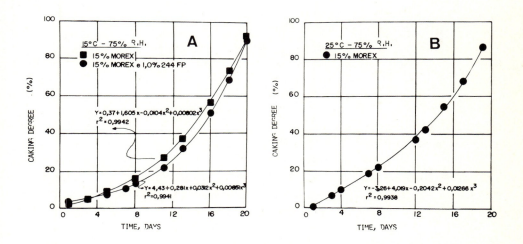

Fig.4. Effect of conditioning time on the caking degree of Spray-dried coconut milk
added morex and conditioned at 15°C (A) and 25°C (B).

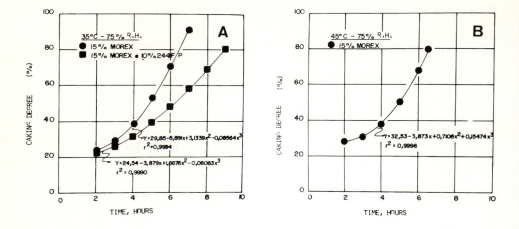

Fig. 5. Effect of conditioning time on the caking degree of spray-dried coconut milk with added morex and conditioned at 35°C (A) and 45°C (B).

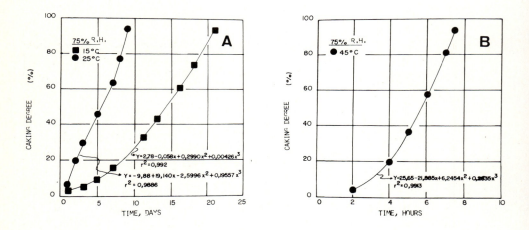

Fig. 6. Effect of conditioning time on the caking degree os spray-dried coconut milk with added morex and conditioned at 15 and 25°C (A) and 45°C (B).

Temperature, Anticaking and Surfactant Concentration Effects

Fig 7 and 8 show the influence of anticaking agents 63FP and 244FP on the caking degree of coconut milk powder at several temperatures and under two different relative humidities. It was observed a higher degree of caking for the

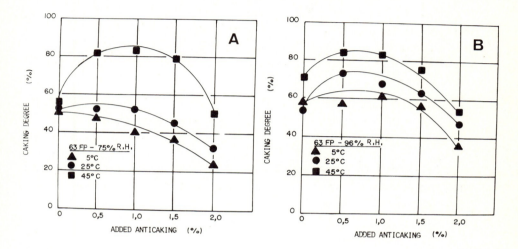

Fig.7. Effect of added anticaking agent 63FP on the caking degree of spray-dried coconut milk conditioned at several temperatures and 75% R.H. (A) and 96% R.H. (B).

high temperatures mainly at 45°C. It can also be noticed that the anticaking concentration plays an important role being its effect more significant at higher concentrations. The increase of the degree of caking with the relative humidity confirms previous reports of the literature (Hamano and Sugimoto, 1978; Lazar et al., 1956; Santos and Cal-Vidal, 1985). The effect of adding a surface active agent is shown in Fig 9. In general the effect is somehow similar to the one presented by the anticaking agents with an increase on the degree of caking at some temperatures at the lower concentrations of the surfactant.

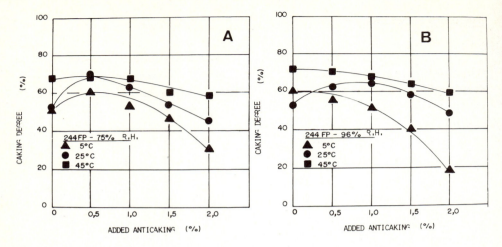

Fig.8. Effect of added anticaking agent 244FP on the caking degree of spray-dried coconut milk conditioned at several temperatures and 75% R.H. (A) and 96% R.H. (B).

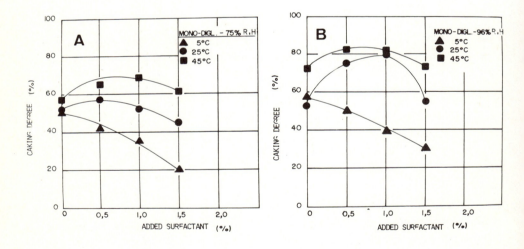

Fig.9. Effect of added surface active agent mono-digliceride on the caking degree of spray-dried coconut milk conditioned at several temperatures and 75% R.H. (A) and 96% R.H. (B).

Processing Conditions Effects

The effect of adding 0.5% of each anticaking and surface active agent
to powders dried at two different air temperatures and conditioned at three
different temperatures and two relative humidities on the corresponding caking
degree is shown in Fig 10 to 12. From the histograms presented it can be
concluded that in some cases the addition of the mentioned substances contributed
to elevate the degree of caking, besides the effect given by the relative
humidity that also made an important contribution to increase the caking degree.

In relation to the effect of the inlet air temperature on the caking
degree it can be concluded that the higher temperature (230°C) favored a
reduction on the degree of caking in most cases. The condioning temperature plays
also an important role promoting an increase on the caking degree as it raises.

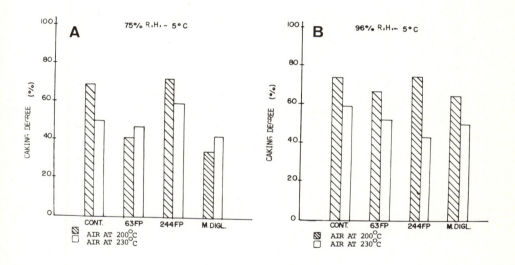

Fig.10. Effect of adding anticaking and surface active agents and of processing
conditions on the caking degree of coconut milk powder conditioned at 75%
R.H. (A) and 96% R.H. (B).

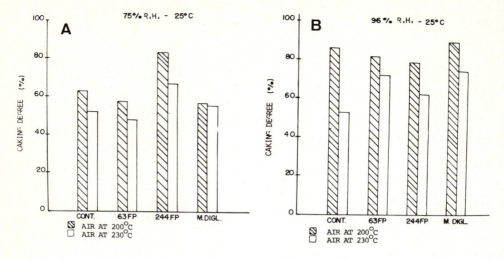

Fig. 11. Effect of adding anticaking and surface active agents and of processing
conditions on the caking degree of coconut milk powder conditioned at 75%
R.H. (A) and 96% R.H. (B).

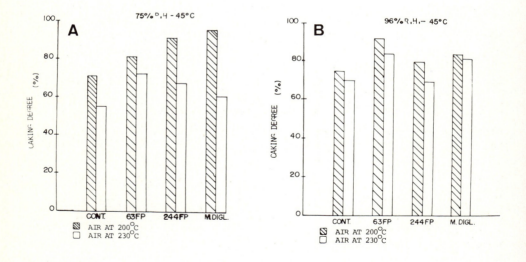

Fig. 12. Effect of adding anticaking and surface active agents and of processing
conditions on the caking degree of coconut milk powder conditioned at 75%
R.H. (A) and 96% R.H. (B).

ACKNOWLEDGEMENTS

Many thanks are due to CNPq (Conselho Nacional de Desenvolvimento Científico e Tecnológico, Brasília, Brazil) for awarding research grants and fellowships to conduct this investigation. The first author also thanks to CAPES (Coordenação de Aperfeiçoamento de Pessoal de Nível Superior, Brasília, Brazil) for the fellowship awarded to develop a M.Sc. Program.

REFERENCES

De Gois, V.A. 1981. M.Sc. Thesis, ESAL. Lavras, Brazil.

Hamano, M. and Sugimoto. 1978. J.Fd. Processing and Preservation 2, 185.

Karnaushenko, L.I. 1984. Pishchevaya Tekhonologiya 2, 97.

Lazar, M.E.; Brown, A.H.; Smith, G.S.; Wong, F.F. and Lindquist, F.E. 1956. Food Technology, 10, 129.

Lazar, M.E. and Morgan Jr., A.I. 1966. Food Technology 20, 179.

Makower, B. and Dye, W.B. 1956. Agr. and Food Chem. 4, 72.

Mannheim, C.H. 1974. Research Report 080-037 Techniun-Israel Institute of Technology, Haifa, Israel.

Moreyra, R. and Peleg, M. 1980. J. Food Science, 45, 865.

Neuman, B.S. 1958. In: Hermans, J.J., ed. Flow properties of disperse systems. North Holland p. 382.

Niro Atomizer (A/S). 1978. Analytical Methods for Dry Milk Products A/S Niro Atomizer. Copenhagen, Denmark. 109p.

O'Brien, F.E.M. 1948. J. Science Instrumental 25, 73.

Pazola, A. and Janjun, J. 1982. Lebensmittelindustrie 29, 248.

Peleg, M. 1977. J. Food Process and Engineering 1, 303.

Peleg, M. and Mannheim, C.H. 1969. J. Food Technology 4, 157.

Peleg, M. and Mannheim, C.H. 1977. J. Food Processing and Preservation 1, 3.

Peleg, M. Mannheim, C.H. and Passy, N. 1973. J. Food Science 38, 959

Pruthi, J.S.; Singh, L.J. and Lal, G. 1959. J. of Science of Food and Agriculture 10, 359.

Rockland, L.B. 1960. Analytical Chemistry 32, 1375.

Santos, S.C.S. and Cal-Vidal, J. 1985. Pesquisa Agropecuária Brasileira 20, 615

Santos, S.C.S. and Cal-Vidal, J. 1986. Proceedings of World Congress III of Chemical Engineering. Tokyo, Japan.

Scoville, E. and Peleg, M. 1981. J. Food Science 46, 174.

Shoton, E. and Harb, N. 1966. J. Pharmacy and Pharmacology 18, 175.

Preconcentration and Drying of Food Materials, edited by S. Bruin
Elsevier Science Publishers B.V., Amsterdam, 1988 — Printed in The Netherlands

DRYING OF AGRICULTURAL PRODUCTS IN A TWO-COMPONENT FLUIDIZED BED

G.DONSI'[1] , G.FERRARI[1] and L.OLIVIERI[2]

[1]Istituto di Ingegneria Chimico-Alimentare, Facoltà di Ingegneria
Università di Salerno - 84081 Baronissi (SA) (Italy)

[2]Kinetics Technology International S.p.A., via Monte Carmelo 5
00166 Roma (Italy)

SUMMARY
    The possibility of performing drying processes of wooden shells fruits in two-component fluidized beds is analyzed, on the basis of experimental results from laboratory-scale apparatus. A predictive model is also developed and tested and results are discussed on its basis.

INTRODUCTION

    The utilization of fluid bed technique in drying processes of agricultural products has been often recommended, due to the high mass and heat transfer rates attainable and to the intrinsic excellent thermal control capability, in respect to conventional air driers (ref.1). However, relatively few fluidized bed drying plants have been put into operation in food industry, due to the poor fluidization properties exhibited by most agricultural products.

    Coarse and odd-shaped solids, such as most fruits and vegetables, require high gas velocities to be sustained and, when fluidized, give rise to disuniformities in gas permeation as well as in solids circulation. This somewhat damps the predicted excellency of transfer properties of a properly fluidized bed.

    For such products, the use of spouted beds has been proposed, in order to reduce the fluidizing flow rate, but the lack of uniformity in transport properties and temperature persists and may be also enhanced (ref.2).

    The use of a fluidized bed made out of inert fine material to suspend, as a freely floating phase, the coarse product to be dried, is also possible, on the basis of well known properties of so called two-component fluidized beds (refs.3 and 4). This technique has been also presented as a general purpose gas-solid contact device in food preservation processes (ref.5).

    This work aims at characterizing experimentally the application of this technique to drying processes of specific agricultural products, and at setting up a model in view of the scale up of the apparatus. The experimental work performed so far is concerned with the drying of fresh hazelnuts, as a first preservation stage before industrial processing.

Hazelnuts are a primary agricultural product in internal regions of Southern Italy. Fresh fruits used to be sun-dried from an initial water content of about 20% down to about 6%, which is the moisture level suitable for a medium term preservation. Actually, mechanical collecting devices tend to recover a somewhat wetter product, due to its longer residence time on the ground. Moreover, being nuts also dirtier, a washing stage must be often added. All together, this requires a more effective and less weather-dependent drying process. Hazelnuts are, then, artificially dried in ovens or fixed bed apparatus.

Actual drying techniques require long processing times, due both to poor contact conditions and to low process temperatures, whose level is damped by thermal disuniformities of these apparatus.

Two-component fluidized bed dryers are supposed to be a suitable alternative process. The presence of a fine inert material as supporting bed makes for a plain operation at low gas velocities; moreover the attrition produced by fine particles on the shells, has a cleaning effect. The washing stage can thus be removed, and all process can be accomplished in a single apparatus.

Experimental results demonstrate that fluid bed processing is an effective technique for hazelnuts drying. A critical discussion of results and the development of a predictive model allows to draw some more general conclusion about possible applications of two-component fluidized bed driers to other products and about the way of carrying out feasibility analysis for such processes.

EXPERIMENTAL

The laboratory scale fluid bed drying apparatus, sketched in Figure 1, consists of a stainless steel vessel, 140 mm ID, 800 mm high. Air is admitted through a perforated double plate distributor; a cyclone is inserted on the gas outlet line, in order to perform the separation of entrained fine particles. Pressure drop through the bed is measured by a water manometer. The fluidizing air, fed by a screw compressor, is metered by a rotameter and then heated by an electrical heat exchanger. Electrical power is regulated by an electronic controller, whose set point can be adjusted in a wide temperature range; the regulation thermocouple is fitted at the exchanger outlet, while a second thermocouple monitors bed temperature. Also the relative humidity of the gas stream at the bed outlet is monitored and recorded, together with bed temperature, on a multichannel recorder.

Silica sand (200-400 μm sieve size) is used as inert bed material; a suitable fluidization velocity of 25 cm/s, corresponding to about twice the sand minimum fluidization velocity, is kept in all experiments. A wide mesh net basket is employed to extract hazelnuts samples from the apparatus without removing the inert bed.

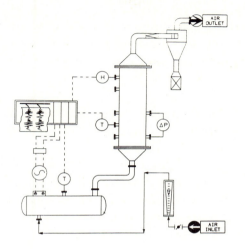

LEGENDA
1) Fluidization vessel
2) Cyclone
3) Rotameter
4) Electronic controller
5) Multichannel recorder
6) Heat exchanger

Fig.1 Experimental apparatus

Experiments are performed as follows: the inert bed is fluidized with hot air, up to the moment when bed temperature reaches the desidered steady-state value. Now the basket containing a weighed sample of hazelnuts is immersed into the fluidized bed (and test time is started on a stop watch). Periodically, the sample is extracted and weighted. Each sample contains also some marked nut, which is weighted separately in order to follow also the individual drying behavior.

A comparison sample, taken from the same batch, is paralelly dried in a high temperature oven, kept at 100 °C, to get the value of total water content to be used as reference value for each test.

Also drying tests in a natural convection oven, at the same temperature as the fluid bed, are carried out in order to simulate natural drying for each sample.

Separate drying tests on shelled nuts and shells are also performed in the same oven, to check water distribution inside hazelnuts and to get more information on the different transfer resistences involved in drying. Occasionally fixed bed drying tests are carried out, using the fluid bed apparatus after removing the inert bed; gas velocity is kept at the same value as in fluidized bed experiments. Temperature of all experiments is alwais kept below 50 °C, which is considered as the limiting value for the product degeneration.

RESULTS

Different hazelnuts batches have been used, belonging to the more diffused commercial cultivated varieties. Accordingly, also in dependance of the time elapsed since fruits have been collected and on atmospheric conditions prevailing in the collection period. Being the objective of the drying process that of bringing nuts down to a water content of about 6% (dry basis), which ensures long preservation before direct industrial processing, different process conditions must be accounted for.

In order to get informations on water distribution inside the nuts for different samples, initial water contents of shells and fruits have been separately determined. For most samples, shells contain almost twice water as inner fruits do, with the only exception of very fresh hazelnuts. This kind of determination as been perfomed also for samples at different drying stages, under different process conditions, and the value of the ratio of shell to fruit water contents is confirmed to be always close to two. On this basis, it is inferred that natural as well as artificial drying of hazelnuts takes place under quasi-equilibrium conditions between shells and inner fruits, which are the same for all samples.

This following data are treated irrespectively of the cultivated variety, but just on the basis of the initial moisture. Figure 2 shows some typical drying curve, represented as average water contents at different temperature and same fluidization conditions. The shape of these curves confirms that drying is alwais carried out under unsteady state conditions, even for higher initial humidities.

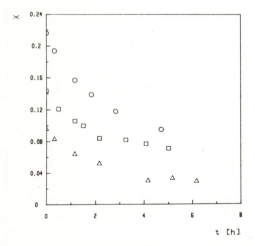

Fig.2 Moisture content vs. time for fluid bed tests for different initial values of moisture. (○) T=47°C X_o=0.216; (□) T=40°C X_o=0.144; (△) T=47°C X_o=0.096

Figures 3 and 4 show drying data in dimensionless form, as the ratio of current water content X to initial value X_o, as a function of time. Data refer to two temperature levels, 40 °C and 47 °C and differnt samples, treated at the same fluidization conditions.

For sake of comparison, also results from tests performed in the oven at the same temperature are reported and, for the higher temperature, also from fixed bed experiment.

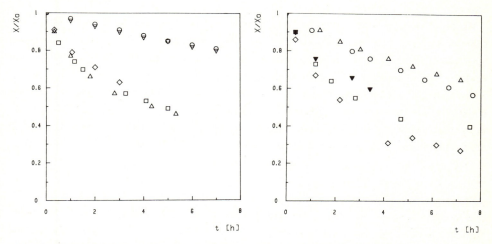

Fig.3 Dimensionless moisture content
       vs. time at T= 40°C
       (∇,$\bigcirc$) Oven; ($\triangle$,$\square$,$\diamond$) Fluid bed

Fig.4 Dimensionless moisture content
       vs. time at T=47°C ($\triangle$,$\bigcirc$) Oven;
       ($\blacktriangledown$) Fixed bed; ($\square$,$\diamond$) Fluid bed

Data obtained at the same temperature collect well on the same line, irrespective of the initial water content.

The temperature effect is rather sensitive, and drying appears to proceed much faster at 47 °C for fluid bed as well as for oven experiments. Changing fluidization conditions does not produce any appreciable effect on the drying curves; this is explained in the following on the basis of the proposed model.

MODEL INTERPRETATION OF THE RESULTS

In setting up the model of the drying process, the following experimental evidences are taken into consideration:
a) oven tests on shelled nuts and shells suggest that equilibrium between their water contents is attained, independently on drying conditions. This indicates that water transfer from the inner fruit to the shell is faster than mass transfer thought the shell.
b) Increasing drying temperature strongly enhances the overall drying rate, as shown by data in Figures 3 and 4. This suggests that a gas phase transfer

resistance exists.

c) The transition from oven tests to fluid bed experiments also produces a relevant increase in mass transfer rate, as shown by the same Figures. This suggests that also an external resistence to mass transfer plays a definite role on the process.

On the basis of previous observations, a model based on a two-steps transfer resistence is developed and the following model hypotheses are formulated:

- Water transfer from the inner fruit toward the shell is fast in respect to the transfer from the shell to the external gas. During the process, equilibrium extablishes between water fractions of the fruits, X_f, and of the shells, X_s, according to a relationship $X_s/X_f = m$.

- Shells are porous and gaseous diffusion of water vapor takes place within pores. Relative humidity Y at the inner end of the pores is at the equilibrium with X_s, according to a linear adsorption isotherm: $Y = \gamma X_s$ Accordingly, the following mass transfer equation can be written across the shell:

$$N_w = - \frac{\alpha \mathbb{D}}{RTs} (P_{ws} - P_{wi}) = k_g (P_{wi} - P_{wg}) \qquad (1)$$

being N_w the water molar flux, P_w the water partial pressure at the inner shell side (s), at the outer shell (i) and in the bulk of drying gas (g), $\mathbb{D}$ the water diffusion coefficient in air, α the shell porosity and k_g the external mass transfer coefficient. On the basis of the hypothesis above, it is possible to express water partial pressure as a function of the average hazelnuts water fraction, $\overline{X}$. Accounting for the water mass balance on the whole fruit:

$$- N_w = \frac{W_s}{AM_w} \frac{d\overline{X}}{dt} \qquad (2)$$

were W_s/A is mass per unit external area of the nuts and M_w water molar weight, it is possible to obtain the following first order differential equation

$$- \frac{d\overline{X}}{dt} = \frac{A M_w}{W_s} k p^{\circ}_w (m \gamma \overline{X} - Y_g) \qquad (3)$$

being k the overall mass transfer coefficient defined from

$$\frac{1}{k} = \frac{1}{k_g} + \frac{sRT}{\mathbb{D}\alpha}$$

p°_w the water vapor pressure and Y_g the bulk relative humidity of the drying gas. Equation (3) is solved

$$\overline{X} = \overline{X}_e + (\overline{X}_o - \overline{X}_e) \exp (- k \frac{A}{W_s} M_w p^{\circ}_w m \gamma t) \qquad (4)$$

having defined $\overline{X}_e$ as $Y_g/m\gamma$, i.e. the average water fraction for a given gas humidity. Equation (4) predicts time evolution of the average water fraction of hazelnuts, as a function of temperature (whose effect, in a limited range, is embodied in $p°_w$), fluid dynamic conditions (k_g), properties of the drying gas ($\overline{X}_e$), of sorption isotherm (γ) and fruit physical properties (A/W_s, α and s).

The model is, in principle fully deterministic. Some input parameters, such as shell porosity α or isotherm slope γ can be determined in a more precise way by means of dedicated experimental work. On the basis of a set of input parameters defined as follows from $\alpha = 0.1$; $\gamma = 3.3$; m = 2 model equation is compared with experimental data, worked out in terms of the ratio $(\overline{X} - \overline{X}_e)/(\overline{X}_o - \overline{X}_e)$.

Figure 5 represents drying data for all conditions tested, compared with model lines. It is assumed that, in the first minutes of the drying process, a greater drop in nuts weight takes place due to removal of liquid water or, simply, of a little ground from the shell. On this basis model straight lines are not forced through the point 1,0. This is the only fitting adjustment considered.

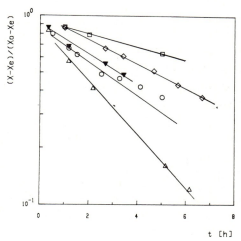

Fig.5 Drying   data   compared   with   model   equations
(□) Oven T=40°C; (◇) Oven T=47°C; (▼) Fixed bed T=47°C
(○) Fluid bed T=40°C;   (△) Fluid bed T=47°C

In order to confirm model hypothesis (a), also drying data for shells and shelled nuts are worked out for evaluating mass transfer coefficient in Figure 6. Considering that transfer rate for shells is now referred to a surface double as for whole fruits, the following values for k are obtained: 0.052, 0.140 and 0.056 respectively for whole fruits, shelled nuts and shells. It is demonstrated that almost all transfer resistence is concetrated within the shells, as supposed in model equations.

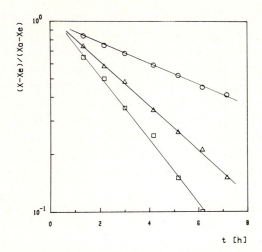

Fig.6   Drying data compared with model equations for oven tests
        at T=47°C   (O) Whole nuts; (△) Shells; (□) Inner fruits

        In order to validate further the model, data have been also represented by
embodying temperature effects within ordinate values through a correction
factor O defined as the ratio between water vapor pressures at test temperature
and reference temperature 40 °C.

        Figure 7 shows the same data as Figure 5, corrected as stated above. Data
collect all on three straight lines, corresponding to the three fluid dynamic
conditions tested. All other effects are taken in proper account by the model.

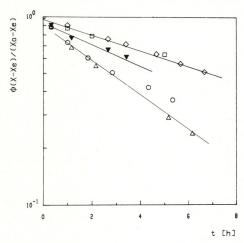

Fig.7   Drying data referred to T=40°C compared with model
        equations (□,◇) Oven; (▼) Fixed bed; (△,O) Fluid bed

From this data, values of mass transfer coefficients k and k$_g$ are calculated and reported in table 1. They compare favourably with values of k_g calculated from classic correlations for the relevant drying system.

TABLE 1.   Values of overall (k) and convective (k_g) mass transfer coefficients

	Oven tests	Fixed bed tests	Fluid bed tests
k	0.056	0.087	0.144
k_g	0.088	0.200	2.200

It can be noted that, for fluid bed operation, $1/k_g$ is negligible in respect to diffusional resistence. This means that no further emprevement can be achieved by fluid dynamic effects.

CONCLUSIONS

The use of two-component fluidized beds as driers appears promising for some application in processing agricultural products. In particular wooden shell fruits, as nuts, chestnuts and so on, can be profitably treated by this type of dryer, while cannot be properly fluidized. In these cases also product cleaning is performed as secondary effect by the apparatus and product wetting in washing tanks can be omitted.

Experiments for hazelnuts demonstate that the reduction of drying times in respect to conventional apparatus is remarkable. Also the use of fine sand as inert bed material appears a sound choice.

The proposed model fits fairly well experimental data and allows to predict dryer performances at different operative conditions. It can also be used to set up design criteria for industrial plants. The model also explains, on the basis of two serial resistances, why second order effects, such as changing fluidization velocity or inert material sieve size, are uneffective on dryer operation mode.

As a more general conclusion, the work performed suggests that, even if external mass transfer coefficients are always enhanced by fluid bed operation, not always the overall drying rate is enhanced by the a comparable factor in respect to that achieved in different apparatus for a given product.

The presence, in natural products, of internal mass transfer resistances due to gaseous or capillary diffusion, may limit the effectiveness of moving to the fluid bed technique. Preliminary analysis and setting up a proper transfer model should always precede the consideration of possible applications of fluid bed drying to specific process.

LIST OF SYMBOLS

A	External surface area	m^2
$\mathbb{D}$	Diffusion coefficient	$m^2 s^{-1}$
k_g	Convective mass transfer coefficient	$kmoles\ m^{-2}\ h^{-1}\ atm^{-1}$
k	Overall mass transfer coefficient	$kmoles\ m^{-2}\ h^{-1}\ atm^{-1}$
m	Water distribution coefficient between shells and inner fruits	
M_w	Molar weight of water	$kg\ kmoles^{-1}$
N_w	Molar flux	$kmoles\ m^{-2}\ h^{-1}$
p^o_w	Water vapor pressure	atm
p_w	Water partial pressure	atm
R	Gas constant	$kmoles\ atm^{-1}\ m^{-3}\ {}^\circ K^{-1}$
s	Shell thickness	m
t	Time	h
T	Temperature	$^\circ K$
X	Weight water fraction	
Y	Relative humidity	
α	Shell porosity	
γ	Slope of water adsorption isotherm	

SUBSCRIPTS

e	At equilibrium conditions
i	At the interface
g	At the bulk gas conditions
s	At inner shell conditions

LITERATURE

1) Vanecek V., Markvart M., Drbohlav R. : Fluidized Bed Drying, Leonard-Hill, London 1976
2) Rowe P.N., Nienow A.W., Agbim A.J., "The Mechanism by which Particles Segregate in Gas Fluidized Beds-Binary Systems of Near Spherical Particles", Trans.Instn.Chem.Engrs., 50, 310, 1972
3) Rice R.N., Brainovich J.F., "Mixing/Segregation in Two and Three Dimensional Fluidized Beds: Binary System of Equilibrium Spherical Particles", AIChE Journal, 32, n.1, 7, 1986
4) Mathur K.B. and Epstein N.: Spouted Beds, Academic Press, New York 1974
5) Rios G.M., Gilbert H., Baxerres J.L.,"Potential Applications of Fluidization to Food Preservation", in Development in Food Preservation, S.Thorne ed., Applied Science Pub., 1983

CLOSING REMARKS

Preconcentration and Drying of Food Materials, edited by S. Bruin
Elsevier Science Publishers B.V., Amsterdam, 1988 — Printed in The Netherlands

ARTI FOR AN ARCHAT

Prof.dr.ir. W.J. Beek*
*Unilever N.V., Postbus 760, 3000 DK Rotterdam (The Netherlands)

For my closing remarks of this memorial symposium, I have chosen the title "arti for an archat". This needs an explanation, because here I use two words derived from Hindi.

Aratti means misfortune or pain. Arti is a ceremony or an art to teach oneself how to live with misfortune. In the Greek tradition it gave rise to the word experilment, now experiment, that is: an act which alleviates the consequences of peril.

An archat is a wise man, literally one who has killed the enemy, especially the enemy within.

Today we as friends of Hans have gathered here to perform arti, in the manner of learned men. We expressed our belief that the things he stood for, are still valid today. The Hindu would say: "no, there is no nothing".

It was a sunny day in 1964 when Tops and I first met Hans and Titi, in a setting very similar to this one. His inaugural address at this university led to many exciting discussions between us, both within and outside the scope of our cooperation in the Royal Council of Engineering Institutions, of which I will now briefly recall three of the topics we discussed.

During the reception, after his first address, we were discussing with De Gruyter the need for the food industry to become more knowledgeable with respect to its major enabling technologies. The business-man De Gruyter was full of pride of what his company had contributed to the university and a bit annoyed that those present showed a higher esteem for an ability to generate technologically sound ideas than for an ability to be commercially successful. The issue was on the one hand that processing costs in the food industry contribute generally less than 10% of the ex-factory costs, ranging third after raw material costs (50-60%) and packaging costs (15-20%) and on the other hand, that ex-factory quality determined to a large extent the ultimate success in the market. Hans had a hard time to stress the latter in commercial terms, and we would experience the same quite often in the years to come. For this reason, Hans kept economic evaluations of novel ideas always in perspective, as Marcus Karel has elucidated. We shared the belief that the food industry would become more and more sensitive to technological skill. Hans grew into a very practical innovator, for whom the university offered the right climate for generating ideas and the industry the right circumstances to work to some purpose. For that reason, he would have been a most successful research director for a company with a strong technical and economic mission. He came close to that when Douwe Egberts and Jacobs decided on joint cooperation and later with TNO, before it had been reorganised, but in both cases the time was not right yet and the circumstances were against it. Entrepreneurial as he was, he achieved the right mix for himself, as a part-time professor, an advisor to the KNGSF and a private consultant, activities which ended so abruptly with his sudden death.

The second subject we discussed concerned the basic differences between processing of food and feed and chemical engineering as it had developed under the impact of a growing petrochemical industry. In fact, Hans said to me, "There are two very basic differences between these two process industries. The raw materials of the agricultural industries have binding energies which are much smaller than those of petrochemicals, because food has to be broken down under very mild conditions in several, quite different metabolic pathways, belonging to various food chains. Hence, quality and variation in quality are here different from those in classical chemical engineering. Related to that," he continued, "but of an importance in its own right, is the way in which water is present and available in the food material. In fact, there is in everything we are doing in the food industry, but one leading thought, that is: how to create functional interfaces. That is so, when we talk about aroma retention; or about stable aerated product formulations; or about food grade methods for sequestering constituents which should not be lost, for instance by making use of already available mono- and diglycerides or fatty alcohols. There is a lot to be learned here from the tricks played by nature itself for similar purposes. Cell wall material as such is a case for study."

So far, I quoted Hans and I have little to add to that what Loncin and Marcus Karel have already said on the same subject. Only, that by the same reasoning, Hans expressed a need for research in two other directions, on which he never embarked himself. The need to look upon the packaging operation of the food industry as providing wall material with specific barrier functions, to be designed by process engineering properties; and the need to gain insight into the relationship between water binding and mechanical properties of foodstuffs, especially with regard to fracture as it occurs in drying or as it might occur in cheeses or sausages when drying out. Judson King rightly so addressed the influence of morphological change on drying, a fact well-known for instance with detergent manufacturers.

The third and last item of dialogue between Hans and myself to be quoted on the occasion of this symposium was on the design of process equipment for the food industry.

Hans had observed that nearly every branch of this industry kept almost exclusively to one type of dryer, leaving for instance the beet sugar manufacturers with a completely different assessment of what they were doing than the dairy industries. Sometimes, this could be understood, quite often not, but the two would never meet. Their suppliers of equipment, with an image of being specialised, in fact offered at best no more insight than that of an overall heat and mass balance, assuming almost equilibrium between the outgoing streams. Consequently, energy losses were high and quality considerations an area of experience and rules of thumb.

We had, of course, already past the stage of talking in terms of pseudo-thermodynamical equilibrium and theoretical plates, but the wish to talk in terms of dynamics, rate processes and hence, transfer units, did not look too promising either for describing current practice.

Hans said: "Wiero, take an extruder or a spray dryer. In terms of hardware they are compact and cost effective. In terms of mechanical design they are up to standard. But they try to achieve everything in a single piece of equipment, without leaving the manufacturer much scope to change formulations without the need to modify parts of his equipment or to allow the operator any flexibility for operating conditions. The extruder has to pump, to mix, to exchange heat and sometimes to vent vapour. The spray dryer has to form droplets of the right size distribution, to mix radially well but not so much axially, to entrain little, to handle a solid powder well at its exit, to limit heat loss and to be explosion-proof. They are specimens of high adaptation to a very specific task, but very little adaptable to a change in task. Should chemical engineers not be challenged to find ways and means to separate these different functions just so much, that they could be influenced more individually, such that the operating versatility of the equipment becomes larger? Or, turning this around, would your firm ever see an advantage in combining the blanching and drying step in vegetable processing into one piece of equipment?"

Hans was right, we would not. From such considerations, Hans developed his thoughts on optimal pressures for pressure atomizers, on which Judson King reported, and on the possible advantage of injecting the feed at different heights, an idea which fell into obscurity much too soon.

His main topic, however, became preconcentration, as a logical conse-quence of the same train of thought and still with the ultimate objective of enhancing food quality by processing tools which retain aroma, are hygienic and avoid degradation in all its aspects. Our first symposium day was alsmost completely devoted to this topic, with keynote talks by Hallstrøm and Van Pelt. Hans' basic thinking behind this was given in one of the slides shown by Marcus Karel. All well-known drying techniques lie within a relatively small margin of equal thermal degradation, when they are plotted in a regime-diagram showing the virtual temperature of the process versus the residence time. Improvements in this respect can only be achieved if we pursue completely novel ways.

This has been taken up, recently, by a group of leading institutions in The Netherlands: the Gas Institute (VEG), the Dutch Energy Development Foundation (NEOM) and the Dutch Agricultural Research Council (HRLO), who plan for an effort to enhance the knowledge within our industry on drying, effective energy use and end-product quality improvement. To this, Hans' school will make a considerable contribution. It is about time that his achievements were translated in such a way that they become consolidated knowledge for the professional plant manager and equipment designer.

So, rightly and happily, emerging from sadness, we may conclude with what I said in the beginning. His beliefs have remained with us and hence "there is no nothing".

POSTER SESSIONS

Preconcentration and Drying of Food Materials, edited by S. Bruin
Elsevier Science Publishers B.V., Amsterdam, 1988 — Printed in The Netherlands

295

AROMA RETENTION DURING AIR-DRYING OF POLYMER SOLUTIONS

A. VOILLEY

Laboratoire de Biologie Physico-Chimique, ENS.BANA, Campus Universitaire, 21100 Dijon (France)

ABSTRACT
In food products, volatiles in definite proportion and at very low concentration give a characteristic aroma. Changes in the composition during processing can be due to chemical reactions ; but in general, during drying, for example, the organoleptic quality is more affected by physical loss of aroma.
The aim of this work is to explain and try to predict the retention of some aroma compounds in model systems during air-drying. Model systems composed of water, five volatiles and substrates were used.
The behavior of volatiles during drying is different in presence of polyethylene glycols (PEG) or glucides and casein. With PEG, the retention decreases linearly with the water loss. With glucides or casein, the retention of volatiles is not negligible at the end of drying. There is a critical water content below which there is no more loss of volatiles. This phenomenon can be explained greatly by the theory of selective diffusion. At the end of drying, volatiles are trapped in the dried product by adsorption. In all cases, the same order of retention is observed.
Direct measurements of diffusivity and activity coefficients of volatiles were used to predict the aroma retention during drying. Other technique was developped in our laboratory to determine the interactions between aroma compounds and casein. Nature of interactions varies with the volatiles and the substrate.

INTRODUCTION

In food products, volatiles in definite proportion and at very low concentration give a characteristic aroma. Changes in the composition during processing can be due to chemical reactions ; but in general, during drying, for example, the organoleptic quality is more affected by physical loss of aroma. The aim of this work is to explain and try to predict the retention of some aroma compounds in model systems during air drying.

METHODS

Model systems composed of water, five volatiles (acetone, ethyl acetate, 2-propanol, diacetyl, n-hexanol) and substrates were used. The volatiles, each at 1000 ppm, were dissolved in concentrated solutions of polymers (glucides, polyethylene glycols or casein) with different molecular weights.

All the solutions were dried in the same experimental conditions in a laboratory drier.

- volatile diffusivity : the technique of concentration profile was used (Voilley, 1986).
- Activity coefficient of volatiles was measured at infinite dilution by inert gas

stripping method (Richon et al., 1985). Another technique equilibrium dialysis was tested to know the strenght of interaction between casein and volatiles (Farès, 1987).

RESULTS

The behavior of volatiles during drying is different in presence of polyethylene glycols (PEG) or glucides and casein.

With PEG, the retention of all volatiles decreases linearly with the water loss. With glucides or casein, the retention of volatiles is not negligible at the end of drying and can be explained by selective diffusion (Thijssen and Rulkens, 1968 ; Kerkhof, 1975) and different types of interactions ; for example, 3.4 moles of diacetyl are strongly fixed per mole of casein. For all substrates, the retention decreases in order : n-hexanol, 2-propanol, diacetyl, ethyl acetate and acetone.

All the results are explained by the diffusivity of the volatiles (which depends strongly on the water content) and the water activity at the surface of the product during air drying. During air drying, for a given relative humidity of the air, a_w at the interface is relatively constant (molar fraction of substrates = constant, for example 0.75). If molecular weight of the substrates increase, their mass fraction increase, mass fraction of water decreases and aroma retention decreases.

Substrates	retention (%) after drying of a solution at 50 % to 40 %		Diffusivity (D) $(x10^{10} m^2.s^{-1})$ water content : 50 % 30 %		$a_w = 0.75$ (25°C) water content (%)
PEG	600	47.3	5.89 (60°C)	8.7	24
	1500	52.8	4.90	-	11
	6000	60.9	3.39	8.7	4.5
	10000	60.7	-	8.4	4
	20000	68.9	2.65	-	5
	35000	67.2	-	8.4	2
Glucose		38.5	1.21 (25°C)	14.7	37
Maltose		71.0	1.25	11.7	15
MD 63		66.0	1.32	12.1	28
MD 33		74.5	1.17	-	20
MD 05		78.7	0.97	10.9	16.5

CONCLUSION

This work of aroma retention in different aqueous solutions during drying suggest the importance of : Characteristics of substrates. In presence of polyethylene glycols, the linear decrease of retention is explained by the PEG's fluidity. With glucides or casein, at the beginning of drying, the retention depends largely on water concentration ; below a critical value, the retention is constant. This phenomenon can be explained greatly by selective diffusion and interactions : Characteristics of volatiles. The same order of retention is related to molecular weight, solubility, volatility and diffusivity of aroma compounds.

Aroma retention as a function of water content can be simulated rather well with the variation of aroma activity and diffusivity.

REFERENCES

1. H.A.C. Thijssen and W.H. Rulkens. Retention of aromas in drying food liquids. De Ingenieur 80, 47, 1968, pp 45-56.
2. P.J.A.M. Kerkhof. A quantitative study of the effect of process variables on the retention of volatile trace components in drying. Thesis, Eindhoven, The Netherlands, 1975.
3. A. Voilley. Etude de la mobilité de solutés en milieux aqueux concentrés. Diffusivité et activité de composés volatils. Thèse d'Etat, Dijon, France, 1986.
4. K. Farès. Comportement de substances d'arôme dans des solutions de caséines. Thèse 3ème Cycle, Dijon, France, 1987.
5. D. Richon, F. Sorrentino, A. Voilley. Infinite dilution activity coefficients by inert gas stripping method : Extension to the study of viscous and foaming mixtures. Ind. Eng. Chem. Process Des. Dev. 24, 4, 1160-1165.

Preconcentration and Drying of Food Materials, edited by S. Bruin
Elsevier Science Publishers B.V., Amsterdam, 1988 — Printed in The Netherlands

THE CONDENSATION OF DILUTE VOLATILE FLAVOUR COMPOUND - WATER VAPOUR MIXTURES

R.J. CLARKE, Chichester, Sussex, U.K., PO20 7PW

SUMMARY

Volatile compounds in dilute mixtures with water vapour from stripping/condensation, are lost to varying degrees under conventional condensing conditions, especially vacuum, as pointed out by Thijssen. A practical equation for quantifying this loss for different conditions and volatile components of flavour interest, is presented. Brief reference is also made to a recently patented method of condensation with economic use of cooling water.

INTRODUCTION

The condensation of steam in power stations has been widely considered in the literature; but not of dilute mixtures of steam-noncondensible gases-volatile flavour compounds. The latter arise in various stripping and evaporative steps used in the food industry, especially fruit juices and coffee extracts, practised on the laboratory and large scale. Thijssen (1) considered the losses of volatile flavour compounds that can occur in condensation, though without exact quantification. Clarke and Wragg (2) presented a working equation for losses under different condensing conditions.

Such vapours can be condensed in a number of ways; 1), single stage condensation usually under vacuum (vacuum will be used in a stripping stage) with various coolants from cooling water to refrigerants; 2), two stage condensation, in which the major part of the water is condensed and removed at a relatively high temperature, followed by condensation at a lower temperature, as illustrated in a number of patents (3) for handling coffee volatiles; and 3), a two stage operation involving the use of cheap tower cooled water, generally still warm, followed by re-contacting with residual vapours/gases in an absorption column with condensate which has been further cooled by smaller quantities of more expensive chilled water at a lower temperature and a final condensate withdrawn. In this way, losses of volatile compounds are reduced in an economical manner (4).

CALCULATION OF PERCENTAGE LOSS OF VOLATILES TO ATMOSPHERE

The equation originally presented (2) has been slightly modified for litre/kg units. The losses of volatile compounds in a typical condensing system decreases with a higher pressure in the condenser, but obviously increases with a higher temperature, and higher quantity of vent gases, and is of course related to the volatility characteristics of the compound in question. The percentage loss is given by,

$$\frac{7.35 \times k_{j\omega} \times A/B \times 10^{-4}}{7.35 \times k_{j\omega} \times A/B \times 10^{-4} + 1} \times 100\%$$

where $K_{j\omega}$ is the air-water partition coefficient of a volatile compound (j), which is related to the relative volatility, usually taken at infinite dilution (α); and A/B, the ratio of the pumping rate of non-condensible gases at NTP (litres per sec) and condensation rate of liquid (kg per sec). A loss of 40% of such a compound as acetone ($k_{j\omega}$ = 8.8) at 25°C from a dilute steam-vapour stream is indicated where equilibrium condensation is occurring at this temperature, under a pressure of 203 Hg Abs. pressure, when the pumping rate is 30 litres per min and condensation rate, 0.25kg per min.

For any particular condensation rate, it is clearly desirable to lower the temperature as far as possible (economics of cooling water), to reduce the volume of non-condensible gases (e.g. reduce leakage in the system) and to increase the pressure (but this is usually determined by that in the preceding stripping/evaporating stage).

REFERENCES

1. Bomben, J.L., Bruin, S., Thijssen, H.A.C., and Merson, L., in C.O.Chichester (Ed.), Advances in Food Research, Vol. 20, Academic Press, New York, 1973, p. 32,
2. Clarke, R.J. and Wragg, A., in C. Canterelli and C. Peri (Eds.), Progress in Food Engineering, Forster-Verlag, Kusnacht, 1983, pp 519-21,
3. GB patent 1 366 331 (1978), Nestle,
4. GB patent 2 086 743B (1983), A. Wragg and J.C. Healey, General Foods Ltd.

Preconcentration and Drying of Food Materials, edited by S. Bruin
Elsevier Science Publishers B.V., Amsterdam, 1988 — Printed in The Netherlands

MODELING HOLLOW-FIBER ULTRAFILTRATION WITH CONCENTRATION-DEPENDENT
THERMODYNAMIC AND TRANSPORT EFFECTS

C. H. GOODING and Y. S. HSU
Chemical Engineering Department, Clemson University, Clemson, SC 29634 USA

SUMMARY
    A numerical solution of the continuity equation is used to model mass
transfer on the inside of a hollow-fiber ultrafilter. Allowances are made for
the concentration dependencies of osmotic pressure, viscosity, and solute
diffusivity. The model yields solute concentration profiles and permeate
fluxes for steady or unsteady conditions. Feed solute concentration, flow
rate, and pressure as well as fiber dimensions can be changed to study their
effects. Comparison of flux predictions with experimental results for a protein system indicate good agreement, but more experimental data are needed
for further validation. Once it is more thoroughly tested, the model can be
used to study osmotic limitations and gel formation in hollow-fiber systems.

INTRODUCTION AND OBJECTIVES
    The overall purpose of this work is to develop an ultrafiltration model
that can be used to aid in the design and application of hollow-fiber systems.
To be of maximum use the model should rigorously account for fluid dynamics,
convective and diffusive mass transfer, and solution thermodynamics. It should
predict permeate fluxes under steady or unsteady conditions, and it should
predict solute concentration profiles, which can be used with solubility data
to evaluate the likelihood of gel formation. To do this the model must be
capable of representing the system under conditions in which the solute
becomes relatively concentrated. This requires taking into account the concentration dependencies of osmotic pressure, solution viscosity, and solute
diffusivity.

MODEL EQUATIONS AND SOLUTION
    The primary equation to be solved is

$$\frac{\partial C}{\partial T} + U\frac{\partial C}{\partial Z} + V\frac{\partial C}{\partial R} = \frac{1}{R}\frac{\partial}{\partial R}\left(\frac{R}{Pe}\frac{\partial C}{\partial R}\right) \qquad (1)$$

which is the solute continuity equation in dimensionless form. Equation (1)
does not assume constant diffusivity as did an earlier version of the model
(ref. 1). The initial and boundary conditions, the laminar velocity profiles,
and the permeation velocity equations used in the earlier work are retained.
Osmotic pressure and axial pressure drop are taken into account. The constant
viscosity assumption in the velocity profiles can be relaxed for axial steps
through the fiber to allow for concentration effects, but this has little
effect on the results.
    The model is solved numerically using a finite difference approach. Specifi-
cally, modified centered difference analogs are written for the axial and time

derivatives. The radial diffusion term with concentration-dependent diffusivity is split into three terms by the product rule of differentiation. The radial first derivative coefficients are then grouped, and modified Crank-Nicolson analogs are written for both the first and second radial derivatives. The numerical solution is accomplished at each axial step of each time increment by estimating the permeation velocity and radial concentration profile and iterating to convergence by direct substitution. Split axial and radial grids are used to handle the steep concentration profiles near the fiber entrance and near the membrane.

RESULTS

Experimental data reported by Wendt, et al. (ref. 2) for bovine albumin concentration were used to test the model. A major limitation to the model verification using these data was uncertainty in the dependence of protein diffusivity on concentration. Two literature sources report opposite trends (refs. 3 and 4), one indicating that diffusivity increases with concentration and the other that it decreases. Given this discrepancy, an empirical diffusivity-concentration expression was fit to one set of data at constant feed concentration and velocity but varying transmembrane pressure drop. The expression indicated an increase in diffusivity with concentration, consistent with the data of Phillies, et al. (ref. 3). The other data at different feed conditions were then predicted using the same diffusivity expression. The results were satisfactory over a range of feed concentrations from 5 to 195 g/l, feed velocities from 0.7 to 1.4 cm/s, and pressure drops up 0.9 atm. The model also yields radial and axial concentration profiles that indicate surface solute concentrations up to several times the bulk average.

CONCLUSIONS

A model and solution technique have been developed to rigorously account for fluid dynamics, convective and diffusive mass transfer, and solution thermodynamics in a laminar flow, hollow-fiber ultrafiltration unit. The model predicts permeate flux as a function of axial position and radial as well as axial solute concentration profiles. It can also be used to model unsteady-state conditions. The model has been tested successfully with one data set, but uncertainty in the diffusivity-concentration relationship prevented complete verification. Additional data are needed to further verify the flux prediction capabilty and to test the model as a tool to distinguish between osmotic flux reduction and gel resistance.

REFERENCES

1 R.P. Ma, C.H. Gooding, and W.K. Alexander, A dynamic model for low-pressure, hollow-fiber ultrafiltration, AIChE J., 31 (1985) 1728-1732.
2 R.P. Wendt, E. Klein, F.F. Holland, and K.E. Eberle, Hollow-fiber ultrafiltration of calf serum and albumin in the pregel uniform-wall-flux region, Chem. Engrg. Commun., 8 (1981) 251-262.
3 G.D.J. Phillies, G.B. Benedek, and N.A. Mazar, Diffusion in protein solutions at high concentrations: a study by quasielastic light scattering spectroscopy, J. Chem. Phys., 65 (1976) 1883-1892.
4 K.H. Keller, E.R. Canales, and S.I. Yum, Tracer and mutual diffusion coefficients of proteins, J. Phys. Chem., 75 (1971) 379-387.

Preconcentration and Drying of Food Materials, edited by S. Bruin
Elsevier Science Publishers B.V., Amsterdam, 1988 — Printed in The Netherlands

MASS TRANSFER IN OSMOTIC PROCESSES

M. Le MAGUER[1] and R.N. BISWAL[2]

[1]Food Science Department, The University of Alberta, Edmonton, Alberta, Canada, T6G 2P5

[2]Food Technology and Science Department, The University of Tennessee, P.O. Box 1671, Knoxville, TN 37901, U.S.A.

SUMMARY

Multicomponent mass transfer in a dehydrocooling process has been modeled using the principles of thermodynamics of irreversible processes. The relationship between the individual fluxes and the independent forces has been found to be non-linear.

INTRODUCTION

Partial dehydration of vegetables and fruits using various osmotic agents has been studied by several workers. In our study, the aqueous freezant AF(15-15) (15% NaCl and 15% ethanol in water) has been used (Ref. 1).

Most of the diffusional mass transfer studies on food systems reported in the literature deal with either binary processes (Fick's law description) or assume independence of the movement of each species in multicomponent systems (Ref. 2,3,4,5,6). To our best knowledge, the only literature to date in food systems where interaction between components has been taken into account is that of Chandrasekar and King (Ref. 7). Their study of the multicomponent diffusion in a ternary system of sugar ethanol and water was based on the thermodynamics of irreversible processes (Ref. 8,9).

Our model uses the same principles to characterize the diffusional mass transfer. As a first approximation, the system has been analysed on a pseudo-ternary basis. The three components of interest are (1) the solute (NaCl or ethanol), (2) the solvent (water), and (3) the total solids (non-salt). It has been assumed that there is no interaction between the total solids and the internal solution, so that the physical and thermodynamic properties of the aqueous solutions are obtainable on a pseudo-binary basis.

MATHEMATICAL MODELING

Flux and Forces

Non-linear relations. A pseudolinear form as suggested by Sauer (Ref. 10) to represent the non-linear relation between the flux and the forces is the following:

$$J_i(\alpha,Y_j) = \sum_{k=0}^{n} L_{ik} (\alpha,Y_j) \times Y_k$$

where the phenomenological coefficients L_{ik} are a function of the reference state α and the forces Y_j. These coefficients are regarded as the generalized Onsager coefficient, and they do possess the symmetry property. As shown in Eq. 1.70 of Sauer (1973) L_{ik} can be expressed as a polynomial in Y_j.

These models have been used to estimate the phenomenological coefficients for mass transfer in a dehydrocooling contacter using carrots as the working materials.

EXPERIMENTAL METHODS

Carrots (cultivar Gold Pak) were hand peeled, trimmed at both ends, and cut into 1 cm cubes. The cubes were graded, washed, and standardized by soaking them in tap water for one hour (full turgor). Experiments were conducted using salt-water and ethanol-water solutions separately.

The designated time levels were 0, 5, 15, 45 and 60 minutes, at which time the following measurements were taken: (1) mass of carrots, (2) mass of solution, (3) weight fraction of salt/ethanol in carrots, (4) weight fraction of water in carrots, (5) weight fraction of salt/ethanol in the solution, and (6) density of solution.

VALIDATION OF MODEL

The diffusional fluxes $(kg/m^2.s)$ with respect to a volume average velocity were calculated. Assuming paroblic concentration profiles for salt and water, Y_1 and Y_2 were calculated. Information on surface concentrations of salt and water in carrots was obtained experimentally by equilibrating carrot cubes with salt solutions. Parameters of the non-linear were obtained and the following two equations represent the fluxes for salt and water respectively:

$$J_1 = -\left[0.012(X_1) + 0.00002 (X_2)^2 + 0.00004 (X_1)(X_2)\right]*10^{-4}$$
$$J_2 = \left[-0.036(X_2) - 0.03 (X_1) + 0.00022 (X_2)^2 + 0.0127 (X_1)^2 + 0.00306(X_1)(X_2)\right]$$
$$*10^{-4}$$

REFERENCES

1 M. Le Maguer and R.N. Biswal, Some engineering properties of aqueous solutions of ethanol and sodium chloride, Engineering and Food - 85 (in press), (M. Le Maguer and P. Jelen, Eds.), Elsevier Applied Science Publishers, London and New York (1985).
2 I.J. Pflug, P.J. Fellers and D. Gurevitz, Diffusion rate in desalting of pickles, Food Technology, 21 (1967) 1635-1638.

3 F.R. Del Valle and J.T.R. Nickerson, Studies on salting and drying of fish, II, Dynamic aspects of the salting of fish, Journal of Food Science, 32 (1967) 218-224.
4 L.C. Menting, B. Hoogstad and H.A.C. Thijssen, Diffusion coefficients of water and organic volatiles in carbohydrate systems, J. Food Technology 5 (1970) 111-126.
5 T.J. Geurts, P. Walstra and H. Mulder, Transport of salt and water during salting of cheese, 1, Analysis of the process involved, Neth. Milk Dairy J. 28 (1974) 102-129.
6 T.J. Geurts, P. Walstra and H. Mulder, Transport of salt and water during salting of cheese, 2, Quantities of salt taken up and moisture lost, Neth. Milk Dairy J. 34 (1980) 229-254.
7 S.K. Chandrasekaran and C.J. King, Multicomponent diffusion and vapor-liquid equilibria of dilute organic components in aqueous sugar solutions, AIChE Journal 8(3) (1972) 513-519.
8 D.G. Miller, Thermodynamics of irreversible processes, Chem. Rev. 60 (1960) 15-37
9 S. Wisniewski, B. Staniszewski and R. Szymanik, Thermodynamics of Non-equilibrium Processes, D. Reidel Publishing Company, Dordrecht-Holland/ Boston (1976).
10 F. Sauer, Non equilibrium thermodynamics of kidney tubule transport. In: Handbook of Physiology, Sec. 8, Renal physiology (appendix), J. Orloff and R.W. Berliner, Eds., Amer. Physiol. Soc. (1973) pp. 399-414.

Preconcentration and Drying of Food Materials, edited by S. Bruin
Elsevier Science Publishers B.V., Amsterdam, 1988 — Printed in The Netherlands

OSMOTIC PRECONCENTRATION OF CARROT TISSUE FOLLOWED BY CONVECTION DRYING

A. LENART and P. P. LEWICKI

Department of Food Technology, Warsaw Agricultural University
02-766 Warsaw, ul. Nowoursynowska 166 (Poland)

SUMMARY
    The kinetics of the osmotic dehydration of carrot in a stationary system
using selected osmoticactive substances was analysed. In the experiments reported here, optimum conditions for osmotic dehydration of carrot have been established, as a pretreatment before convection drying. Solutions of hydrolyzed starch
syrup, saccharose, glucose and sodium chloride were used. Initial osmotic dehydration shortens drying time depending on the kind of osmoticactive substance
used, the time of osmotic preconcentration and final water content of the dried
product. Osmo-convection drying is significantly more effective than the convection drying itself, in the range of certain final water content of dried
material.

INTRODUCTION
    The osmotic dehydration can be use to reduce water content of materials to
30-70% of the original amount and leads to a modification of the chemical composition of the dry matter. Water activity of the material is also reduced but do
not drops below 0.9. Because of this osmotically dehydrated food at longer storage periods calls for an additional preservation procedure (ref. 1-3).
    The aim of the work was to analyse the kinetic of the osmotic dehydration of
carrot using selected osmoticactive substances. Optimum conditions for process
have been established, as a pretreatment befor convection drying. Apart form
that, influence of a kind of osmoticactive substance on the convection drying
rate was analysed.

METHODS
    Carrot of "Nantejska" variety was used as a material of investigations. The
following osmoticactive substances were used: hydrolyzed starch syrup, saccharose, glucose and sodium chloride. The osmotic dehydration was done at a temperature of 30°C and the time range from 0.5 to 10.0 hours. Convection drying of
the pretreated material was done in the cabinet dryer, at a temperature of 80°C
and air velocity 1.6 m/s with the single layer of carrot cubes spread on the
screen. The change of mass, water content and water activity in the carrot were
determined. The results were used to calculate the osmoticactive substance diffusion and dehydration rate (ref. 3-4).

RESULTS

The osmotic dehydration of carrot is accompanied by the penetration of osmoticactive substances into the dehydrated tissue. Independently of the kind of
the applied osmoticactive substance the amount of the removed water always sur-
pass the amount of the substance which penetrated the tissue. The most advantageous relation between water loss and solid gain was found in carrot dehydrated
in a starch syrup. The least advantageous one is the case of dehydration in
sodium chloride solution. The osmotic dehydration of carrot proceeds most intensively during the first hours of the process. For carrot dehydrated in a
saccharose solution a decrease of water content from 6.5 to 1.2 g/g d.m. and
water activity from 0.985 to 0.950 is observed after 3 hours. In the case of
the dehydration carried out in a sodium chloride solution, however, the water
content decreases to 2.7 g/g d.m. and water activity decreases to 0.960 during
0.5 hour.

In a convection drying, following initial osmotic preconcentration, no constant rate period of drying was observed. Initial osmotic dehydration in sugar
solution decreases the rate of convection drying by 20-40% as compared with drying rate of raw carrot. Starch syrup decreases drying rate of carrot even more.
No significant influence of osmotic dehydration in sodium chloride solution on
drying rate of carrot has been found.

Initial osmotic dehydration shortens drying time by 10-60% depending on the
kind of osmotic substance used, the time of osmotic preconcentration and final
water content.

CONCLUSIONS

Osmotic preconcentration of carrot affects the course of convection drying
of the material. Time of osmotic dehydration and kind of osmoticactive substance
have a significant influence on the kinetic of osmo-convection drying. The optimum time for osmotic dehydration of carrot, as a pretreatment before convection
drying, is 2-3 hours at temperature 30°C and the best osmoactive substances are
saccharose and starch syrup.

REFERENCES

1 C. R. Lerici, G. Pinnavaia, M. Dalla Rosa and L. Bartolucci, Osmotic dehydration of fruit. Influence of osmotic agents on drying behaviour and product
   quality, J. Food Sci., 50 (1985) 1217-1219.
2 M. Tomasicchino, R. Andreotti, A. De Giorgi, Desidratazione parziale della
   frutta per osmosi, Ind. Conserve, 61(2) (1986) 108-114.
3 A. Lenart, J. M. Flink, Osmotic concentration of potato. I. Criteria for the
   end-point of the osmosis process, J. Food Technol., 19 (1984) 65-89.
4 G. Mazza, Dehydration of carrot. Effects of pre-drying treatments on moisture
   transport and product quality, J. Food Technol., 18 (1983) 113-123.

HEAT TRANSFER IN A SCRAPED SURFACE HEAT EXCHANGER OPERATING IN THE TURBULENT
FLOW REGIME

R. DE GOEDE and E.J. DE JONG

Delft University of Technology, Laboratory for Process Equipment,
Leeghwaterstraat 44, 2628 CA Delft (The Netherlands)

SUMMARY
    The heat transfer properties of a scraped surface heat exchanger operating in
the turbulent region have been investigated. Comparison of experimental data
with a model based on penetration theory learnt that the measured enhancement
due to the scraper action is much stronger than the enhancement according to the
model. This effect is probably due to the induction of vortices by the moving
scraper blades. The amount of scaling turned out to be independent of scraper
rotational speed and throughput.

OBJECTIVES

    Investigation of heat transfer phenomena in a scraped surface heat exchanger
used in a paraxylene crystallization process.

MODELLING OF HEAT TRANSFER

    In the literature, a theoretical approach for the heat transfer coefficient
has been found only for laminar flow in axial direction [1]. This description is
based on penetration theory and the resulting equation is:

$$\alpha = \frac{2}{\sqrt{\pi}} (\lambda \rho \, C_p \, n \, N)^{0.5} \tag{1}$$

with λ, ρ, C_p respectively the thermal conductivity, density and heat capacity
of the process medium and n and N being the number of rows of scraper blades and
the rotational frequency.

    In the case of crystallization of p-xylene the flow is turbulent in axial di-
rection (Re $\approx 10^5$) which implies that equation (1) can not be used here. A model
has been developed based on the following assumptions: (i) The laminar boundary
layer is completely removed by the scraper action. (ii) Heat transfer can be
described by penetration theory until the laminar boundary layer has been penetrated; (iii) After penetration of the laminar boundary layer the situation is
identical with turbulent pipe flow until the next scraper action.
This leads to the following equation:

$$\alpha \, (\phi_v, N) = \frac{\lambda \rho \, C_p \, n \, N}{\pi \, \alpha_t \, (\phi_v)} + \alpha_t \, (\phi_v) \tag{2}$$

    In equation (2) $\alpha_t \, (\phi_v)$ represents the heat transfer coefficient for turbu-
lent pipe flow which only depends on the volumetric throughput ϕ_v for a given
configuration and given physical properties of the medium. For this quantity the

approximation proposed by Gnielinski [2] has been used.

The formation of a crystal layer on the wall results in an additional resistance against heat transfer. The total resistance at the xylene side can be regarded as the sum of hydrodynamic and scaling resistance according to [4,5]

$$\frac{1}{\alpha_x} = \frac{1}{\alpha(\phi_v, N)} + \frac{d_{cr}}{\lambda_{cr}} \tag{3}$$

with α_x the inside heat transfer coefficient, d_{cr} the thickness of the crystal layer and λ_{cr} the thermal conductivity of the layer.

EXPERIMENTAL

A scraped surface heat exchanger consists of two coaxial cylinders. The coolant flows throught the annular space. An axis equipped with scraper blades is mounted in the inner cylinder. The blades are pressed against the wall by springs.

A bench-scale unit with a length of 1 m, axis ϕ = 30 mm, inner cylinder inside ϕ = 50 mm has been used to determine the influence of flow and scraper rotational speed on $\alpha(\phi_v, N)$. A pilot plant unit with L = 6 m, ϕ axis = 75 mm and inside cylinder ϕ of 207.2 mm has been used to investigate the influence of the process variables on scaling.

RESULTS AND DISCUSSION

A comparison between bench-scale data and equation (2) has been presented in figure 1. It appears that Gnielinski's equation gives an adequate description in the situation with non-moving scraper blades. The enhancement due to the scraper action turns out to be much more pronounced than the model predicts; this is probably due to the induction of vortices by the movement of the scraper blades.

The thickness of the crystal layer has been presented in figures 2a and 2b. No significant dependence on scraper rotational speed and flow rate seems to exist, but the thickness of the crystal layer appears to depend strongly on the wall temperature T_w. This effect is due to crystal growth phenomena at the solid-liquid interface.

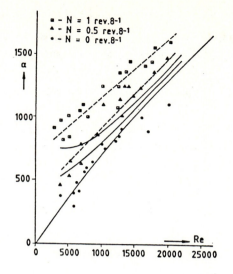

Fig. 1. A comparison between eq. (2) and
experimental data
——————— eq. (2)
----------- fit through experimental data

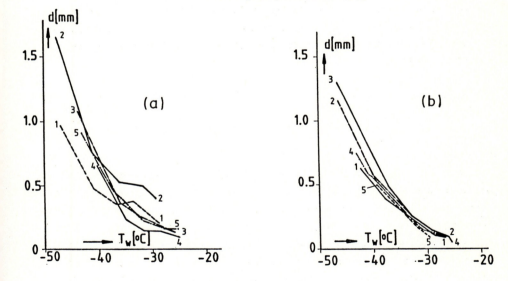

Fig. 2. The heat transfer coefficient as a function of the wall temperature at
five different flow rates at N = 0 (a) and N = 35 (b) (rev. min^{-1}).

312

REFERENCES

1. Latinen, A.G., Chem. Eng. Sci. $\underline{9}$ (1958) pp. 263.
2. VDI - Wärmeatlas, Berechnungsblätter für den Wärmeübergang, Düsseldorf, VDI Verlag.
3. R. de Goede, A.B. Hadimoeljono, E.J. de Jong, to be published.
4. R. de Goede, J.L.E.M. Polet, E.J. de Jong, to be published.
5. R. de Goede, Thesis, Delft University of Technology, in preparation.

Preconcentration and Drying of Food Materials, edited by S. Bruin
Elsevier Science Publishers B.V., Amsterdam, 1988 — Printed in The Netherlands

DETERMINATION OF WATER DIFFUSIVITY IN MODEL GELS OF POLYACRYLAMIDE STUDIED BY OSCILLATORY SORPTION EXPERIMENTS

A. CAIRAULT; H. BIZOT and M. ROQUES[*]
L.P.C.M., I.N.R.A., Rue de la Géraudière, 44072 Nantes, France
[*] L.P.C.I., E.N.S.I.C., 1 rue Grandville, 54042 Nancy, France

SUMMARY
      A polyacrylamide gel was used as a model for the study of the drying behavior of non-porous and swelling materials, simulating food products. The following oscillatory diffusion experiment was devised to analyze the water transfert within the polymer: an electronic microbalance was used to measure the weight of a polyacrylamide gel sphere placed in an oscillatory humidity air stream controlled by a bithermic loop. The observed periodic steady state indicated the fickian diffusion domains, the influence of concentration on the diffusion coefficient, and the relaxation of the polymer matrix.

INTRODUCTION

      In order to obtain a better insight about the specific behavior of swelling gels in drying processes, a model synthetic gel of polyacrylamide has been chosen for its non-spoiling, non-ageing, and non-melting capabilities, as opposed to common biogels like gelatin (ref.1) or starch films (ref.2). A newly proposed oscillatory sorption technique (ref.3) has been applied and improved to determine water diffusivities, while avoiding transitory perturbed regimes and allowing future viscoelastic analysis of diffusion.

MODEL GEL CHARACTERISTICS

      Free radical polymerization of solution of 50% w.w. acrylamide and 0.03% w.w. of bisacrylamide (crosslinker) at 10˚C, produced a strong rubbery material containing 538% H_2O d.b. upon natural swelling in pure water at 25˚C. The intimate network structure corresponds most likely to a very entangled but scarcely crosslinked matrix. The sorption behavior of this material is similar to common food polysaccharides or proteins gels (ref.4) with a hysteresis loop present up to $a_w \approx 0.7$ at 25˚C (fig.1). The closure point corresponds to a clear change of state between glassy and rubbery domains commonly found in amorphous polymers, but occuring here at an interrelated set of temperature-concentration values, in connection with the plasticizing effect of water (ref.5). Thin shells (e=0.5mm) of gel have been molded on the surface of glass spheres (⌀=6mm) to allow isotropic shrinkage.

PRINCIPLE AND INTERPRETATION OF OSCILLATORY SORPTION

      The principle of diffusion experiments under oscillatory conditions consists in analysing the mass response of a sorbate submitted to time dependent sinusoidal variations of surface concentration. Easier interpretation is obtained from the analysis of the steady periodic regime. This method avoids uncertainties linked to the transitory phase; the uniform frequency imposed to every regions of the material eases the interpretation in terms of characteristic relaxation times (ref.6).

Presently we limit the analysis to a classical fickian description and for each oscillation, we assume that the amplitudes are small enough to neglect volume changes, and that sorption isotherms can be approximated by a linear relationship over the span of each experiment: $C(Re,t)=K1 \cdot p(t)+K2$ with Re=external radius of the sphere; $C(r,t)$=water concentration; $p(t)$=pressure; K1, K2=constants at $\theta °C$.

Second Ficks'law written in spherical coordinates for isotropic media with constant diffusivity (D) writes (ref.7): $(\partial^2 C/\partial r^2)+(2/r) \cdot (\partial C/\partial r)=(1/D) \cdot (\partial C/\partial t)$ the boundary conditions being: $(\partial C/\partial r)_{r=R0}=0$ at the inner surface of the isolated spherical shell and $C(Re,t)=Ci+Ac \cdot \sin(\omega \cdot t)$ for the surface imposed concentration change, with Ci=mean concentration; Ac=concentration amplitude ω=angular frequency.

After decomposing the total mass changes into a transient (Mt) and a steady periodic (Me) contribution, we obtain: $Me(t)=Am \cdot \sin(\omega \cdot t+\psi)$ with Am=mass amplitude and ψ=phase angle. The method of complex concentrations yields upon solving the differential equation: $tg(\psi)=I/R$ with $\nu=\sqrt{\omega/2D}$,

L=Re-R0; (ch,sh,cos,sin) being fonctions of $(2 \cdot \nu \cdot L)$ in:

$I=2\nu^3 R0^2 Re(-sh+sin)-2\nu^2 R0L(ch+cos)-\nu L(sh+cos)+R0\nu(sh+sin)+ch-cos$

$R=2\nu^3 R0^2 Re(sh+sin)+2\nu^2 R0Re(ch-cos)+\nu L(sh-sin)+R0\nu(sh-sin)$

Diffusivities are then deduced from the phase angle ψ.

EXPERIMENTAL LAYOUT

Mass changes were measured by an electronic microbalance (CAHN R 100) protected from unwanted sorption in its mechanism. Based on the bithermal relative humidity regulation principle, a controlled steam of moist air was circulated around the suspended sample (ref.8). A microcomputer (Apple II) monitored parameters such as temperature, R.H. and mass, together with vapor pressure changes, through temperature controllers for the boiler and the sample environment.

RESULTS

The phase shift angle between pressure and mass responses are better calculated from integration over a complete cycle ($T=2 \cdot \pi/\omega$) than by fitting procedures. The following equations are used (ref.3): $cos\psi=|A/(B \cdot C)^{1/2}|$ where $A=\int_t^{t+T}p(t') \cdot Me(t')dt'$; $B=\int_t^{t+T}p(t')^2dt'$; $C=\int_t^{t+T}Me(t')^2dt'$. Using a period of 5400 sec, and amplitude of 0.05 a_w at 40°C, the water mutual diffusion coefficients calculated for our polyacrylamide gel give similar results as those reported for gelatin $D\approx10^{-11}$ m^2/s (ref.1)(fig.2). However, since distortions in the mass response appear near and over the glass transition domain, a non-fickian treatment (ref.9) incorporating the viscoelastic characteristics of the material (shear modulus and relaxation times) becomes necessary. Moreover, the differences observed between samples originally conditioned in sorption or desorption show a clear influence of hysteresis which may eventually be connected to shifts in maxima of diffusivity-concentration relations.

CONCLUSION

Covalent polyacrylamide gels are good models for the study of food gels behavior during drying processes, although they shrink isotropically. Viscoelastic diffusion studies have recently become more accessible to experiment and also to theoretical analysis particularly using oscillatory sorption. An automatized sorption equipment as used here allows such studies as well as measurement of isosteres, of frequency induced transitions and of pseudo-equilibrium stability.

ACKNOWLEDGMENT

This work was supported by G.R.E.C.O.72 and M.R.E.S. n° 86 G 0707 research contracts.

REFERENCES

1 D.Gehrmann and W.Kast, First Int.Drying Symp., Ed.Mujumdar, (1978), 239-246.
2 B.P.Fish, Food Investigation Technical Paper, H.M.S.O., London, (1957).
3 J.S.Vrentas, J.L.Duda, S.T.Ju and L.W.NI, J.of Memb. Sci., 18, (1984), 161-175.
4 H.A.Iglesias and J.Chirife, "Handbook of food isotherms", Academic Press, (1982).
5 L.Slade and H.Levine, "Water as plasticiser". In"Water Science Review", 3,
   Cambridge Univ.Press.F.Franks Ed. (in preparation), (1987).
6 J.S.Vrentas, J.L.Duda and W.J.Huang, Macromolecules, 19, 6, (1986), 1718-1724.
7 J.Crank, "Mathematics of Diffusion", 2nd ed., Oxford Univ.Press, London, (1975).
8 W.Bolliger, S.Gal and R.Signer, Helv.Chim.Acta, 55, 7, (1972), 2659-2663.
9 C.J.Durning and M.Tabor, Macromolecules, 19, 8, (1986), 2220-2232.

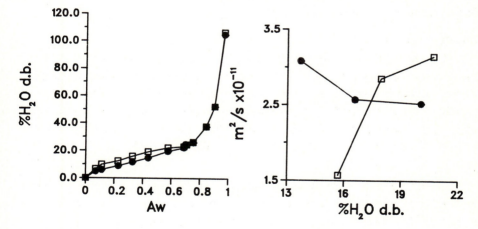

Fig.1.Isotherm of polyacrylamide gel (50%) at 25°C.
○ sorption
□ desorption

Fig.2.Water diffusion coefficient of polyacrylamide gel (50%) at 40°C.
○ sorption
□ desorption

Preconcentration and Drying of Food Materials, edited by S. Bruin
Elsevier Science Publishers B.V., Amsterdam, 1988 — Printed in The Netherlands

EVALUATION OF DIFFUSION COEFFICIENTS IN A SHRINKING SYSTEM.

V. GEKAS, Y. MOTARJEMI, I. LAMBERG and B. HALLSTRÖM
Department of Food Engineering, University of Lund, P.O.Box 124, S-221 00 Lund
(Sweden)

INTRODUCTION

The present study is concerned with the analysis of the diffusion coefficient
in shrinking systems. We first analyze and compare the Crank and the Fish-
Danckwerts approaches and then we present our own proposal to correct the diffusion coefficient for the shrinkage.

The Crank approach

Crank[1] introduces a moving coordinate system, following the volume change
rate of the medium. Both diffusion and volume change occur in one (and the same)
direction. The constant-mass diffusion coefficient, D^M, defined in this coordinate system, is proved to be related to the constant-volume diffusion coefficient, D^V, as follows:

$$\frac{D^M}{D^V} = \left(\frac{\text{Total-mass basic volume}}{\text{Total actual volume}}\right)^2 \tag{1}$$

The total-mass basic volume is expressed as $(A+B)V_B^0$, where: A is the mass of the
diffusing substance (example: water). B is the mass of the medium (example: dry
substance). V_B^0 is the specific volume of the medium in its dry condition.
$(A+B) V_B^0$ then, would be the initial total volume if the medium had the same
specific volume as the water. Furthermore, D^M remains independent of the volume
change during an experiment.

The Fish-Danckwerts approach

A 'pseudo' diffusion coefficient, D_ψ, is defined in a moving (following shrinkage) coordinate system. Uni-axial diffusion is assumed while the volume change
occurs isotropically in three dimensions. D_ψ is proved to be related to the proper diffusion coefficient, D_{proper}, as follows:

$$\frac{D_\psi}{D_{proper}} = \left(\frac{\text{Volume of dry substance}}{\text{Total actual volume}}\right)^{2/3} \tag{2}$$

If the volume change is uniaxial, then the exponent 2/3 should be replaced by 2. $D_{\bar{\psi}}$ is also independent from shrinkage during an experiment.

While the two approaches have much in common, there is an important difference: While Crank uses the total basic volume (A+B) V_B^o, Fish-Danckwerts use the dry medium volume B V_B^o as the reference basic volume. Therefore $D_{\bar{\psi}}$ and D^M are not the same.

Our proposal

The above approaches make use of ratios of volumes and this leads to different forms of eqs (1) and (2), depending on the kind of volume change.

To overcome this problem, we define the diffusion coefficient of reference, D^*, as follows:

$$\frac{D^*}{D} = (\frac{\text{Initial thickness}}{\text{Actual thickness}})^2 \equiv (\frac{\ell_i}{\ell_t})^2 \tag{3}$$

D corresponds to D^V of Crank or D_{proper} of Fish. Use of eq (3) can be extented in cases of any kind of volume change, provided that diffusion is uniaxial.

It can be shown that a relationship between the ratio of thickness and the volume change ratio exists having the general formula

$$(\frac{\ell_i}{\ell_t})^2 = (\frac{V_i}{V_t})^{2/n} \tag{4}$$

V_i is the initial total volume, V_t the final total volume and n a factor varying in the range 0-3.

At values of n=1 and 3, similar relationships to those derived by Crank and Fish-Danckwerts, are obtained.

We have followed the shrinkage of slabs of minced meat and potato during drying. Our study shows that the thickness of the slab as well as the surface area decrease considerably with decreasing moisture content. On the table below we present the extent of the decrease of the thickness $(\frac{\ell_i}{\ell_t})$ at a moisture content of 1g/g dry matter and also the effect of this shrinkage on the diffusion coefficient. D^*, the diffusion coefficient of reference, is estimated from the solution of second law of Fick and D is obtained through eq (3).

Furthermore, the value n in the table shows that the shrinkage is anisotropic and three-dimensional.

TABLE

Examples of diffusion coefficients

	Temp. $^{\circ}C$	$\dfrac{\ell_i}{\ell_t}$	D* $10^{10}m^2/s$	D $10^{10}m^2/s$	n
Raw minced beef	30	1.63	1.6	0.6	2.48
	40	1.54	1.9	0.8	2.3
Heat treated beef	30	1.19	2.0	1.4	2.4
	40	1.17	2.2	1.6	2.2
Unblanched potato	60	2.24	-	-	1.8
Blanched potato	60	2.75	8.0	1.1	1.5

REFERENCES

1 J. Crank, Some mathematical diffusion studies relevant to dehydration. In
   Fundamental Aspects of the Dehydration of Foodstuffs, Soc. Chem. Ind., London,
   1958, pp. 37-41.
2 B.P. Fish, Diffusion and thermodynamic of water in potato starch. Fundamental
   Aspects of the Dehydration of Foodstuffs, Soc. of Chem. Ind., London, 1958,
   pp. 143-157.

Preconcentration and Drying of Food Materials, edited by S. Bruin
Elsevier Science Publishers B.V., Amsterdam, 1988 — Printed in The Netherlands

DIFUSION IN SYSTEMS WITH MULTIDIRECTIONAL SHRINKAGE

PASCUAL E. VIOLLAZ[1]

[1]Departamento de Industrias, Facultad de Ciencias Exactas y
Naturales, Ciudad Universitaria, (1428) Buenos Aires, Argentina

SUMMARY

The differential equation which predicts the diffusant
variation as a function of time, for a slab with unidirectional
diffusion but multidirectional shrinkage, is given and its
numerical solution presented. The variation in the lateral area
(with the corresponding increase in the dry halfthickness) is a
very important parameter which can cause the appearance of a
second falling drying rate as well as erratic results, owing to
different shrinkage behaviour as a function of time.

INTRODUCTION

The traditional approach in studying diffusion in shrinking or
swelling bodies is to use Fick's second law with concentration of
diffusant expressed on a dry basis. But, the diffusion coefficients
obtained from this model, have been difficult to understand and
have lead to seemingly anomalous results. The main anomalies are:
1) Erratic results that vary greatly from study to study
2) Drying rates that vary with the first or the second power of the
   drying slab.
3) Different diffusion coefficient for absortion or desorption.
4) Very low values of the diffusion coefficients, characteristic
   of diffusion in liquid phase, but presure effects that suggest
   vapor phase diffusion.

In view of the above mentioned difficulties of drying theory, it
was felt that a careful revision of the basic differential equation
of drying by a diffusional mechanism was in order. From previous
works, Viollaz and Suarez[1] and Viollaz and Suarez[2], it appears
that Sherwood's differential equation (Sherwood[3],1929), is not
correct for a shrinking or swelling body. In order to explain these
anomalies it was proposed to use Fick's second law with a variable
domain of integration, which for an infinite slab becomes:

$$\partial \rho_A / \partial \theta = D \partial^2 \rho_A / \partial^2 x \tag{1}$$

where ρ_A is the concentration of diffusant (which will be assumed
to be water) measured as weight of diffusant per unit total volume,

θ denotes time, x is the coordinate along the diffusion path and D is the mutual diffusion coefficient which was assumed to be constant. The component B was considered to be the solid without moisture of the slab which is drying.

It was found that the numerical solution of equation (1) differs significatively from the standard solution of Fick's second law with a fixed domain of integration. Furthermore, in a recent work Viollaz and Suarez[2] obtained the numerical solution of the following equation for drying with unidirectional shrinkage:

$$\partial u/\partial\theta = \partial/\partial\xi (D_A^B \; \partial u/\partial\xi) \tag{2}$$

where u is the moisture on a dry basis and ξ is a variable defined by Crank in order to fix the domain of integration in a slab which is drying with shrinking. Physically, ξ is the volume of dry solid B per unit trasversal area, being the maximum value of this variable equal to the dry halfthickness of the slab, $D_A^B = D(\rho_B/\rho_S)^2$, is the diffusion coefficient with reference to a plane fixed to component B, ρ_B is the concentration of solid measured as weight of solid B per unit of total volume and ρ_S is the mass density of fully dried solid. Eqn. (2) has a fixed domain of integration when shrinkage is unidirectional and its numerical solutions coincide with the numerical solution of equation (1).

Performing a differential balance, following the same procedure as given in (2) it is obtained that equation (2) is valid for unidirectional drying and multidirectional shrinkage, but now the domain of integration is variable.

By adopting different law of area variation, we can obtain the numerical solution of equation (2) with a variable domain of integration. It can be observed that there are significant differences in the results owing to the different stories in area variation. Besides, the interception is no longer $8/\pi^2$ and in some curves appears a second falling rate period. The real variation in area could be different in adsorption or desorption, so it can be expected different values of the apparent diffusion coefficient for both processes. Also, the results can be a function of the initial halfthickness, because the center of the slab has a high moisture content that avoid the lateral shrinkage.

The results can be of interest in drying, ion-exchange, dyeing, solid-liquid extraction, and theories for predicting diffusion coefficients.

REFERENCES

1 Pascual. E. Viollaz and C. Suárez, An equation for diffusion in shrinking or swelling bodies, J. of Polymer Science Physics Ed., 22, (1984), 875-879.
2 Pascual E. Viollaz and C. Suárez, Drying of shrinking bodies, Aiche J., 31, (1985), 1566-1568.
3 T.K. Sherwood, The drying of solids, Ind. Eng. Chem., 21, (1929), 12.

EXPERIMENTAL STUDY OF THE DIFFUSION BEHAVIOUR OF ELECTROLYTES IN POLYMER STRUCTURES

W.E.L. SPIESS AND Ch.L. CHU

Bundesforschungsanstalt für Ernährung, Karlsruhe, FRG

During diffusion processes in a protein matrix, the environmental conditions are frequently subjected to changes of pH, water activity and temperature. Those changes cause not only variations of the diffusion coefficient itself but also change the physico-chemical properties of the substrates (protein denaturation). The present work is concerned with measurement of the effective diffusion coefficients of lactic acid in protein entrapped in a gel (polyacrylamide) and its dependence upon the pH-values. The primary objective is to investigate the diffusion behaviour of small electrolyte molecules at pI of protein.

Preconcentration and Drying of Food Materials, edited by S. Bruin
Elsevier Science Publishers B.V., Amsterdam, 1988 — Printed in The Netherlands

MEASURING DROPLET SIZES
FROM ROTARY ATOMIZERS

A. Hallström

APV ANHYDRO A/S

Østmarken 7, 2860 Søborg, Denmark

INTRODUCTION

A large number of droplet size measurements have been made in sprays from spray dryer rotary atomizers. A Malvern laser-diffraction particle sizer was used. The laser beam was directed vertically through the horizontal spray at some distance from the atomizer.

Measurements of this kind have a number of problems, and the most serious ones are related to the flow pattern in the spray. This paper focuses on some of these problems and reports on investigations of potential measuring errors.

VELOCITY GRADIENTS

Laser diffraction is a method which examines the droplets present in a defined measuring volume. Droplets passing through the volume with a high velocity will have a short residence time in the measuring volume, and they will therefore be underrated in the measured size distribution. Low-velocity droplets will be overrated. In other words, the spatial (measured) size distribution is not only a function of the temporal ("true") distribution. It is also a function of the velocity distribution. The two size distributions are equivalent only when all droplets have the same velocity. Small droplets will always accomodate to the gas velocity in a shorter time than large ones, so there will always be velocity gradients near the atomizer.

The influence of particle velocities is often ignored in experimental investigations. Only recently, a number of publications have dealt with the problem - see, e.g., Ref. 1. No ways to circumvent the problem are put forward, except for measuring where there are no velocity gradients, or measuring velocities and concentrations simultaneously.

Fig. 1a shows a typical set of measured size distributions at four different distances from the atomizer centre-line. There is a significant increase with increasing distance in measured droplet size.

Fig. 1b shows results of calculations using a simplified model for droplet movements. A constant temporal size distribution was assumed, and spatial distributions were calculated using the one-dimensional continuity equation in cylindrical coordinates for each class of droplets. Droplet velocities were calculated from a one-dimensional equation of motion and a standard drag coefficient curve for spheres. A constant gas velocity was assumed.

Even though this is a rough model, there is evidently good agreement in order of magnitude. Most of the observed variation in droplet size can be explained by velocity gradients.

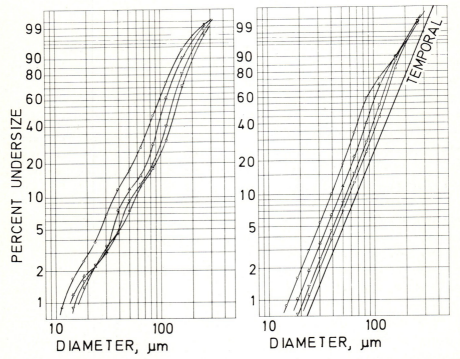

Fig. 1. Size distributions for water droplets in air at 20°C at (from left to right) 500, 700, 950, and 1200 mm from the atomizer. Atomizer wheel diameter 250 mm, peripheral speed 82 m/s, liquid flowrate 366 kg/h. (a) Measured distributions. (b) Calculated distributions assuming a temporal Rosin-Rammler distribution and 2.75 m/s gas velocity.

In reality, the flow pattern around the atomizer depends on wheel characteristics and on the liquid flowrate. Therefore, when measuring at a fixed distance from the atomizer, an observed variation in droplet size may be a function of varying flow patterns in the spray as well as of a true variation in

size. For example, when varying the liquid flowrate, a variation in droplet
size may be measured that is partly due to varying velocity gradients. This may
account for some divergent reports in the literature on the flowrate dependence
of particle size.

In consequence of what has been said above, experimental data should be
based on measurements at a series of distances from the atomizer. If possible,
measurements should only be accepted at a "sufficiently long" distance, where
data have stabilized. Another possibility is to use droplet velocity simulations to calculate backwards from the measured data. A more sophisticated flow
model is then needed.

OTHER FACTORS RELATED TO THE FLOW PATTERN

There is inevitably some degree of segregation in a spray. Therefore, it is
desirable to measure through the whole spray rather than cutting a part of it.
Measurements have shown that this does not have to be a problem in this application.

Recirculation of small droplets may cause an increase in the amount of such
droplets in the measuring volume, and it may cause time dependent measurements.
Table 1 shows results of three consecutive measurements that were made without
stopping the atomization. In the final tests, measurements were always made
about 3 minutes after the atomization was started.

TABLE 1.

Results from consecutive measurements with a 250 mm wheel at 366 kg water per
hour. Atomizer-to-laser distance 0.95 m.

Time from start, minutes	Rosin-Rammler diam, μm	spread	Droplet conc. in beam, Pct.
3	89	2.24	0.0015
7	85	2.31	0.0014
10	88	2.08	0.0017

FACTORS RELATED TO THE MEASURING PRINCIPLE

An investigation of the instrument accuracy of ten Malvern instruments was
published in Ref. 2. Measuring results varied within wide ranges, but the variation could be brought down by individual calibration of each instrument. The
achieved accuracy would be sufficient for our purpose. Malvern Instruments
claim that all instruments are now calibrated individually.

When the spray becomes more and more dense, an increasing portion of the
light sees more than one droplet on its way to the detector. Above a certain

limit in beam obscuration, the results become inaccurate. Correction factors can be used (3), but these are only applicable to Rosin-Rammler parameters. However, we have found that high beam obscuration is not normally a problem in this application. We have found the maximum allowable flowrate to be from 300 kg/h to well over 2000 kg/h for water, depending on the wheel type, the speed of rotation, and the measuring distance.

The most obvious practical problem is to keep the optical lenses free of droplets. Solving this problem involves dry and clean air streams passing over the lenses. These streams may cause enough density variations in the air to refract the beam and divert it from the centre of the detector. Beam refraction may become a serious problem when large temperature gradients are involved. In cold atomization tests without a significant amount of evaporation, the effects of this phenomenon may be avoided.

CONCLUSIONS

Laser diffraction can be used to measure droplet size distributions from rotary atomizers. It has some drawbacks, but it is simple to use and readily available. The results can be fairly detailed and they can form a good basis for mathematical simulation of the drying process.

The measured spatial size distributions are functions of the distance from the atomizer. Most of this variation with distance is likely to be due to velocity gradients. Measurements should always be made at a number of distances.

REFERENCES

1. Chin, JS, Nickolaus, D, Lefebvre, AH, Influence of Downstream Distance on the Spray Characteristics of Pressure-Swirl Atomizers, Trans. ASME J. Engng Gas Turbines and Power, 108, 219 (1986).
2. Hirleman, ED, Dodge, LG, Performance Comparison of Malvern Instruments Laser Diffraction Drop Size Analyzers, Proc. ICLASS-85, IVA/3 (1985).
3. Felton, PG, Hamidi, AA, Aigal, AK, Measurement of Drop Size Distribution in Dense Sprays by Laser Diffraction, Proc. ICLASS-85, IVA/4 (1985).

Preconcentration and Drying of Food Materials, edited by S. Bruin
Elsevier Science Publishers B.V., Amsterdam, 1988 — Printed in The Netherlands

DROP VELOCITIES AND AIR INCORPORATION IN NOZZLE ATOMIZER SPRAYS

A. BJERNSTAD[1], A. PEDERSEN[1] AND H. SCHWARTZBERG[2]

[1]Food Engineering Dept., University of Lund, Lund, Sweden
[2]Food Engineering Dept. Univ. of Massachusetts, Amherst, MA, U.S.A.

SUMMARY

Drop sizes and velocities for whirljet atomizer sprays were
measured using high speed television. Momentum transferred to air
and air velocities and mass flow rates in the spray envelope were
calculated from decreases in drop velocities. The air flows in the
envelope were too small to permit rapid drying near the nozzle.

INTRODUCTION

Aroma retention in spray drying is greatly influenced by
initial rates of drying. These rates depend on drop velocities
relative to the air in the spray envelope and the air's mass flow
rate. A method for determining these quantities is described.

METHODS

Sections of hollow-cone water sprays produced a whirljet nozzle
were illuminated by 0.3 μs, 6 MW Xenon light flashes and pairs of
flashes 43 to 68 μs apart using Bete Fog Nozzle Inc. equipment.
140 to 13,000 recorded TV images of the drops were obtained at each
locale. Bete's computer and software measured the image areas;
calculated equivalent diameters, D; classified the D into D_i
ranges; counted N_i, the numbers of drops in each range, computed
average D and measures of spread in D; measured distances between
centers of pairs that agreed in size, pointed the right way and
were far enough apart, divided the distances by the time between
flashes to obtain drop velocities, V, and computed V_i, the average
V, for each D_i:

Still photos of the spray were used to determine the spray
boundary. The spray flow pattern was determined by collecting the
spray for one minute periods in a radial array of tubes Air velocities just outside the spray envelope were measured with a hot
wire anemometer

The nozzle sprayed 0.087 kg of water/s at velocity, V_o, of 15.9 m/s. D_i, N_i and V_i measured at seven traverses 38 to 352-mm downstream from the nozzle.

RESULTS

The spray moved in almost straight lines for 100 mm, then slowly curved downward. $V_m = \Sigma N_i D_i{}^3 V_i{}^2 / \Sigma N_i D_i{}^3 V_i$, the local momentum-based drop velocity based on fixed coordinates, decreased with distance as shown in Table 3. D_{sm}, the Sauter mean drop size and the spray flow rate index, $F = \Sigma N_i D_i{}^3 V_i$ varied with position as shown below for a typical traverse 65 mm from the nozzle.

Table 1   Drop size and liquid flow rate vs position in traverse

Radial pos. (mm)	24	28	30	34	39	42	45
Local D_{sm} (mm)	78	112	144	267	216	204	180
F, (m^4/s x 10^9)	1.5	–	10	–	25	–	–

The air velocity was virtually zero 5-mm outside the spray. A typical distribution of V_i and N_i vs D_i is presented below.

Table 2 V_i vs drop D_i 171 mm from nozzle

Diameter (mm)	200–316	125–199	100–125	63–100	50–63	20–32
Velocity (m/s)	8.8	7.7	7.2	6.6	6.5	5.7
No. image pairs	25	54	60	332	198	208

Probably because of intense turbulence, V varied markedly within D_i ranges. This variation was larger than the change in V_i due to changes in D_i. The computed V also occasionally varied because the software used images that were not true pairs. The change in V_i with D_i was much smaller than occurs for isolated drops. The large drops moved faster than the air in the envelope causing it to accelerate, which, in turn, accelerated the small drops or reduced their deceleration. Momentum transfer to the air caused air to flow into the spray envelope.

Gravitational acceleration caused slight increases in momentum in the spray. The external air velocity was zero. Therefore, the combined momentum flow of air and liquid in the spray equalled the momentum flow of the liquid leaving the nozzle. The air temperature was low, virtually no evaporation occurred and L, the liquid mass-flow rate, remained constant. Consequently, U, the local mean air velocity in the spray, roughly $= \sqrt{L(V_o-V_m)/\rho A_c}$. ρ is the air density, A_c the cross sectional area of the spray. U was corrected to account for momentum input due to gravity acting on the spray droplets. W_a, the air-mass flow rates in the spray $= U\rho A_c$ The corrected U and W_a at various distances from the nozzle are listed below. Maximum extents of drying that would occur due to complete adiabatic heat transfer between the liquid and the air in the spray envelope for a hypothetical case where 250°C air is used are also listed.

Table 3 V_m, U, W_a and estimated maximum extents of drying
(for 250°C air use) vs distance from nozzle

Distance (mm)	38	65	110	173	352
V_m (m/s)	12.1	10.5	9.2	8.3	6.7
U (m/s)	11.4	9.8	6.3	4.5	3.6
V_m-U (m/s)	0.7	0.7	2.9	3.8	3.1
Air flow rate (kg/s)	0.029	0.049	0.097	0.160	0.264
Maximum fraction dried	0.025	0.042	0.082	0.135	0.225

CONCLUSIONS

Drops in compact sprays decelerate much slower than isolated drops do. The slip velocity, (V_m-U), may increase first, then decrease rather than steadily decreasing as occurs for isolated drops. If normal heat- and mass-transfer coefficient equations apply, only 0.076 of the water content of 200µm drops would evaporate in the 0.044 s it takes the spray to travel 0.35 m. This evaporation may be too slow to induce formation of selectively permeable films that enhance aroma retention. The spray-air interaction can be changed by changing how the inlet air is applied. Such changes can profitably be studied using the methods employed in this work.

Preconcentration and Drying of Food Materials, edited by S. Bruin
Elsevier Science Publishers B.V., Amsterdam, 1988 — Printed in The Netherlands

SIMULATION OF DEEP-BED DRYING OF PARTICLES

O. RATTANAPANT, A. LEBERT, J.J. BIMBENET

Ecole Nationale Supérieure des Industries Agricoles et Alimentaires, Institut National de la Recherche Agronomique - 91305 MASSY (FRANCE)

SUMMARY

Attempts are made to simulate deep-bed drying of particles by hot air, on the basis of :

1. experimental drying kinetics expressed as a function of external drying conditions and product moisture content

2. energy and mass balances of thin layers and flowing air.

The simulation has been used for the drying of plums. The agreement between calculated results and experimental ones was fair.

INTRODUCTION

Many authors studied the water migration within the particles. But this requires a number of physical parameters. It also obliges to take simplified hypothesis.

Thompson et al (1) developed a mathematical model for corn drying in deep beds. They first calculated an equilibrium drying temperature based on the sensible heat balance between air and grain. The equilibrium moisture content and the drying rate of the grain were then estimated using this temperature. Bakker – Arkema (2) developed the model for corn drying based on a system of 4 partial differential equations involving air temperature, grain temperature, humidity ratio and the grain moisture.

In recent years a number of researchers have developed simulation programs, mainly for cereals drying based on the Thompson (3,4,5) and Bakker-Arkema (6,7) approachs.

Objective of this study is to simulate the drying granular biological materials in deep beds percolated by hot air, using experimental drying kinetics.

SIMULATION MODEL

For the simulation of deep bed drying, we consider the deep bed as a series of thin layers. We required a mathematical expression for the kinetics of thin layer drying and balance equations.

1.1. mathematical expression of the kinetics of thin layer drying

We developed this expression by using the experimental result of thin layer drying, carried out at various conditions, such as temperature, moisture content and air velocity. After trying different types of formula, we selected the following form :

$$x = a.exp(-b.t)$$

We used the simplex method and multiple regression to correlate "a" and "b" with the drying conditions.

For drying of plum :

$$a = 1.112Xo-100.7(Va/Ta)-0.261X10^{-2}$$
$$b = (0.5136X10^{-7}.Ta^3+0.6586X10^{-3}.Ta.Va-1.9205)X10^{-4}$$

(air temperature is in ° Kelvin)

1.2. three balance equations

These equations are derived from the mass and energy conservation principles :

$$d(\int a.(Ca+Y.Cv).Ta)/dt = -div(\overrightarrow{Va.\int a.Ta.(Ca+Y.Cv)}) ----(1)$$
$$d(\int a.Y)/dt = -div(\overrightarrow{Va.\int a.Y}) ----(2)$$
$$d(\int s.(Cms+X.Cw).Ts)/dt = -div(\lambda s.grad \ Ts+ \overrightarrow{\Phi ms.Cw.Ts})--(3)$$

The temperature of the product is important for the color, texture and flavor. Heating of product is taken into account on a simplified way assuming the temperature profil of the product is parabolic.

COMPARISON BETWEEN THE MODELSATION AND EXPERIMENTAL DRYING OF PLUM IN A PILOT DRYER

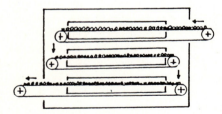

Fig.1 Pilot dryer

The dryer is made of 3 compartments.
Air flows through the product layers.
Product thickness is two fruit layers.
Comparison between simulation results
and experimental ones are given in the
figures 2,3,4.

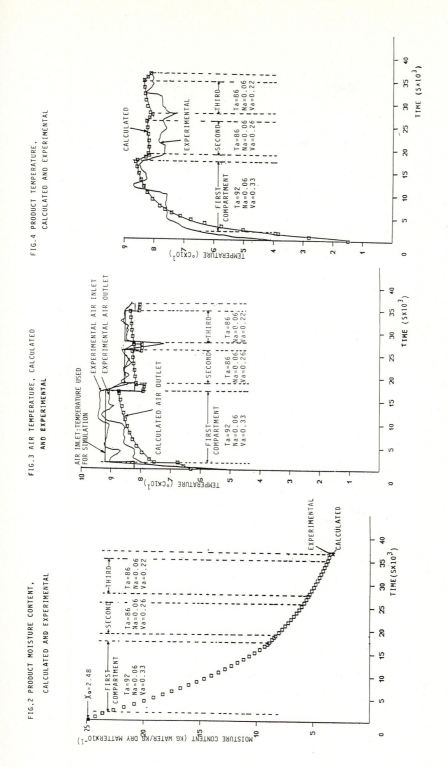

FIG.2 PRODUCT MOISTURE CONTENT,
CALCULATED AND EXPERIMENTAL

FIG.3 AIR TEMPERATURE, CALCULATED
AND EXPERIMENTAL

FIG.4 PRODUCT TEMPERATURE,
CALCULATED AND EXPERIMENTAL

CONCLUSION

Our model gives a good agreement with the experimental moisture content of product. However, the calculated air temperature is slightly lower than the experimental one and the product temperature is slightly higher than the experimental values. This may due to the experimental errors caused by measuremental difficulties of temperature in the pilot conditions as well as the oversimplification of the model compared to the real situation (channeling, radiation etc.).

NOTATIONS

a,b   coefficients

C   specific heat j/(kg.°C) ; Ca of dry air ; Cv of water vapour ;
      Cw of water ; Cms of dry matter

t   time s

T   temperature °C ; Ta of air ; Ts of product

Va   air velocity m/s

X   product moisture content kg water/kg dry matter ; Xo initial

Y   air moisture content   kg water/kg dry air

ρ density kg/m^3 ; ρa of air ; ρs of product

λs   product conductivity W/(m.°C)

Φms mass flux in product kg water/(m^2.s)

REFERENCES

1. Thompson T.L., Peart R.M., Foster G.H. (1968), Mathematical simulation of corn drying : a new model, Trans.ASAE, v.11, pp582-586.

2. Bakker-Arkama F.W., DeBoer S.F., Lerew L.E., Roth M.G. (1974), Grain dryer simulation. Michigan State University, Agricultural Experimental Station, Research Report 224.

3. Allen J.R. (1960), Application of grain drying : theory to the drying of maize and rice. J.of Agri.Eng.Res., v.5, pp363-385.

4. Paulsen M.R., Thompson T.L. (1973), Drying analysis of grain sorghum, Trans.ASAE, v.16, pp.537-540.

5. Roberts D.E., Brooker D.B. (1975), Grain drying with recirculation, Trans.ASAE, v.18, pp181-184.

6. Patil N., Lehoczky L. (1985), Drying analysis of recirculating crossflow dryer design using computer simulation, Int. Agrophysics, v.1, n3-4, pp269-288.

- This work was supported by CTIFL/DIAA
- The laboratory is a member of groupe de recherches coordonnées (GRECO) Nr.72 of C.N.R.S.

Preconcentration and Drying of Food Materials, edited by S. Bruin
Elsevier Science Publishers B.V., Amsterdam, 1988 — Printed in The Netherlands

A FEW METHODS OF EVALUATING PRODUCT TEMPERATURE DURING THIN BED DRYING.

F. BERA, J.L. DELADRIERE, H. RENAULD, Cl. DEROANNE

Food Department of the Agricultural Sciences Faculty of Gembloux (Belgium).

SUMMARY
   With the two methods we present, we can calculate the product temperature
during drying. Each of the methods uses a particularity of the drying mecanisms,
the wet equilibrium of the air and the product for the Coppens model, and the
heat transfer characteristics at the interface air-product for the heat transfer model. The first model don't take into account the influence of slow diffusion of water in the product on its temperature rising during drying. To
limit product temperature, this curve can be considered as an objectif to reach
using the heat transfer model temperature. During the described experiments,
the models show the improvement of the drying conditions when the rice is milled
before drying.

INTRODUCTION
   During drying, the product temperature is the most important and the most
difficult parameter to control. The rate of quality degradation of the biological product is higher when the product temperature is high during the adiabatic
and hygroscopic drying phase. The aim of this study is the models development
of product temperature prediction during drying.

THE LABORATORY DRYER
   The experimental device consist of a drying room in which rice is fluidized
by a vibrating sieve. The air temperature at the input, the air wet and dry
temperatures at the outlet are measured. The air flow is measured using a thermal mass flow meter.

METHODS
   A few assumptions are to be respected to applicate the models. The particulates bed is homogeneous and isotropic. The water activity at the product surface can be estimated with its water content and its desorption curve. According
with Alzamora (ref. 1) and Vaccarezza (ref. 6), we assume that the temperature
gradient is insignificant in the product. The geometrical properties of the
product are constant.
   The first method was theoretically exposed by Coppens (ref. 3) and used by
the authors (ref. 2, 4 and 5). It is useful for drying study of product in which
the water flow is easy.
In the method of the convective heat transfer coefficient, the sensible heat
exchanges between the air and the product may be represented by the equation :

$$G \cdot (Cp^{air} + Cp^{steam} \cdot X_{Input}) \cdot (T_{Input} - T_{Output}) \cdot dt =$$

$$\alpha \cdot S \cdot \left[(T_{Input} + T_{Output})/2 - T_{Product} \right] \cdot dt \qquad (1)$$

The value of the heat transfer coefficient α . S can be estimated at the drying beginning, during the adiabatic phase when $T_{Product}$ is known.

RESULTS

The figure 1 describes dryings of intact rice kernels and of a rice milling The two experiences were made in similar working conditions.

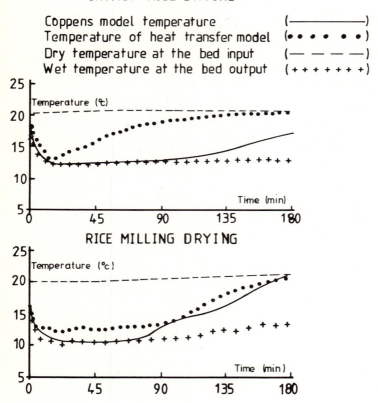

INTACT RICE DRYING

Coppens model temperature	(—————)
Temperature of heat transfer model	(• • • • • •)
Dry temperature at the bed input	(— — — —)
Wet temperature at the bed output	(+ + + + + +)

RICE MILLING DRYING

Fig. 1. Temperatures evolution versus time.

For the intact rice, the Coppens model temperatures rise after an important time with regard to the temperatures calculated with the second model. The Coppens model do not take into account the "pseudo-hygroscopicity" notion because the superficial water activity is lower than the calculated water activity with the desorption isotherm and the dry matter content. The Coppens temperatures curve begins to rise when the average water activity of the product diminishs. The water flow in the product is difficult. There is a big hysteresis between the Coppens temperature curve and the temperatures estimated with the heat transfer model. During all the dryings, the dry temperatures of the air at the output and the temperatures of the heat transfer model were always near each other. As we can see with the relative humidity of the output air, the adiabatic drying phase is much more evident for the drying of rice milling than intact rice.

CONCLUSIONS

The heat transfer model can be used as an indirect measure device of the product temperature. The Coppens model gives us a minimum temperature curve of the product. This function can be considered as an objectif for an optimized management of the drying.

REFERENCES
1. ALZAMORA S.M. and al., A simplified model for predicting the temperatures of foods during air dehydratation, J. Fd Technol., 1979, 14, 369–380.

2. BERA F., Evaluating product temperature during thin bed drying, Sensors and measurement of product properties – Instrumentation and process control, February 1987, Berichte der Bundesforschungsanstalt für Ernährung.

3. COPPENS R., Cours de séchage, Faculté des Sciences Agronomiques de Gembloux, Belgique, 1970.

4. DELADRIERE J.L., Estimation de l'évolution de la température du produit lors du séchage, Travail de fin d'étude, Faculté des Sciences Agronomiques de Gembloux, Belgique, 1987.

5. RENAULD H., Etude de la perte d'activité enzymatique de cellulases en fonction des conditions de séchage, Travail de fin d'étude, Faculté des Sciences Agronomiques de Gembloux, Belgique, 1986.

6. VACCAREZZA L.M. and al., Kinetics of moisture movement during air drying of sugar beet root, J. Fd Technol., 1974, 9, 317–327.

Preconcentration and Drying of Food Materials, edited by S. Bruin
Elsevier Science Publishers B.V., Amsterdam, 1988 — Printed in The Netherlands

TRANSITION FLOW OF A GAS IN POROUS FREEZE-DRIED FOODS

J.D. MELLOR

Hibberd Pressed Metal and Tooling Pty Ltd, P.O. Box 177, Mortdale, N.S.W.
2223, Australia

SUMMARY
    A minimum diffusivity of a gas flowing along straight capillaries in
freeze-dried foods is reached at a particular low pressure. This minimum
diffusivity, which has also been observed in a number of porous materials such
as sintered glass and ceramics, is considered to be due to a transition from
viscous to molecular flow. An analysis of the transition in terms of
molecular collision theory is given and it is shown how a high gas flow
diffusivity is obtained at low pressures, especially for slow frozen liquid
foods. These findings have important implications for predicting freeze-
drying rates.

TRANSITION FLOW

    Gas diffusion in porous materials varies from viscous flow in large pores
to molecular flow (Knudsen) in small pores. In viscous flow the mean free
path of molecules (average distance traversed by gas molecules between
successive collisions) is determined by collisions between molecules, and
collisions with the walls is regarded as negligible. In molecular flow the
situation is just the opposite, collisions with the walls are predominant and
hence it is the pore size that determines the mean free path of the molecules.
Between viscous and molecular flows there is transition flow with inter-
molecular as well as wall collisions occurring with comparable frequency. The
three types of gas flow may be specified by limiting values to Knudsen's
number, $\lambda/2r$, where λ is the mean free path and r the equivalent pore radius.
Thus, if $\lambda/2r < 0.01$, the flow is viscous, if $\lambda/2r > 1$, the flow is molecular
and, if $0.01 < \lambda/2r < 1$, it is transition flow.

    Transition flow occurs at intermediate vacuum pressures and has been
modelled in several ways, Bosanquet's formula for the effective diffusivity
for transition flow in a tube assumed the gas diffusion process as a random
"walk" in which the successive steps of the individual molecules are term-
inated either by collisions with other molecules or with the tube wall.
However, transition flow was not appreciated until Knudsen observed a minimum
in the flow rate for a gas at low pressures flowing in a long straight
capillary. He considered the minimum to be the transition from viscous to

molecular flow and not simply to viscous flow with slip. After Knudsen's discovery, minima were observed for long narrow slits and for some porous materials by Barrer (ref. 1) and for freeze-dried foods by Mellor (ref. 2). Various theoretical models for transition flow with low-pressure minima have been published, one by Mellor (ref. 3) applies to freeze-dried foods in terms of the effective diffusivity as a function of the gas pressure which varies inversely as the mean free path. The latter model is examined here in the light of experimental data.

THEORY AND EXPERIMENTAL DATA

The effective diffusivities D_e of freeze-dried foods at different pressures P were determined and plotted giving a transition curve which approaches an asymptote in the medium pressure range. The slope and the asymptote intercept on the D_e-axis yield the equivalent pore radius r and the diffusion ratio (porosity ε to the tortuosity factor $(L_e/L)^2$ of the porous material). These quantities can be deduced by developing an equation for the asymptote in terms of an equivalent cylindrical model (ref. 3) for the porous material, giving

$$\text{slope} = \frac{\varepsilon r^2}{8k(L_e/L)^2 \eta} \quad , \tag{1}$$

$$\text{intercept} = \frac{2\delta_1 \varepsilon r \bar{v}}{3k'(L_e/L)^2} \quad , \tag{2}$$

where structural constants, $k = 2.5$, $k' = 1$, $\delta_1 = 3\pi/16$ (rough pores) or $\delta_1 = \pi/4$ (smooth pores), L_e is the actual flow path, L is the sample thickness, η is the gas viscosity and molecular gas velocity $\bar{v} = (8RT/\pi M)^{1/2}$.

The equivalent pore radius can therefore be found from

$$r = \frac{16\delta_1 \bar{v} \eta k}{3k'} \quad \frac{\text{slope}}{\text{intercept}} \quad . \tag{3}$$

And the diffusion ratio $\varepsilon/(L_e/L)^2$ can be obtained from either the slope or the intercept.

Diffusivity-pressure curves for freeze-dried beef and egg pulp are shown in Fig. 1. The minima occur in the range of pressure P, 0.5 to 2 Torr, and the calculated average pore radii for beef and egg pulp are approximately equal to the mean free path at the minimum. This can be expected from kinetic theory.

The asymptotes derived from the above curves involve molecular collisions between successive wall collisions, whereas under the conditions where the capillary radius equals the mean free path, a considerable number of molecules

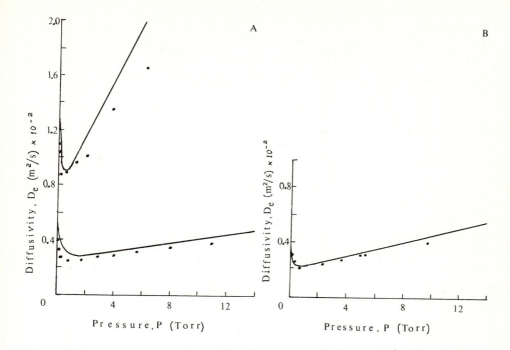

Fig. 1. Diffusivity-pressure relationships for freeze-dried products. (a) Slow frozen egg (top curve), fast frozen egg (bottom curve). (b) Slow frozen beef. Theoretical curve shown as a plain line, experimental data as dots.

do not behave in this way. These data suggest that a model for the complete curve should be given. If the fraction of the molecules that, on the average, do collide with other molecules between two wall collisions in a transition flow term and the fraction that do not collide in an additional molecular flow term are considered, an equation (ref. 3) from kinetic theory for the effective diffusivity D_e in terms of the mean free path λ, gives eqn. 4:

$$D_e = \frac{\varepsilon}{(L_e/L)^2} \ D_K \left[(-\frac{3}{32k} \ \frac{2r}{\lambda} + \delta_1)(1-e^{-2r/\lambda}) + e^{-2r/\lambda} \right], \tag{4}$$

where $D_K = (2/3) \ r\bar{v}$ is Knudsen's diffusivity.

DISCUSSION

Equation (4) with structural constants $k = 2.5$, $\delta_1 = 3\pi/16$ is found to fit the experimental data for freeze-dried beef to within a few percent and for freeze-dried egg in a reasonable way. The cylindrical model may be less appropriate for freeze-dried egg because of its amorphous ultrastructure.

344

In freeze-drying the rate at which preliminary freezing is carried out is important since it determines the size and location of the ice crystals, which in turn affects the structure and therefore the water vapour diffusivity of the freeze-dried product. The slower the freezing rate the larger the ice crystals, consequently an open porous structure occurs on freeze-drying, and this is beneficial for the rate of drying. Comparing the diffusivity-pressure curves (Fig. 1) for egg it is clear the diffusivity for the slow frozen product is 3 times that for the fast frozen product.

Overall, the effective diffusivity D for water vapour flowing in the product together with air and vapour flowing in the space of a freeze-drying system, while depending on the porous structure of the product, also depends on the diffusivity of the air and vapour D_a. The latter has a value of 0.25 x 10^{-4} m^2/s at atmospheric pressure and $20^{\circ}C$. Corrected for freeze-drying conditions, $D_a = 0.25 \times 10^{-4} (760/P)(T/293)^{1.75}$. According to Bosanquet it can be written $1/D = 1/D_e + 1/D_a$.

Typical calculated D values are:

Beef: D = 0.0033, 0.0032 and 0.0027 m^2/s for P = 0.005, 0.013 and 1 Torr respectively.

Fast frozen egg: D = 0.0039, 0.0031 and 0.0026 m^2/s for P = 0.1, 0.5 and 1 Torr respectively.

Thus, freeze-drying of these two products could be effective in the pressure range 0.005 to 1 Torr.

Slow frozen egg: D = 0.0069 and 0.0059 m^2/s for P = 0.5 to 1 Torr respectively.

There are advantages operating a freeze-dryer in the pressure range 0.5 to 1 Torr rather than at 0.05 Torr and lower where the diffusivity would be doubled. The real advantage for this product is the marked increase in diffusivity because of its open porous structure as explained above.

ACKNOWLEDGEMENTS

I am grateful to Dr Graham Bell, CSIRO Division of Food Research, North Ryde, N.S.W. 2113, Australia for reading the manuscript.

REFERENCES

1   R.M. Barrer, Diffusion in porous media, App. Mat. Res., 2 (1963) 129.
2   J.D. Mellor and D.A. Lovett, Flow of gases through channels with reference to porous materials, Vacuum, 18 (1968) 625-627.
3   J.D. Mellor, Fundamentals of Freeze-Drying, Academic Press, London, 1978, pp. 99-101, 121-125.

Preconcentration and Drying of Food Materials, edited by S. Bruin
Elsevier Science Publishers B.V., Amsterdam, 1988 — Printed in The Netherlands

EXPERIMENTAL STUDY ON SUBLIMATION FLUX OF TYLOSE AT ATMOSPHERIC PRESSURE

M. SAKLY[1], J. AGUIRRE-PUENTE[1], G. LAMBRINOS[2] and P. BERNARD[1]

[1]Laboratoire d'Aérothermique du CNRS, 4ter Route des Gardes, 92190 Meudon (France)

[2]Superior School of Agriculture of Athens, 75 Iera Odos, 11855 Athens (Greece)

INTRODUCTION

Ice and frozen dispersed media sublimation is a complex problem of heat and mass transfer with change of phase which concerns many scientific research and technical applications. Classical freeze drying and interstellar ice behaviour are concerned by sublimation at low pressures. Weight losses of frozen stored foodstuff , new technics of freeze drying and wall protection in underground cavities for cryogenic storage are concerned by sublimation at atmospheric pressure "(ref. 1)".

Certain problems in geotechnical, polar engineering and physical and mathematical models need information about the behaviour of pure ice. On the other hand, investigations about dispersed media are necessary to resolve many food engineering problems and to evaluate the thermal balance of frozen ground surface.

A part of the research we conducted treated the frozen meat behaviour during storage. Nevertheless, in order to conduct experiments upon reproductible media and to work under good conditions of manipulation and measure a simulation substance, the tylose, has been choosen for certain experiments. Indeed, in many aspects, tylose presents similar properties to those of meat, principally water content and thermophysical parameters.

Previous publications give details about the methods used to approach the problem "(ref. 2)". We recall that for experiments done upon cylinders located in a wind tunnel, the average sublimation flux was calculated taking into account the mass loss measured and the total exposed surface. In this paper, we present results about measurements done upon cylinders from which the surface was partially hidden in order to estimate with more precision the sublimation flux on different zones (upstream and downstream).

EXPERIMENTAL METHOD

Loss of mass experiments have been conducted upon 25 mm diameter, 50 mm high vertical cylinder located in the center of the 20 cm x 20 cm experimental section of a wind tunnel. Half of the surface of the cylinders was

346

covered by an aluminium sheet, upstream or downstream. Cylinders were made on
tylose and frozen prior the experiments. A thermocouple was placed in the
center. The ends of the samples were fixed to the wind tunnel walls with the
help of cylindrical extensions made on brass in view to eliminate the hydrodynamic and mass transfer indesirable board effects.

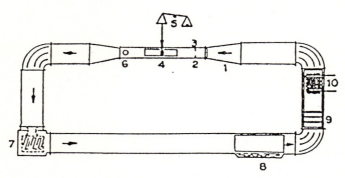

Fig. 1. Wind tunnel plant.

1. Convergent flow ; 2. Platinium resistance probe ; 3. Hot-wire probe ; 4. Test
section ; 5. Balance ; 6. Hygrometer ; 7. Blower ; 8. Saturated solution ;
9. Drying agent ; 10. Heat exchanger.

Samples were exposed to a steady flow of air at -5°C for   about 9 hours. The
mean relative humidity was calculated for each run taking into account measures
made, at different instants, with the help of a calibrate hygrometer. The
values of mean relative humidity of the different runs varies from 35 to 50% and
the used velocities were 0,9, 1,5 and 2,3 m.s^{-1}.

RESULTS

The flux sublimation curves are plotted on figures 2 to 4. In every case the
flux magnitude decreases with time. The creation of a superficial dried layer
is probably the reason of this evolution due to a supplementary resistance to
the diffusion mechanism.

For the low velocity, i.e. 0,9 m.s^{-1}, the sublimation flux is more important
in the forward part of the cylinder. For the intermediate value of the velocity,
i.e. 1,5 m.s^{-1}, the two curves representing the forward and backward sublimation
are crossed : the flux being more important backward during the first half time
of the experiment.

For the highest velocity, i.e 2,3 m.s^{-1}, concerning the backward part of the
cylinder, the flux becomes more important than that on the other side.

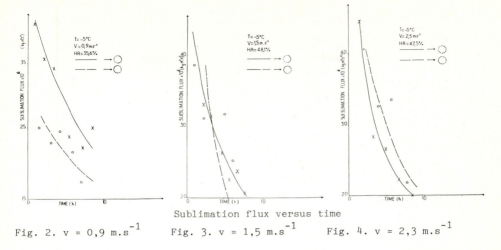

Sublimation flux versus time

Fig. 2. v = 0,9 m.s^{-1} Fig. 3. v = 1,5 m.s^{-1} Fig. 4. v = 2,3 m.s^{-1}

The above remarks can be explained by the evolution of the hydrodynamic regime around the cylinder. For the small velocities (Re ≃ 1740) the regime is similar to a no-sticking out flow, and for high velocities (Re ≃ 4450) the near of the cylinder undergoes a turbulent regime where eddies enhance the mass loss.

On examination of the figure 3, the crossing of the curves in the middle of the experiment can   lead to the hypothesis that a dried layer first is created at the stagnation point, the more exposed to the air flow, and that this layer, then is propagated upon each side from the stagnation point. The sublimation flux decreases more and more due to the progressive creation upstream of the dried layer, while the flux decreasing is more regular downstream due to the regular distribution of the eddies at any moment.

In view of a best appreciation of the mass transfer phenomenon, we are evaluating the forward and backward Sherwood number in fonction of the Reynolds number. Results will be published in a next paper.

REFERENCES

1   M. Sakly, Sublimation non convective de la glace à de bas niveaux de température et d'hygrométrie. Expérimentation. Modélisation. Calcul. Thèse de Doctorat, Université Paris VI, décembre 1986.
2   G. Lambrinos, M. Sakly et J. Aguirre-Puente Prévision de la sublimation de la glace, _XVIIème Congrès Int. du Froid, Août 1987, Vienne (Autriche).

Preconcentration and Drying of Food Materials, edited by S. Bruin
Elsevier Science Publishers B.V., Amsterdam, 1988 — Printed in The Netherlands

THE IMPORTANCE OF LACTOSE CRYSTALLIZATION IN DEHYDRATED DAIRY PRODUCTS

T. TABOURET

Reactivity of Solids Laboratory B.P. 138 21004 DIJON CEDEX FRANCE
and/or Institut Universitaire de Technologie B.P. 510 21014 DIJON CEDEX FRANCE

SUMMARY

As a major component of dairy products, lactose has a strong tendency for crystallizing upon their dehydrating. Research work is suggested in order to find out and to achieve the most convenient cristalline state for each application.

INTRODUCTION

The lactose percentage (of total Solids) is high in all common dairy products especially in wheys. Lactose therefore has a strong tendency for crystallizing upon dehydrating of those products. However, its graining is rarely well control led... (if it is !)

DIRECTED CRYSTALLIZATION

Is common practice only for a) lactose recovery from whey ; b) sweetened condensed whole and skimmed milk ; and c) whey powder manufacture.

Although its main factors are rather well known, some improvement could be explored chiefly in the fields of seeding and temperature monitoring.

CONTROLLING OF THE RESULTS

It should not rely only on the refractive index of the mother liquor, but should include also microscopic observations and photos of the crystals (as shown in congress).

OTHER GRAINING OCCURRENCES

In liquid materials (-especially before drying-) the chances for self nucleation and growing into uncontrolled crystals may be sometimes estimated : two quoted examples have been compared. During drying, lactose is said to keep its mutarotational equilibrium until the glassy state.

Post-graining may also take place in powders after humidity take up, but the precise extent of this cristallinity and its consequences remain obscure.

LACTOSE CRYSTALLINITY INFLUENCE

Besides sandiness in some foods, and increased yield in drying, this influ-ence is more or less well defined in powders, for instance on powder hygrosco-picity as related to other hygroscopic components such as dehydrated proteins and minerals. This is all the more important as hygroscopicity in turn acts on practically all the handling properties of powders.

Consequently, it is clearly shown, as an example, how Lactose.graining in whey must be directed according to two distinct purposes : either lactose re-covery or chocolate making.

CONCLUSION

Obviously, it would be worth to look further into the role of lactose crys-tallization in order to achieve the most suited state for each application.

Preconcentration and Drying of Food Materials, edited by S. Bruin   351
Elsevier Science Publishers B.V., Amsterdam, 1988 — Printed in The Netherlands

OPTIMAL DRYING PROFILES FOR VEGETABLES IN AN AIR SUCTION DRYER

G.DALL'AGLIO[1], G. CARPI[1], M. DAVIDE[2], L. PALMIERI[2], B. DE CINDIO[3] and G.IORIO[3].

[1]Stazione Sperimentale per l'Industria delle Conserve Alimentari, Via F. Tanara 31/A, 43100 Parma (Italy)

[2]Nuovo Crai, Piana di Monte Verna, 81015 Caserta (Italy)

[3]Dipartimento di Ingegneria Chimica, Università di Napoli, Piazzale Tecchio 25, 80125 Napoli (Italy)

SUMMARY

In dehydration plants with air circulation pattern which is directed vertically onto the product, it is possible to operate with high air velocities and thick product layers in each dehydration stage. Layer thickness, air pressure loss and air velocity are closely interdependent parameters and their control allows the dehydratation process to be optimized. A practical example of the importance of these parameters in optimizing the air suction process is given by the results obtained with dehydration tests on diced carrots with a multi-stage feeding technique. A simulation of the process has been developed. Results have shown that the pilot plant can improve its production, utilizing an optimal fresh product load distribution.

INTRODUCTION

Food plant industry has developed new different air circulation dryers for dehydration of vegetables in pieces.

After trolley and tray dryers in equi/counter corrent, air suction multi-layers have been designed in order to improve mass and energy exchange between product and air (refs. 1-2).

In this paper dehydration process has been optimized, by simulation of an air suction dryer, to obtain an improvement of the average production.

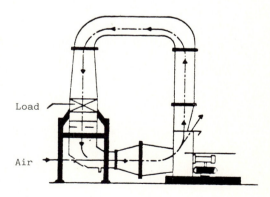

Fig. 1. Pilot plant (static air suction dryer.

METHODS

Experiments were carried out, with a pilot plant (Fig. 1), on diced carrots (1x1x1 cm) obtained by traditional preparation method of the products to be dehydrated (ref. 3). Air temperature was 115° C and air replacement was 5%.

Multi-layers feed was carried out putting a layer on the previous one at defined intervals of time up to 5 stages (ref.4).

RESULTS AND DISCUSSION

Experiments have shown that during the dehydration process the product structure is modified progressively with a continual fall of pressure loss and a rise of air velocity (Fig. 2). Therefore fresh product has been added on predried to obtain again optimal condition of pressure drop and air velocity.

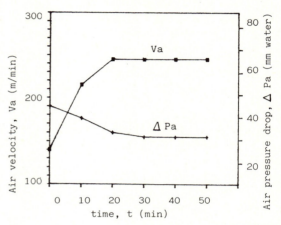

Fig. 2. Diagram showing the air velocity (Va) and the air pressure drop (Δ Pa) vs time for a single layer.

Fig. 3 shows the change of drying rate curves with time for different loads. The following relationship links load (P) and drying rate (v) during the costant rate period:

$$v = 0.7 - 3.13 \times 10^{-2} \cdot P - 1.56 \times 10^{-3} \cdot P^2$$

with $1 < P < 10$ Kg.

Optimization of process has been studied taking into account:

1) maximum load of pilot plant;

2) minimum and maximum moisture

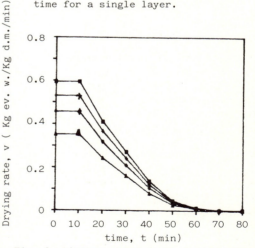

Fig. 3. Diagram showing the drying rate (v) vs time at different layer load (P): ■ 3.0 Kg; ✚ 4.5 Kg; ◆ 6.0 Kg; ▲ 8.0 Kg.

content for each layer;

3) absence of interactions among pieces of different layers;

4) fixed time of loading (10 min.).

The criterium of optimization has been applied estimating the best load distribution (Tab. 1).

TABLE 1
Optimal load condition - Total drying time 120 min.

LAYER	LOAD	FINAL WEIGHT	MOISTURE CONTENT
n	Kg	Kg	Kg water/Kg dry matter
1	5.7	0.6	0.5
2	2.1	0.3	0.6
3	2.2	0.3	0.7
4	2.3	0.3	0.9
5	2.1	0.3	0.9
TOTAL	14.4	1.8	0.7

NOMENCLATURE

v	drying rate (Kg evaporated water/Kg dry matter/min)
P	fresh product load (Kg)
t	time (min)
Va	air velocity (m/min)
Δ Pa	air pressure drop (mm water)
M	moisture content (Kg water/Kg dry matter)

REFERENCES
1 M. Greensmith, Practical dehydration, Food Trade Press, London 1971.
2 G. Dall'Aglio, A. Porretta and G. Carpi, Dehydration plant with air suction, Medicina e Vita (Ed.), Proc. Int. Meeting on Food Microbiology and Technology, Tabiano B. (Parma), Italia, April 20-23, 1978, pp. 161-173.
3 G. Carpi, G. Dall'Aglio, A. Porretta, A. Versitano, Dehydration of vegetables with air suction drier, Industria Conserve, 52 (1977), 215-221.
4 G. F. Dall'Aglio, G. Carpi, A. Versitano, Dehydration with air-suction: study on processing parameters and their optimization, E. A. Fiera di Parma, Contributi della ricerca per l'automazione del controllo di processo nell'industria delle conserve vegetali , Parma, Italia, October 29, 1987.